The Wilson Sisters' HORSE AND PONY GUIDE

THE ESSENTIAL HANDBOOK
FOR RIDERS OF ALL AGES

KELLY WILSON & AMANDA WILSON

PENGUIN BOOKS

Contents

INTRODUCTION   4

PRINCIPLES OF HORSE OWNERSHIP • THE BENEFITS OF OWNING A HORSE • THE COSTS OF OWNING A HORSE • HOW TO FIND THE RIGHT HORSE

SECTION 1: HORSES AND PONIES   17

A SHORT HISTORY OF THE HORSE • HORSE BREEDS • COLOURS • MARKINGS • IDENTIFICATION REQUIREMENTS • HORSE VS PONY • AGE AND GENDER • POINTS OF THE HORSE • INTERNAL SYSTEMS OF THE HORSE • DEVELOPMENT OF THE EQUINE SKELETON • CONFORMATION • EQUINE BODY LANGUAGE • INSTINCTIVE EQUINE BEHAVIOUR: FLIGHT, FIGHT, FREEZE, FAWN

SECTION 2: CARING FOR YOUR HORSE OR PONY   63

PADDOCKING YOUR HORSE • PADDOCK MAINTENANCE • FEEDING YOUR HORSE • KEEPING YOUR HORSE HEALTHY • DENTAL CARE • HOOF CARE • ILLNESS AND INJURY

SECTION 3: HANDLING YOUR HORSE   141

HANDLING BASICS • GROUND MANNERS • TIMING AND FEEL: THE FOUNDATION OF GREAT HORSEMANSHIP • GROOMING AND OTHER CARE • RUGGING YOUR HORSE • TRANSPORTING YOUR HORSE

SECTION 4: SADDLERY AND CLOTHING   203

SADDLES • BRIDLES AND BITS • TACKING UP YOUR HORSE •
SADDLE AND BRIDLE MAINTENANCE • RIDER CLOTHING

SECTION 5: RIDING YOUR HORSE   253

MOUNTING AND DISMOUNTING • RIDING POSITION • WHERE
TO RIDE • BRINGING A HORSE INTO WORK • FLATWORK • AIDS •
GAITS • TRANSITIONS • BASIC EXERCISES ON THE FLAT •
ADVANCED FOOTWORK • OBSTACLE TRAINING • JUMPING •
COMPETITION • EPILOGUE

ABOUT THE WILSON SISTERS   331

ACKNOWLEDGEMENTS   335

GLOSSARY   337

INDEX   344

Introduction

We have put together *The Wilson Sisters' Horse and Pony Guide* in the hope it will promote better horse welfare and give you, the reader, an insight into what it takes to own and care for horses, as well as the skills to further your horsemanship, riding and competition ambitions.

Whatever your age, future aspirations or level of experience, the information, photographs and illustrations in this book will help give you a greater understanding about the health, well-being and comfort of your horse, and show you how to establish safe and correct handling and riding practices.

While many practices in the equestrian world can produce satisfactory results, far too many overlook the welfare of the horse. While this is sometimes done intentionally, oftentimes it is done through ignorance and inexperience. Regardless, it is the horse that suffers. When it comes to owning, riding and training horses, we firmly believe that love on its own is simply not enough; to truly give your horse a good life, it's vital you gain in-depth and comprehensive understanding of every facet of the horse's physical, mental and emotional well-being.

As owners, trainers and competitors, our aim is to become a voice for horses on a global scale; not just setting a standard for what is acceptable now, but for what will be the standard for the future. Our journey with horses is ongoing: how we train today may not be how we train tomorrow, and what we believe now may not be what we believe in the future, but that is the beauty of our journey. It is one based on progression and a never-ending desire to put the welfare of our horses first.

With this in mind, we have spent our lives constantly striving to increase our knowledge and understanding of all things equine so we can offer our horses a stimulating, safe and nurturing environment — whether they are wild horses or World Cup showjumpers. With over 25 years of competition experience, more than 15 years spent coaching thousands of riders around the country, and being clinicians and ambassadors at leading equestrian events in New Zealand and internationally, we have seen first-hand the need for horse welfare to improve on a global scale.

This book is our love letter to the horse, collating fundamental principles and skills that we believe every horse owner should have, as well as tried-and-true methods that have been transformative in our own journey. We hope it educates and inspires you to become the type of owner your horse deserves, and that like us, you become committed to improving horse welfare from the grassroots, to the highest levels of competition.

Top: Amanda (left) on Blackstone Fattori NZPH and Kelly on Showtym Sinatra, enjoying a ride through the forest.

Bottom, from left: Heather (Mum), Vicki, Amanda and Kelly, after Showtym Cassanova won the 1.30 metre Derby at 2017 Equifest. Vicki won the same class in 2015 on Showtym Girl.

> **THE WILSON SISTERS' MISSION STATEMENT**
>
> To increase the standard of horse welfare worldwide, and to establish empathetic and ethical practices for horse management, handling and riding.

PRINCIPLES OF HORSE OWNERSHIP

When it comes to owning and caring for horses, our code of ethics follows a holistic approach, taking into consideration the horse's physical, mental and emotional well-being.

TREAT EVERY HORSE AS AN INDIVIDUAL: To get the best from your horse, it's important to customise your training methods to suit its unique personality, talents, experience and way of going.

SET YOUR HORSE UP FOR SUCCESS: Your horse needs to have a solid understanding of basic skills before it is ready to learn more complex questions; much like teaching a kid to recognise the letters of the alphabet, then sound out words, before they are expected to read or write. During training sessions, break down each milestone into achievable steps so your horse can learn in a constructive way.

BUILD A SOLID FOUNDATION: A solid foundation is important for both horse and rider. When things go wrong, especially as you progress up the levels, it is usually a sign that there are holes in your training. In times of struggle, it is important to go back to the basics and refine your horse's education so it has a solid foundation to work from.

HAVE REALISTIC EXPECTATIONS: Don't expect your horse to start where it finished the day before; instead, work through whatever your horse offers you on the day. Having high expectations can cause confusion, frustration, anger or disappointment — all of which can sabotage the relationship you have with your horse.

RELAXATION IS KEY: If your horse becomes tense during a training session, spend the time needed to foster a relaxed state before continuing. A relaxed horse is more likely to give you the correct answer and retain information, while a tense horse is more likely to give you the wrong answer as it will have switched to its survival brain (see page 38) and will likely carry that tension into future sessions.

FRUSTRATION BEGINS WHERE KNOWLEDGE ENDS: If you or your horse become frustrated during a training session, it is likely that one of you has reached the end of your knowledge base. If this happens, it's important not to take your frustration out on the horse; instead, end the session and then take the time needed to pursue further education — you can upskill by getting lessons, studying online, or sending your horse away to a professional for schooling.

CLEAR COMMUNICATION IS KEY: It is important to have clear aids to ensure your horse understands what you are asking of it. If your horse is scared or confused by your communication style, it is unlikely to understand what you are asking and may misbehave or become tense as a result.

LET YOUR HORSE KNOW WHEN IT'S DONE WELL: When your horse does the right thing, it should be immediately rewarded (see pages 164–66) to let it know that it has answered the question correctly. This will not only foster a good relationship with your horse, but also encourage it to repeat the desired behaviour in the future.

FIX SMALL MISTAKES BEFORE THEY BECOME BAD HABITS: Horses learn the wrong thing just as easily as they learn the right thing. Because of this, it's important to correct things when they first happen, while they are only small mistakes. Allowing your horse to repeat an undesirable behaviour even a few times is enough for a bad habit to start forming.

SEARCH FOR SOLUTIONS, DON'T PUNISH THE SYMPTOMS: If you have a horse that's misbehaving, it's important to understand that these behaviours usually come about because the horse is trying to communicate with you. Rather than punishing the horse for 'speaking up', strive to understand what it is trying to tell you. A 'bad' horse is often sore, bored or confused, and unfortunately these behaviours can easily be misinterpreted by people who lack an understanding of equine behaviour.

LESS IS MORE: Train your horse to listen to subtle aids (see pages 158–62) so it is able to respond off the lightest pressure. This will make handling and riding your horse more enjoyable, as it will be attentive and responsive when you ask it to do something, rather than needing to be nagged or hassled.

KEEP IT SHORT AND SWEET: Horses can become bored or fatigued easily, so their work should be varied and stimulating. When horses are learning new skills, especially ones they are struggling with, short sessions are best; finish the session after three positive attempts, rather than repeating the question until they become bored. If you do need to teach your horse a lot in a short time-frame, often two or three short sessions (5 to 15 minutes) per day is better than a single longer session (25 to 40 minutes of intensive learning).

THE BENEFITS OF OWNING A HORSE

The costs of owning and caring for your horse will be well worth it for the many benefits the equestrian lifestyle can provide. Horses can teach you the importance of responsibility, self-discipline and working together as a team, and instil in you a love of the outdoors and adventure, as well as a profound respect and empathy for all living things. They also have the capacity to teach you the art of patience, kindness and good sportsmanship; how to cope with failure and setbacks; have the capacity to ignite your desire to learn and seek continual self-improvement; and, most importantly, give you the grit and work ethic to make your dreams a reality.

The life lessons learnt from horses will not only benefit your horse–human relationships, but will also carry through to your human–human relationships, positively impacting your career and every aspect of your life. There is no doubt you'll benefit from pursuing your passion for horses, and that it will be the start of a life-changing journey.

THE COSTS OF OWNING A HORSE

Horse riding is not a cheap sport, and the cost of buying a horse or pony — as well as the basic saddlery — can seem overwhelming. These start-up costs, however, are only the beginning, so it's important to understand that significant support will be needed in terms of both finances (to pay for your horse's ongoing care) and time (unlike other sports, horses require daily care to enrich, train and exercise them, and they can't be forgotten about during the off-season). The cost and time involved with owning a horse will also significantly increase if you don't own land and your horse has to be grazed at a boarding facility.

Left: Kelly riding Showtym Sinatra bareback and bridleless.

Right: Amanda and Arlento, a young stallion she bred and produced as a showjumper.

WHAT IF YOU CAN'T LEASE OR BUY A PONY?

Don't despair! Horse riding is one of the few sports you can do at any age, so start saving now, spend time furthering your knowledge of all things equine by studying books and videos, and get lessons at a riding school or volunteer at a local stable to gain hands-on experience until you're in the position to own a horse of your own.

HOW TO FIND THE RIGHT HORSE

If you've made the decision to purchase a horse or pony, the easy part is done. Now you need to find that rare unicorn who suits your level of riding experience, as well as your height, weight, aspirations and budget. A lot hinges on making the right choice — including your future enjoyment of the sport, your safety and long-term confidence, and your bank balance; while many horses maintain or increase their value over time, others may have soundness or behavioural issues that a novice purchaser might not notice, which can leave you out of pocket.

Not all *sellers* are upfront when selling a horse or pony and, through inexperience, many novice *purchasers* may misrepresent their own ability and end up with an unsuitable mount. For these reasons, consider doing the following things when looking for a horse or pony.

- **TAKE AN EXPERIENCED HORSEPERSON WITH YOU:** No matter your experience or future ambitions, it is beneficial to take an experienced horseperson, who understands your current riding level and future goals, with you.
- **RIDE THE HORSE MORE THAN ONCE:** You will get a better gauge of a horse's suitability by trying it several times; both in its normal environment (making sure you see it being caught, saddled, handled and ridden) and also at a venue that it's unaccustomed to (to see how it reacts in a new place). If you're planning to do a lot of trail riding, it can also be worth taking the horse for a farm ride with other horses to see how it copes in that type of situation.
- **KEEP A RECORD:** Screenshot the horse's advertisement and keep any email correspondence so you have a copy of how the seller has represented the horse.
- **ASK LOTS OF QUESTIONS:** Ask detailed questions over the phone or by email (to keep a paper trail) so you have a comprehensive understanding of the horse's suitability. It can also be helpful to ask for videos of the horse, especially if you have to travel some distance to view it. This will help you determine whether it's worth trying the horse, without wasting the seller's time.

QUESTIONS TO ASK THE SELLER

GENERAL
- How long has the current owner had the horse?
- Why is the horse being sold?
- What is the horse's history and how many homes has it had?

HANDLING AND CARE
- Is the horse good to catch?
- Does the horse load well on a truck or trailer and travel well?
- Does the horse have any handling vices, including biting, kicking, separation anxiety or being pushy to lead?
- What is the horse's personality like?
- Is it good for the farrier?
- Is the horse good to saddle and bridle?

RIDING
- How often is the horse ridden, and what type of riding does it do in an average week?
- Does the horse have any ridden vices, including bucking, rearing, napping, bolting, head shaking or refusing at jumps?
- Is the horse good to ride out alone and with company?
- Has the horse competed? If so, in what discipline and at what level, and what were the horse's results?
- What type of gear does the horse get ridden in (including the brand and size of the bit and saddle)?
- How does the horse respond to being ridden again after time off?
- How does the horse handle being ridden in new environments?

HEALTH
- Has the horse ever had any accidents, health concerns, or been unsound?
- Has it ever been seen by a vet, or had an X-ray? If so, for what?
- Has it had its teeth done, and, if so, when and by whom?
- Has the horse ever been grass-affected or had grass staggers (see pages 89 and 133)?

Amanda and Showtym Viking competing in the Young Rider of the Year, at the 2013 Horse of the Year Show. KAMPIC

- **WATCH OUT FOR RED FLAGS:** An experienced horseperson will be able to recognise red flags in a horse's advertisement from the jargon and photos used, and more importantly by what *isn't* said. If you're a novice purchaser, these can easily be missed. Below are some classic phrases to watch out for.
  - **PROJECT PONY:** Often an inexperienced or difficult pony that needs an experienced rider to further its education.
  - **GREEN:** An inexperienced horse, often newly started under saddle or young, that needs an experienced rider to continue its training.
  - **FUTURE SCHOOLMASTER:** In this instance, the term 'future' means that the horse has the nature or potential to be a schoolmaster at some point, but doesn't have the current level of training to be one right now. Therefore, the horse needs an experienced rider to further its education.
  - **NEEDS A KNOWLEDGEABLE HOME:** The horse is likely to be difficult to either handle or ride and will need a confident and experienced rider (with horsey parents, if it is for a child).
  - **NEEDS A CAPABLE RIDER:** A horse that needs a brave and experienced rider, with an established riding position, due to it being green or difficult.
  - **VERY FORWARD-MOVING:** These horses are often strong and intimidating for an inexperienced rider, and are usually ridden with strong bits to maintain control. Often, horses rush because of pain-related issues (see page 167), so a pre-purchase examination would be recommended. The advertisement may also say that the horse loves to jump, but in actuality, very forward-moving horses will often rush at jumps because they are trying to escape from pain or because they have been conditioned to jump from speed, due to poor training.
- **BE HONEST ABOUT YOUR EXPERIENCE:** Be honest with the seller about your level of experience, the type of lifestyle you can offer the horse, and your one- to three-year ambitions; an honest seller will be able to tell you whether they think the horse is suitable for you or not.
- **DON'T BUY SIGHT UNSEEN:** It's better to avoid buying a horse or pony that you haven't viewed in person. Far too often you'll end up buying one that isn't suitable, which can result in a loss of confidence or difficulty on-selling it.
- **BE REALISTIC ABOUT YOUR BUDGET:** Take your budget into consideration and remember that if you're limited by how much you can spend, then it's likely you'll only get two of the following three things: cheap, trained (well-trained and safe for your level of experience) or sound (a horse with no lameness, illnesses or injuries). For those on a budget, off-the-track thoroughbreds can be appealing due to their athletic abilities and cheaper price, but this is often a false economy with many requiring extensive feeding, shoeing, rehabilitation and body work, and they can also be more prone to ulcers than other breeds. Often, spending more on a sound, low-maintenance horse can be cheaper in the long run, rather than buying a horse that needs extensive management.

Kelly and Atahu, the stallion she tamed at liberty for the 2022 Kaimanawa Stallion Challenge.

> **CHEAP AND TRAINED = NOT SOUND**
> Some soundness issues may limit a horse from top-level competition, but they may still be suited for a beginner rider with lower ambitions and expectations. More serious soundness issues can mean a horse is totally unsuited for any ridden work or may require expensive maintenance.
>
> **CHEAP AND SOUND = NOT TRAINED**
> These horses are usually suited to capable riders who have experience training young or difficult horses.
>
> **TRAINED AND SOUND = NOT CHEAP**
> Often referred to as schoolmasters (an experienced horse that is used to give confidence to inexperienced riders), these horses and ponies are the real unicorns and their price usually reflects this. They are worth their weight in gold though, as you'll likely reach your ridden aspirations faster and be less likely to have confidence knocks.

Once you've found a horse or pony that matches your needs, it's worth considering the following.

- **GET A PRE-PURCHASE EXAMINATION:** Even the most experienced riders can miss crucial health and soundness issues when they purchase a horse, so it can be beneficial to have the horse checked by an equine veterinarian. The veterinarian works on behalf of the purchaser and reports any abnormalities they find in the horse's eyes, teeth, heart, skin, joints, tendons, ligaments and hooves. The horse is usually observed in motion too, being watched at the walk, trot and canter on the lunge. During a five-stage pre-purchase examination, the horse is also observed under saddle and will undergo further diagnostic tests like X-ray, electrocardiogram of the the heart, blood tests, ultrasound or endoscopy (before and after strenuous exercise) to determine the overall soundness of the horse. A five-stage check is beneficial for horses that compete at higher levels, that are more expensive, or that you are wanting to insure for loss of use (see below), while a one- or two-stage vet check, which includes flexion tests to test the joints in the limbs, might be sufficient for horses that are expected to compete at lower levels, or be used as pleasure mounts.
- **SIGN A CONTRACT:** For your peace of mind you should ask the seller for a sale contract so that you have a written history of the horse and any known health, soundness or behavioural issues, what sort of management it needs, what and how much it is fed, the saddle and bit that it is currently ridden in, and when it was last wormed or seen by an equine dentist.
- **INSURE THE HORSE:** If you've stretched your budget to purchase a horse, or can't afford to replace it if something were to happen, it may be worth insuring your new horse. Horses can be insured for loss of use or death, and

most policies also cover vet costs; claims can be difficult, however, so make sure you read the fine print so you know exactly what the policy covers.
- **GET SADDLERY THAT FITS**: The first thing you should do when your new horse arrives is to have a saddle correctly fitted (see pages 210–11). You should also purchase a suitable and correctly fitting bit — usually the one the horse is accustomed to is recommended (unless the horse has been ridden in a single-jointed bit; in that instance it may be worth changing to a double-jointed bit as we find that these are more comfortable for the horse).

SETTLING IN A NEW HORSE

We have heard many stories of people who have purchased a new horse or pony, then felt the horse was misrepresented in its advertisement because it behaved differently after it arrived at their property. Although misinterpretation can and does happen, often it isn't the case; rather, it is the horse reacting to its new environment and the many changes it is facing. The most common reasons why a horse's behaviour regresses or changes when it moves to a new home are: a change in feed and grass (see page 98), getting ulcers from travelling (see pages 86–87), a different work regimen, confusing rider aids, not having enough work, or being ridden in a poorly fitting saddle (see pages 210–11).

When you are buying a new horse, think of it like a foster child. If you were to adopt a child and take it away from everything it knows, then place it into your family with a completely different set of rules, styles of communication, meal plans and exercise routines, the child would likely feel very lost and confused initially.

Horses are similar. As a general rule, we have found that it usually takes about three to six months for a horse to settle in to its new environment and start to develop a relationship with its rider, and up to two years for a rider to get the most out of their new horse. This time can be greatly reduced, however, by choosing a suitable horse or pony for your level of experience and getting professional advice throughout the initial stages of horse ownership. We hope the information provided in this book will give you the resources you need to help make your new horse's transition as seamless as possible, so that you're able to make the most of your time spent in the saddle.

SECTION 1

Horses and Ponies

Whether you want to learn to ride, or already have your own horse, this section will give you insight into the basics of what a horse is, including different breeds, colours, ages and genders, the difference between horses and ponies, as well as the development of the equine skeleton and conformation faults.

A SHORT HISTORY OF THE HORSE

Horses were domesticated around 6000 years ago, and since then their relationship with humans has been ever-present throughout civilisation; in times of both war and peace. Until the invention of the steam train in the early 1800s, then the internal combustion engine in the industrial age, horses were the only way for people to travel at faster than human pace, making them an essential part of society.

While horses still have cultural significance in many countries, in modern times they are generally used for sport and pleasure. Horse riding is one of the very few sports that can be enjoyed by all ages and levels, across a range of disciplines, and is the only Olympic sport where both women and men can compete as equals.

While most horses are domestic, others remain wild — many of which are descendants of once-tamed horses that have run feral for generations. There are estimated to be up to 1 million wild Brumbies in Australia, 120,000 Mustangs in America (of which 50,000 live in government feed lots), and 2000 to 3000 wild horses in both Canada and New Zealand. While other countries, like France, Portugal and Japan, also have feral horses, their populations generally range between a few dozen to about a thousand horses.

> ### EQUIDAE FAMILY
> Every horse and pony, no matter its size, breed or colour, belongs to a single species, *Equus ferus caballus*. It is one of seven living species that make up the Equidae family, which also includes donkeys as well as several species of zebra and wild ass.

HORSE BREEDS

There are around 400 different breeds of horses and ponies within the horse species, which have all evolved from prehistoric and feral horses. Over the past 6000 years — since horses were first domesticated by humans — they have been selectively bred for specific purposes to create the modern breeds we have today. Each breed has distinctive traits such as size, conformation, colour, disposition and performance ability that are passed on to their offspring.

Gaining knowledge about the different horse breeds is helpful for choosing the right horse for your requirements. While experienced riders might enjoy the athleticism of a Hanoverian or a Holstein, or the speed of a Thoroughbred, these breeds are usually unsuited to young, inexperienced or nervous riders as they are often more sensitive when ridden and can require higher-maintenance care. In comparison, breeds like Clydesdales, American Quarter Horses and Standardbreds are known for their quieter temperaments, making them more suitable for inexperienced riders; however, they are likely to be less suited to a rider wanting to

Top: Vicki's Zangersheide stallion Carpaccio BDV Z TWS, who was imported from Belgium.

Bottom: A band of wild Brumbies in the Snowy Mountains of Australia.

compete in the Olympic disciplines of dressage, showjumping and eventing due to their size, movement or conformation.

> ### STUD BOOKS
> Stud books exist for many horse breeds, with horses able to be registered as either purebreds or partbreds. To be registered as a purebred the horse must have both parents registered as purebreds, while a partbred needs only one registered parent. Some stud books require a DNA test, at the time of registration, for proof of lineage.

Horse breeds are generally grouped, by their type and temperament, into the following three categories.

- **COLD-BLOODED**: Cold-blooded horses include the heavy, working breeds such as the Clydesdale, Suffolk, Shire, Gypsy Cob and Percheron. They have been purpose-bred to carry or pull heavy loads and are known for their calm and steady temperaments. Although their easy nature often makes draught horses gentle to both handle and ride, their size, solid demeanour and heavy weight generally means that they are best suited for pleasure riding, hauling heavy loads or ploughing.
- **HOT-BLOODED**: Hot-blooded horses are the finer, faster breeds such as the Arabian and Thoroughbred. They are purpose-bred for speed, strength and endurance and are known for being sensitive and energetic. Because they are often of a high-strung nature, hot-blooded horses are generally suited to capable, experienced riders; especially Thoroughbreds that have previously raced, as they can be more reactive and less forgiving if the rider doesn't have an established riding position or good timing and feel.
- **WARM-BLOODED**: Warm-blooded horses are derived from the selective breeding of cold-blooded and hot-blooded breeds, resulting in most modern breeds, including the Hanoverian, Andalusian, Selle Francis, Welsh, English Riding Pony and Quarter Horse, as well as crossbreds. Over hundreds of years they have been purpose-bred for both ridden and carriage work, with the aim of combining the athleticism of a hot-blooded horse with the temperament of a cold-blooded horse — this makes them the most popular choice for a sport horse or child's pony. There are, however, hundreds of different warm-blooded breeds, with varying sizes and temperaments: the greater the percentage of hot-blooded heritage a horse has in its lineage, the more sensitive it is likely to be.

Showtym Burrow, a partbred Gyspy Cob that Amanda competed to 1.40m before selling to Australia.

DOES BREED INFLUENCE RIDEABILITY?

While a horse's breed can largely influence its disposition and nature, there are always exceptions to this rule. We have had cold-blooded horses that have been very sensitive and needed confident, capable riders because of how powerful and forward-moving they were; and we have had hot-blooded horses that have been very safe and easy-going.

Other factors that may influence a horse's rideability can include how the horse was trained, how it was raised and managed, how nervous the rider is (horses can sense a rider's anxiety, which can make them anxious themselves), if it has nutritional deficiencies, and if it is in pain.

COLOURS

There are over 60 different horse colours, which are actually all different shades and variations of three base coats: chestnut, black and bay. For example, a palomino, red roan, red dun and rose grey are all variations of a chestnut base coat, with either diluted genes or white hair interspersed with the red; chestnuts can also be affected by a white patterning which will result in chestnut pintos or appaloosas. Variations in colour are based on the horse's base coat and points (muzzle, tips of ears, lower legs, mane and tail).

It's important to know what your horse's colour and markings are so that you can accurately mark them on its identification papers (see page 26) or describe your horse.

DOES COLOUR INFLUENCE TEMPERAMENT?

While there are myths about chestnut mares and black stallions being more temperamental than other colours and genders, a horse's colour actually has no influence on its temperament.

Common colours

The most common horse colours include the following.

BAY: The most common colour is bay, where the horse has a brown coat and black points. Variations are *red or blood bay* (reddish brown), *light bay* (yellowish brown), and *dark bay* (a deep or blackish brown).

CHESTNUT: This is a common colour, seen in most horse breeds. Chestnuts can vary in shade, ranging from orange, to red, to brown. This colour is distinguishable by the absolute absence of true black hairs. Variations include *flaxen chestnut* (the mane and tail are lighter than the horse's coat) and *liver chestnut* (dark-reddish brown). At its darkest shade, a liver chestnut may be hard to distinguish from black without careful inspection.

BLACK: A true black horse has a black coat with no red or brown on the flanks, underbelly or muzzle. This colour is relatively uncommon; dark liver chestnuts or dark bays are often mistakenly described as black.

BROWN: Horses that are brown in colour with brown points.

GREY: Grey horses are nearly always born with a black, bay or chestnut base colour, although some show a grey tinge at birth. As they age, the coat greys out through progressive silvering of their coloured hairs. The adult hair coat is referred to as *grey* (white), *steel grey* (dark hairs are prominent), *dappled grey* (light grey circular patches on the coat), *flea-bitten grey* (brown hairs form in small spots, making the coat appear speckled) or *rose grey* (usually seen when a chestnut horse is greying out, giving it a pinkish tinge). Some horses turn grey very quickly, while others may take several years.

DUN: A dun horse has a golden or cream coat with a black mane and tail, and primitive markings such as zebra striping on the legs and a dorsal strip down the back. The dun dilution gene affects bay, chestnut and black horses differently, and within each colour

---

1. Red roan.
2. Palomino with stripe and snip.
3. Palomino pinto.
4. Liver chestnut with star and snip.
5. Grullo with star.
6. Flea-bitten grey with snip.
7. Dun with dorsal strip.
8. Dapple grey.
9. Chestnut with star.
10. Chestnut pinto, also known as a skewbald.
11. Black.
12. Blue roan.
13. Bay with star and snip.
14. Bay with star.
15. Grey with strip.
16. Leopard spot appaloosa.
CHRISTIANE SLAWIK

there is a variety of different shades. The most common is *yellow dun* (dun dilution of a bay base coat), *red dun* (dun dilution of a chestnut base coat), and *grullo* or *blue dun* (dun dilution of a black base coat).

BUCKSKIN: Buckskins have a golden or cream coat with a black mane and tail. Buckskins get their colour by having one cream dilution gene on a bay base coat. (Two cream dilution genes on a bay base coat will produce a *perlino*, which has the same coat colour but the points will be a darker shade of cream, with pink skin and blue eyes.) Duns are commonly mistaken for buckskins; the easiest way to tell them apart is by the dorsal stripe — if it has one it's a dun, if not it's a buckskin.

ROAN: Roan horses have white hairs intermingled throughout their base coat, with the points mostly solid-coloured. Variations include a *blue roan* (black base coat), a *bay roan* (bay base coat), and a *red* or *strawberry roan* (chestnut base coat).

PINTO: A pinto horse has large patches of white and any other colour on their coat. A black-and-white pinto can also be referred to as a *piebald*, while chestnut or bay pintos are known as *skewbalds*. Regardless of the colour, there are several coat patterns used to describe pintos; the most common are *overo* (a dark-coloured horse with white markings — at least one and often all four legs are dark) and *tobiano* (a white-coloured horse with dark markings — generally all four legs are white).

PALOMINO: A palomino horse has a golden or cream coat with a white mane and tail. Palominos get their colour by having one cream dilution gene on a chestnut base coat. (Two cream dilution genes on a chestnut base coat will produce a *cremello*, which has the same coat colour, but the horse will have pink skin and blue eyes.)

APPALOOSA: The term appaloosa can refer to both a breed and a colour. As a colour, it refers to a horse with distinctive spotted patterns. The most common variations include *leopard spot* (white or dark spots over all or some of the coat) or *blanket* (a white spotted area over the hindquarters).

MARKINGS

Markings are distinctive white areas of hair, usually on the face and legs.

Head markings

STAR: A white marking on the forehead, ranging in size from a few white hairs to covering the entire forehead.

BLAZE: A broad white marking on the horse's forehead that extends down on to the horse's nose.

SNIP: A white marking on the horse's nose, sometimes extending onto the nostrils or lips.

STRIPE/STRIP: A narrow white stripe running down the horse's forehead.

INTERRUPTED STRIPE/STRIP: A disconnected white stripe running down the horse's forehead, often created by a star, stripe and snip combination.

WHITE OR BALD FACE: A large white marking which covers the horse's forehead, eyes, nose and part of the muzzle.

WALL EYE: An eye with partial or full blue colouring, created by a lack of pigmentation in the iris.

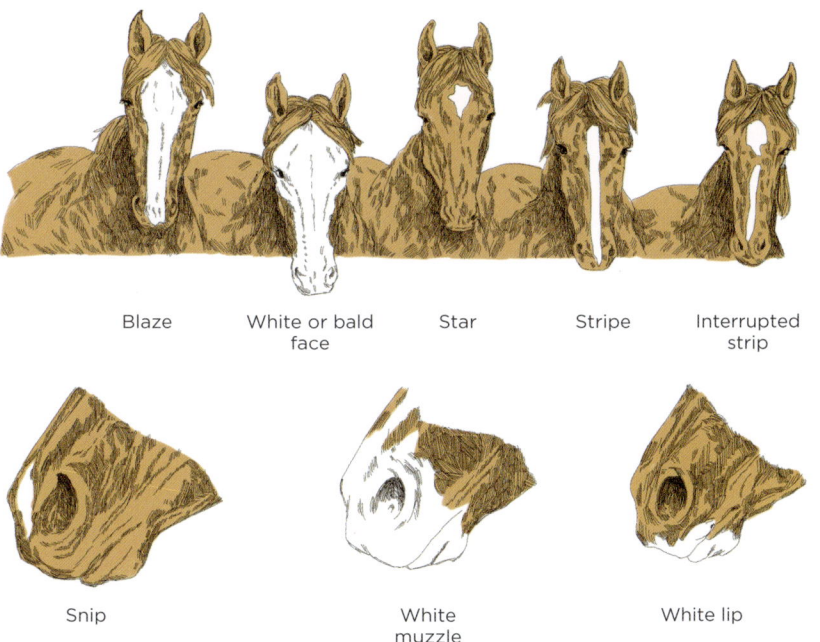

Blaze · White or bald face · Star · Stripe · Interrupted strip

Snip · White muzzle · White lip

Top left: A flaxen chestnut with a blaze and white lip.

Top right: A bay with a bald face, and two blue eyes.

Left: Examples of head markings.

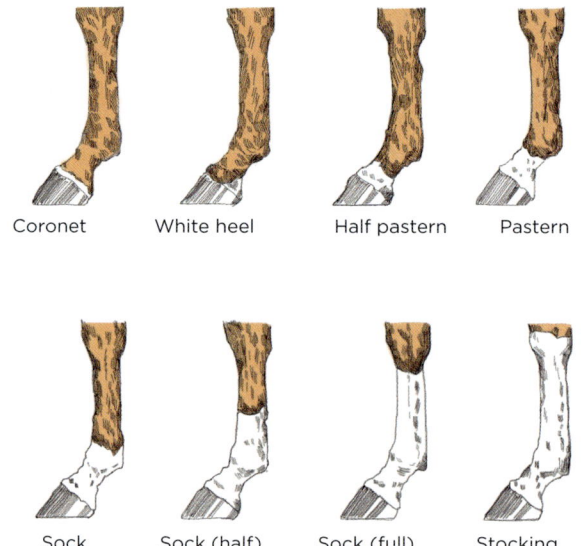

Examples of leg markings.

Leg markings

SOCK: A white marking extending from the hoof up to the base of the knee or hock.

STOCKING: A white marking extending up to the knee or hock, or further. Some stockings finish in a jagged, 'irregular' pattern.

CORONET: A band of white around the top of the hoof, not extending past the pastern. If the band only covers part of the hoof, it's referred to as a partial coronet.

ERMINE: A small coloured spot within any white marking, either on the forehead or the legs.

Whorls

Whorls are distinctive changes in the direction in which the hair grows on the horse's coat. They are usually found on the forehead, flank, belly, neck and chest. The location of whorls is unique to every horse, so they are especially useful for identifying horses with no white markings. Because of this, whorls are recorded on the horse's identification charts in their passports, registration certificates or height certificates.

IDENTIFICATION REQUIREMENTS

For identification purposes, horses and ponies are often branded or microchipped. In some cases, identification papers or a passport are also required.

IDENTIFICATION PAPERS: Most horses registered with a national equestrian federation or a stud register, or those with a height certificate, will require an identification chart to record the horse's height, age, lineage, colour, markings and whorls.

BRANDS: All Thoroughbreds, and several other breeds, require the horses to be branded on both shoulders.

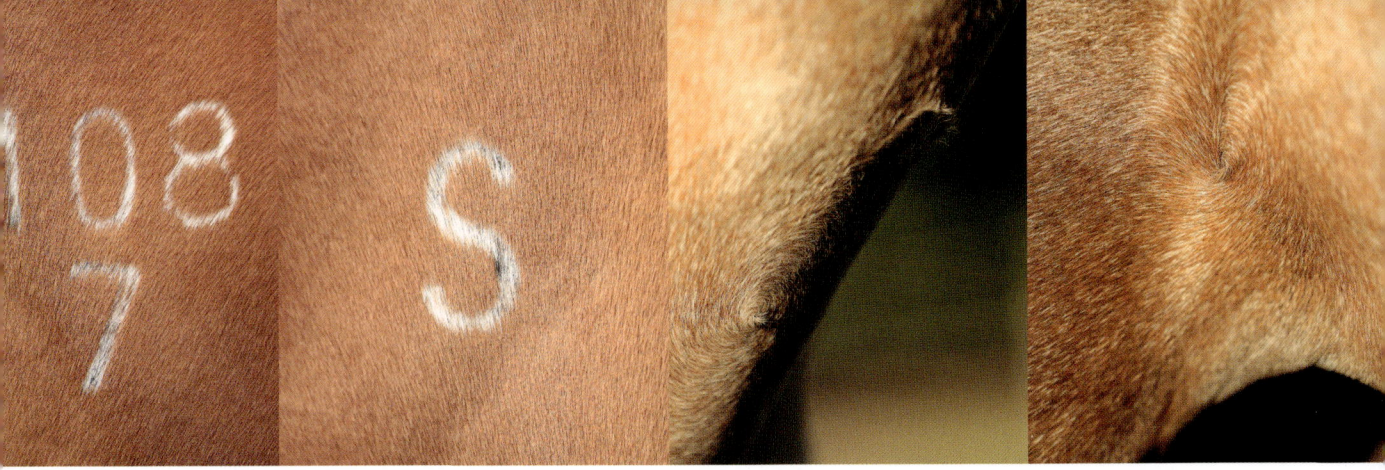

- On the near (left) shoulder, a registered cipher brand (usually a symbol or letters) will indicate which stud the horse was born at or who the attending vet was.
- On the off (right) shoulder there will usually be two numbers. The top one generally indicates the numerical order in which the foal was born, in any given year, to that stud or vet clinic; the bottom number is the last number of the year in which the foal was born (if only one number is present, it indicates the birth year). For example, a horse with the numbers 14 over 5 is the fourteenth horse born to that stud or vet clinic in either 1995, 2005 or 2015; of those options, the actual age will be determined by contacting the stud or vet clinic to check their records against the horse's colour and markings, or by ageing the horse's teeth.

Other breeds, such as American Mustangs, require the horse to be freeze-branded on the neck. Each symbol denotes a different number, allowing you to determine the year the horse was born, the country or origin, and its registration number.

PASSPORTS: All horses registered with the FEI (Fédération Equestre Internationale) are issued with passports which include an identification chart and a vaccination record.

MICROCHIPS: All horses issued with an FEI passport or an RAS Lifetime Certificate are required to be microchipped, as are certain breeds (including Thoroughbreds, Connemaras and Standardbreds), before they can be registered.

HORSE VS PONY

The difference between a horse and pony is height. The height of horses and ponies is measured at the withers (the highest point of the body), and is taken in both centimetres and hands. In New Zealand, a horse measures anything over 148 centimetres or 14.2hh ('hh' means hands high; and one hand is 4 inches (10 centimetres), which originated from the average width of an adult hand).

Some smaller 'pony-sized' breeds like miniature horses or Icelandic horses, and many wild horses — including Mustangs, Brumbies and Kaimanawas — are traditionally referred to as horses due to their type, even if they are pony-sized.

Examples of brands and whorls.

CONVERSIONS FOR HANDS HIGH (HH) TO CENTIMETRES (CM)

HH	CM	PONY OR HORSE?
10.0	103	PONY
10.2	108	
11.0	113	
11.2	118	
12.0	123	
12.2	128	
13.0	133	
13.2	138	
14.0	143	
14.2	148	
15.0	153	HORSE
15.2	158	
16.0	163	
16.2	168	
17.0	173	
17.2	178	
18.0	183	

In most equestrian disciplines, events are divided into horse and pony classes, with ponies allowed to be competed by riders aged 17 years or under. Because of this, many young riders prefer to stay on ponies as long as possible so that they aren't having to compete against adults.

Because children are constantly growing in size and skill, they will often go through several ponies over the course of their riding careers; whereas adults can buy a horse and expect to keep it for many years. Although children are likely to outgrow their ponies, it's important to not 'over-horse' them by buying them a horse or pony that is too big (or too difficult) for their current needs.

The rider's height and weight are also important to ensure the welfare, soundness and longevity of the horse. Many people believe that the taller a horse is, the more weight it can carry, but this isn't always true. A 14hh pony with a heavier build (or more bone — determined by measuring around a horse's cannon bone) and a good topline (see pages 275–77) could easily carry as much, if not more, than a 16hh horse with a finer build (less bone or a weak topline). A horse's ability to carry weight is also influenced by its conformation, fitness, strength, soundness, and fit of the saddle (see pages 210–11).

Research suggests that the weight of the rider and tack combined should be no more than 20% of the horse's bodyweight, and ideally less than 15%. For example, the combined weight of the rider and tack on a 500 kilogram horse should ideally be less than 75 kilograms.

IS MY HORSE THE RIGHT SIZE?

As a rough guide, when you are standing beside your horse or pony's withers it should be no taller than the top of your head and no shorter than the height of your shoulders. Once mounted, your legs should be able to wrap around the horse's sides without hanging below its belly, not only offering you a more secure seat but also ensuring your height doesn't negatively affect your horse's balance.

As always, there are exceptions. Someone who is tall but very light in build may get away with riding a smaller pony, while a smaller rider may enjoy riding a bigger horse if it has a suitable temperament.

HOW TO MEASURE YOUR HORSE

To accurately measure your horse's height, it is important to stand your horse square and on flat ground, then use a measuring tape or stick (a long ruler with a sliding bar that levels onto the horse's withers). You can get an official measure done at a Height Measuring Day, where a level bar or laser will be used. When a horse is officially measured it will be issued with an annual Height Certificate, which will have the horse's height recorded alongside its details (name, age, breed, colour, markings and whorls). In New Zealand, once a horse or pony is 8 years old it is eligible for an RAS Lifetime Certificate, which is valid for the horse's lifetime and requires a vet to be in attendance to microchip the horse and fill out an identification form.

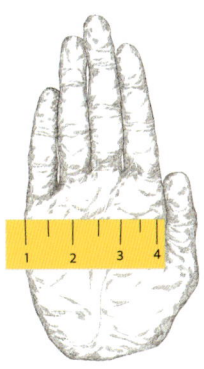
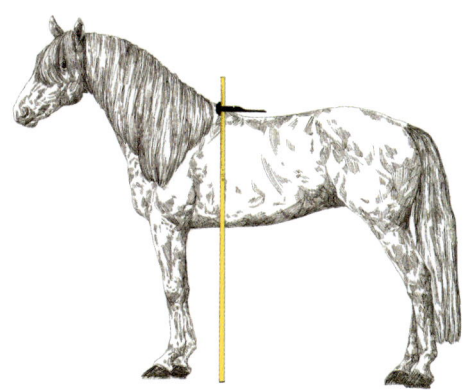

Top tip: When buying a 14.2hh pony for competition purposes, it is a good idea to have it officially measured before you buy it if it doesn't have a current height certificate. A pony that doesn't measure will have to compete in the hack ring (and may struggle to make the longer hack strides when jumping), and its value may also significantly decrease. Remember that a pony won't reach full maturity until its bones have set (see page 42), so if it is already a full-height pony as a 4- to 6-year-old then it may grow into a horse.

> ## WHEN TO UP-HORSE
>
> A tough question that many parents face as their child grows is whether to stay on ponies or make the move to a horse. There are pros and cons for both options, but as a general rule we have found that ponies can be more fun and forgiving, so if your child is size-appropriate for ponies (see page 28), we recommend them staying on ponies for as long as possible.
>
> Moving on to horses early, however, can be beneficial to highly talented and ambitious riders who want to reach the top levels of their chosen discipline (children are legally allowed to compete horses from 12 years of age). This is because riders can get away with making a lot of mistakes on ponies, who tend to be more tolerant and easier to ride, which can sometimes lead to the rider developing bad habits. With horses, you usually have to be much more attuned to how they go, as they can be more powerful and sensitive to work with.
>
> Competing both horses and ponies at the same time can be hard for some riders to juggle, however, as they may find it confusing to change between pony striding and horse striding.

AGE AND GENDER

Choosing the right age and gender of horse for your needs is important to ensure that you're well matched in experience and suitability.

HOW LONG DO HORSES LIVE?

LIFE SPAN: Horses have an average life span of 25 to 30 years.

OFFICIAL BIRTHDAY: Most horses officially change age on 1 August in the southern hemisphere, and 1 January in the northern hemisphere. The only exception is Standardbreds, which officially change age on 1 January, to align with the northern hemisphere.

GESTATION PERIOD: Mares carry their foals for 11 months, and within a couple of hours of being born, foals can stand to nurse and run.

Juvenile horses

The following terms are used for juvenile horses, according to their age and gender.

- **FOAL:** A horse under 1 year old. A foal usually suckles on its mother until about six to nine months of age.
- **WEANLING:** A foal that has just been weaned from its mother, usually between six months and 1 year of age.
- **YEARLING:** A young horse, either male or female, aged between 1 and 2 years old.

- **FILLY**: A female horse under the age of 4 years.
- **COLT**: A male horse, usually uncastrated, under the age of 4 years.

Horses under the age of 4 years are not suited for much ridden work, and they are not allowed at Pony Club or English-style competitions because their skeleton hasn't finished developing. Even once they have matured enough to ride, juvenile or green horses are rarely a good choice for inexperienced or nervous riders as they will require a professional rider to start them under saddle and give them the life experience needed to ensure that they are safe and reliable.

Depending on its breed, temperament and level of education, a young horse may require the guidance of an experienced rider for months, if not years, and some may never be suited to a beginner. Even a young horse with the most biddable and unflappable nature can have its future compromised if it is trained by someone who lacks the skills needed to offer it a well-rounded education.

A colt foal plays with his mother, before resting.

Mature horses

The terms for mature horses are as follows.

- **MARE:** A female horse 4 years or older.
- **GELDING:** A castrated male horse, of any age. Geldings usually have a better quality of life than stallions as they can be paddocked with other horses, and are also safer to handle and ride.
- **STALLION:** An uncastrated male horse 4 years or older. Stallions are never suited to inexperienced or nervous riders as they require very careful management and can be highly dangerous in the wrong hands. Even a good-natured stallion can become unpredictable and potentially dangerous at times, especially during the breeding season or around food.

Horses and ponies 4 years or older are considered mature enough for ridden work, although they don't actually reach physical maturity until about 7 years old, when the growth plates in their bones finish fusing (see page 42). Because of this, it's important to consider your expectations when buying a horse. In many equestrian disciplines, especially jumping, there are limits on how much a young horse can do up until the age of 7 years, to ensure the long-term welfare of the horse and its competition longevity.

When deciding on what age horse to buy, remember that a horse's price usually reflects its level of training and experience. Young, inexperienced, difficult, injured or older horses are often cheaper because they are either limited in their abilities or need additional training. These horses may save you money in the short term, but often cost more if they need to have professional training or if they have behavioural or soundness issues.

The younger a horse is, the less education and life experience it will have had, and the less predictable its reactions are likely to be when things go wrong. Younger horses, therefore, usually require an experienced rider and regular work, to train them into safe and reliable mounts. The ideal rider for an inexperienced horse is someone with the experience to foresee problems developing before they begin — a level of foresight that beginners usually lack. While some young horses can be very quiet and reliable, in the wrong hands they can regress in their training, lose confidence, or even develop bad habits.

In comparison, older horses are usually more reliable and experienced. Horses that have 'been there and done that' are known as *schoolmasters* (geldings) or *schoolmistresses* (mares) and are ideal for giving riders the chance to improve their own skills, gain a competitive edge, and progress faster than they would on something less experienced. Assuming that they are sound and well cared for, horses aged 10 to 20 years of age can still compete at a high level; horses as old as 19 have competed at the Olympics. Even into their mid-20s, a healthy horse can be well suited as a pleasure or beginner mount if its temperament is suitable.

HOW TO AGE A HORSE

If you don't know your horse's date of birth, and it isn't branded or microchipped (see pages 26–27), its age can be determined by examining its teeth. The way horses' teeth erupt and wear can indicate their approximate age. If in doubt, have your equine dentist or vet assess your horse to determine its likely age.

JUVENILE HORSES

FOALS: Baby (temporary) teeth emerge soon after birth, and are whiter, smaller and smoother than permanent teeth. Incisors and premolars appear first.

YEARLINGS: A yearling will usually have 12 temporary incisors, 12 premolars and 4 permanent molars.

2½-YEAR-OLDS: The middle juvenile front incisors will fall out at about 2½ years and the new permanent teeth will erupt and be in full wear by 3 years of age. These permanent teeth are larger and yellower than the baby teeth.

3½-YEAR-OLDS: The next set of temporary incisors are shed at 3½ years; by the time the horse is 4 years old it will have four permanent incisors fully erupted and in full wear at the top and bottom of its jaw.

4½-YEAR-OLDS: The last set of temporary incisors, at the front corners of the horse's mouth, fall out at 4½ years. The horse is said to have a full mouth at 5 years of age, once the permanent incisors are in full wear. Canine teeth, or tushes (which are small, sharp teeth positioned between the horse's incisor and cheek teeth) also emerge from about 4 years of age, although they aren't present in all horses, and seldom in mares.

CAPS: Horses have three sets of four temporary cheek teeth. The first set begins the process of shedding at 2½ years of age, the second set at 3 years of age, and the third set at 3½ years of age. As the horse's caps start to change, bony enlargements under the jaw can indicate that the changes are occurring. If caps don't shed correctly, they can cause long-term damage, including misalignment of the permanent teeth. To ensure the caps are correctly shedding, equine dental work should be done from 2½ years of age (see page 111).

MATURE HORSES

Once a horse has a full set of permanent teeth, its age is estimated by studying the wear on the teeth: including the incisors, cups, ridges, length, shape, slope and grinding surfaces, as well as the Galvayne's groove (which appears in the upper-corner incisors at about 10 years of age). This is only an estimate, however, as wear can vary depending on nutrition, birth defects, environment and genetics.

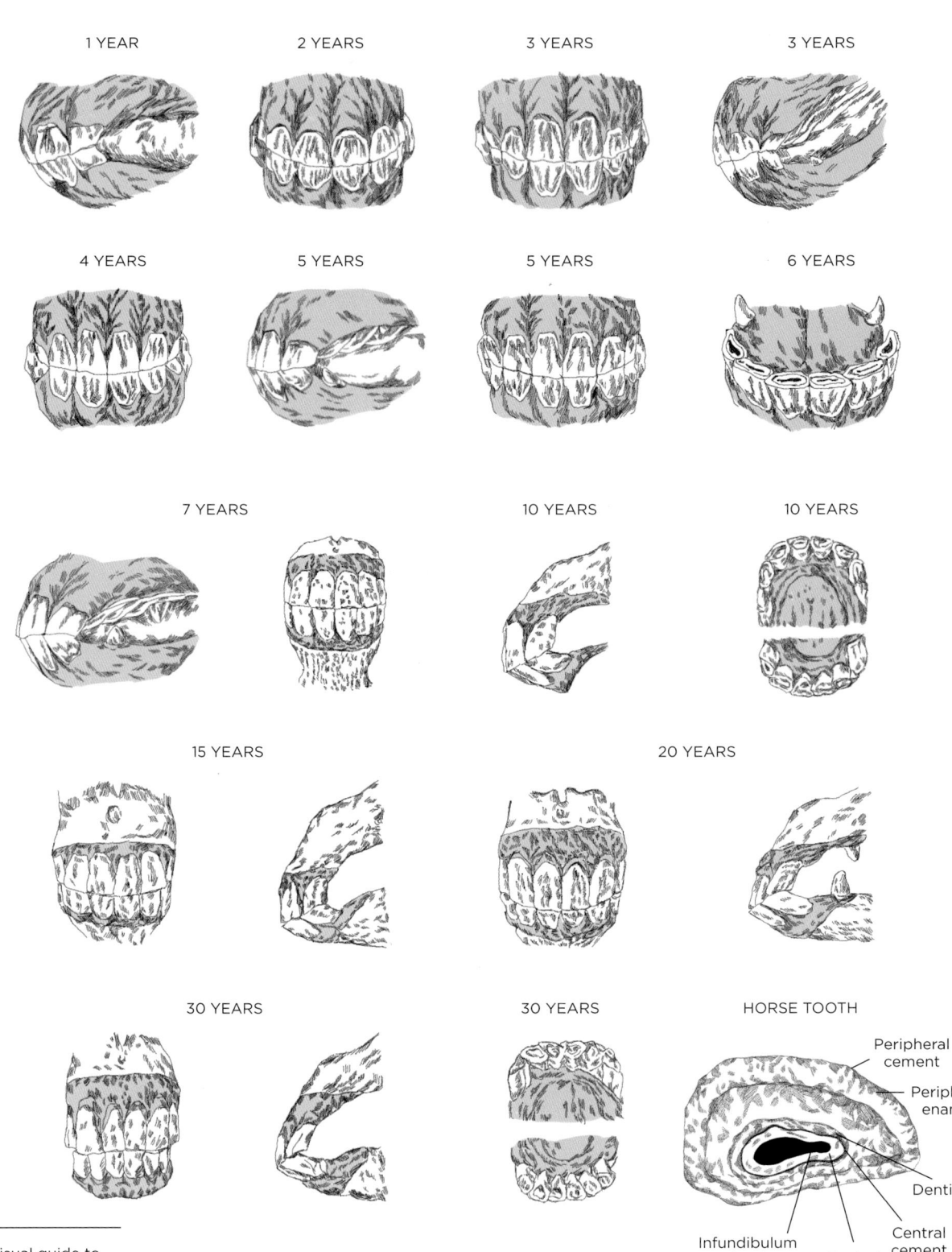

A visual guide to aging horses' teeth.

34

POINTS OF THE HORSE

Knowing the points of the horse (see pages 36–37) is an important part of horse ownership. Not only will this allow you to accurately describe your horse's conformation and identify the location of an injury, but it will also give you an understanding of how a horse's body works, which will positively influence your ability to care for it.

INTERNAL SYSTEMS OF THE HORSE

For greater understanding of your horse's overall health and well-being, it's important to have knowledge about its internal structures.

Musculoskeletal system

Like all animals, a horse's skeleton is made up of bone and cartilage, which creates the framework of the horse and provides protection for its vital organs. Joints are found where bones meet, allowing the skeleton to move.

Unlike humans, two distinct parts of the horse's skeleton are not connected by joints, but rather by muscle and ligaments. These are:

- the axial skeleton, which includes the skull, spine and ribcage; and
- the appendicular skeleton, which includes the shoulders and forelegs, as well as the pelvis and hind legs.

Bones are coated with a strong membrane called periosteum, to which ligaments, muscles and tendons attach. Damage to any of these will affect a horse's soundness.

LIGAMENTS: Rigid bands of fibrous tissue, called ligaments, connect bones to one another and also regulate and support movement in the joints. Two important ligaments are the *suspensory ligament*, which is positioned behind the cannon bone and supports the fetlock joint and tendons, and the *check ligament*, which supports the knee and hock, and regulates their range of motion to prevent overextension.

MUSCLES: The muscular system is made up of soft tissues known as muscle fibres, which flex, extend and contract to allow movement.

TENDONS: Tendons are made up of strong, flexible tissue which can stretch up to 4% of its length, and connect the horse's muscles to its bones. If damaged, tendons heal slowly as they have a poor blood supply, and the replacement tissue will be less elastic. The tendons found at the front of the horse's legs are responsible for extending the leg and are known as *extensor tendons*, while *flexor tendons* are found at the back of the legs and allow them to flex.

Nervous system

The horse's nervous system is made up of the brain, spinal cord and peripheral nerves (which are found throughout the body). These create complex circuits which allow the horse to respond to sensations.

There are three types of action:

- voluntary action — sensory nerve cells (which record sensation) send

information to the brain, which is assessed in relation to the horse's instincts and past experiences, and then motor nerve cells (which regulate movement) signal the appropriate response to trigger an action;
- reflex action — an immediate and involuntary survival response, like flicking a tail or taking flight, which bypasses the brain; and
- automatic action — this happens without conscious effort, and regulates bodily functions like heart rate and digestion.

Fascia system

The fascia system is a network of connective tissue that allows the body to function as an integrated system. It surrounds all muscles, nerves, bones, organs, blood vessels and cells, and connects with the central nervous system to influence both the mechanical and emotional function of the horse.

Endocrine system

The endocrine system influences how horses behave, by releasing hormones into the blood and lymph systems. These hormones are released automatically, with no voluntary control by the horse, and influence their growth, digestion, ageing, natural immunity and reproduction, as well as producing cortisol (to reduce inflammation and inhibit pain during stress) and adrenaline (to prepare the horse for action in times of stress).

Sensory system

Horses rely on the same five senses as humans:

SIGHT: Horses' eyes are set wide on their heads, allowing them to see almost 360 degrees around them. They do have two areas they can't see, known as blind spots; however, with a slight tilt or shift of the head they can see in all directions.

SOUND: Horses can detect low to very high frequencies (from 14 hertz to 25 kilohertz), enabling them to hear noises that can't be detected by humans. They can hear sounds from up to 4 kilometres away, and can swivel their ears 180 degrees to pinpoint a specific direction to listen in.

SMELL: A horse's sense of smell is more developed than that of a human and is used to interpret the world around it, as well as identify familiar horses and humans. Studies have also shown that horses can smell the emotions of humans, through the odours they emit in times of fear and happiness.

TOUCH: Horses have a well-developed sense of touch. The skin is a sensory organ, containing nerve endings that makes horses sensitive to pressure, pain and temperature (including their whiskers, which allow them to feel if they are about to bump into something — especially in the dark). Horses can also feel vibrations through the ground, via their hooves, teeth and jaw, which gives them almost a sixth sense that allows them to anticipate approaching weather patterns and read the emotions of both horses and humans.

TASTE: Horses have taste receptors on their tongue and the roof of their mouth,

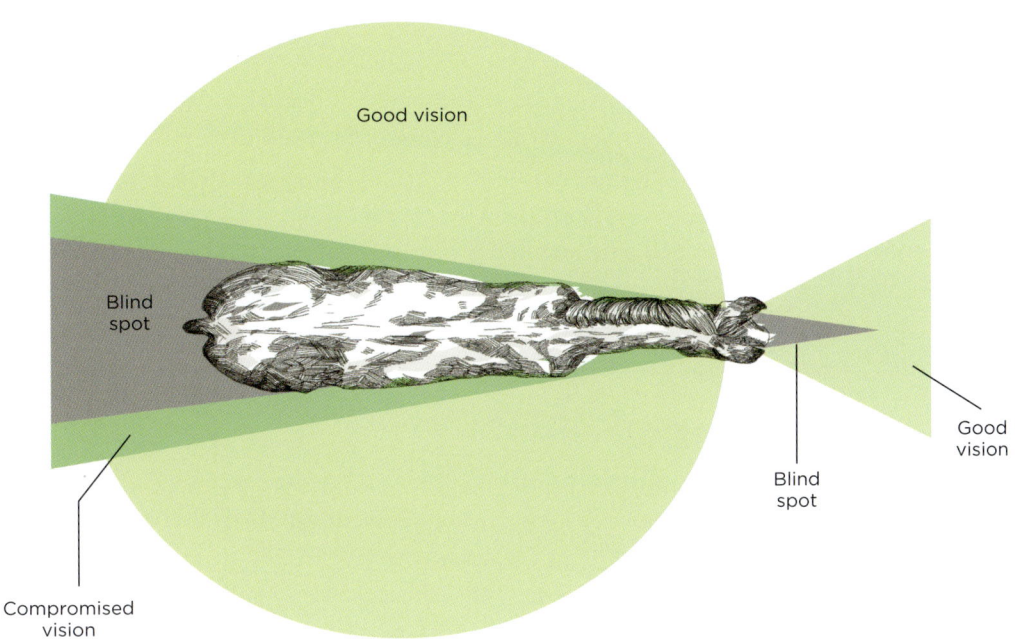

which allows them to differentiate between different flavours, as well as identify and avoid eating anything harmful. If something has an unpleasant taste (including most poisonous plants), the brain sends an impulse to the muscles in the mouth and tongue which makes the horse drop the food (although some horses will eat poisonous plants if they are starving or develop a taste for them). This action is critical for survival, as horses can't throw up to purge harmful food from their bodies once it has been swallowed.

Circulatory system

The circulatory system distributes blood to the horse's cells, providing them with the vital nutrients, oxygen and water needed to survive. It also regulates the horse's body temperature, carries hormones from the endocrine glands, distributes white blood cells to fight infections, promotes healing and prevents blood loss during injury by clotting.

The horse's heart pumps the blood around the body, circulating it through a network of veins and arteries. This pumping action is known as the heartbeat and can be heard if you place a stethoscope behind your horse's left elbow.

EQUINE HEARTBEAT

The heartbeat should be between 35 and 45 beats per minute when the horse is resting, and can increase to 200 beats per minute during a strenuous or fast-paced workout.

The horse's areas of vision and blind spots.

Lymphatic system

The horse's lymphatic system is a network of organs, tissues and blood vessels that move lymph fluid (which contains white blood cells, fat and serum) throughout the body. It supports the circulatory system, helping to fight infection and provide natural immunity, supplies cells with nutrients, absorbs fat from the digestive tract, removes dead or damaged cells, and prevents fluid accumulating (known as oedema) in the horse's body. If the lymphatic system becomes damaged, blocked or inflamed (often through bacterial infection), this can lead to a very painful condition known as lymphangitis, which causes the horse's tissues to swell rapidly.

Respiratory system

The horse's respiratory system carries oxygen, which is breathed in through the nostrils, to the blood. It is also responsible for removing carbon dioxide from the blood, helps to regulate the horse's temperature (by the horse breathing in cold air and breathing out warm air), and also aids the horse's sense of smell, as well as its ability to communicate vocally through snorting, neighing, nickering and squealing. A horse with a defect in the laryngeal nerve or arytenoid cartilage (within the larynx) is known as a roarer; the airway will be compromised, affecting the horse's ability to inhale oxygen during exercise, and a 'roaring' sound may be evident.

Digestive system

The horse's digestive system allows it to digest food and turn it into valuable nutrients and energy. This supports the growth and development of muscle, replaces damaged cells, provides energy for movement, allows the horse to regulate its body temperature and helps it maintain an ideal body condition (see page 101). It is made up of over 30 metres of tubing, in a network of twist and turns, which starts at the mouth and ends at the rectum.

MOUTH/TEETH: Digestion starts in the mouth, where food is taken in, chewed, mixed with saliva and then swallowed. Salivary glands in the mouth and the top of the throat are stimulated by the act of chewing, releasing between 30 to 40 litres of saliva each day. The saliva contains bicarbonate, an essential buffer against the acid that is present in the horse's stomach. To ensure that your horse is able to graze and chew pain-free, good dental health (see pages 111–13) is essential.

STOMACH: A horse's stomach is relatively small in comparison to that of other animals, holding about 8 to 15 litres of food and water at any one time, and works best when it is only about three-quarters full. As a result, horses should not eat large portions of food at one time; instead, they are built to eat small but frequent portions of food for up to 16 to 18 hours throughout the day. Typically, food passes through the stomach in about 12 minutes, which allows horses to graze continuously.

With a natural high-roughage diet, a steady flow of acid is required to digest the chewed food, so a horse's stomach produces acid 24 hours a day. This is normally buffered by both feed and saliva that mixes with the gastric secretions; fibre floats to the top of the horse's stomach, forming a protective layer that helps prevent acid from splashing against the lining of the upper stomach. If a horse is left for longer than five hours without access to roughage, however, there is nothing to buffer the acid, which can result in very painful gastric ulcers (see pages 86–87).

SMALL INTESTINE: Enzymes are released from the pancreas and bile flows from the liver continuously to aid in the digestion of carbohydrate, protein and fat. Once digested, these nutrient particles are absorbed through the wall of the small intestine, as are fat-soluble vitamins and some minerals.

HIND GUT (CAECUM, LARGE COLON, SMALL COLON AND RECTUM): The hind gut is where fermentation of the feed takes place. After passing through the small intestine, the feed enters the caecum, a pouch which holds about 30 litres of feed. Here millions of microbes produce the enzymes needed to ferment the fibre. After about seven hours it is released into the large colon, where it stays for between two and three days while the fermentation and absorption process continues. Excess moisture from the remaining, indigestible feed is then absorbed by the small colon and returned to the body, and the residue forms faecal balls which leave the body as manure through the rectum.

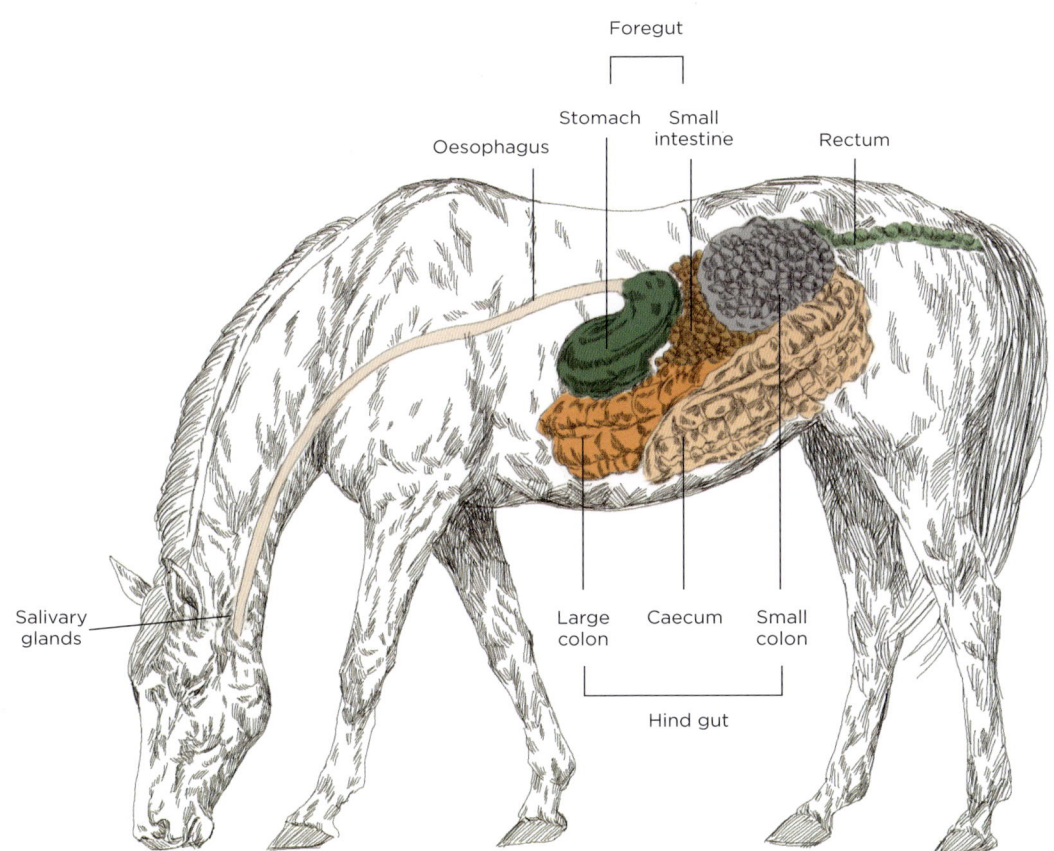

The digestive system of the horse.

Urinary system

The urinary system consists of two kidneys, the bladder and the urethra, and is responsible for expelling excess water from the horse's body as urine, as well as maintaining the correct balance of water and electrolytes, eliminating toxins, maintaining the acid–base status of the blood and regulating blood pressure.

> About 65% of the horse's body is made up of water, so drinking enough water is vital for its internal systems to function correctly. The includes the digestive tract, as dehydration can lead to impaction colic (see page 131).

DEVELOPMENT OF THE EQUINE SKELETON

Knowledge about the development of the equine skeleton is essential, and something that every rider and owner should be aware of to ensure the welfare and longevity of their horse.

A horse's skeleton does not reach physical maturity until about 7 years of age. Even though foals can be up and moving within 20 minutes of birth, a newborn will only have 17% of its mature bone content, and be only about 10% of its eventual body weight. As the horse grows, the growth plates fuse from the hoof up, with the bones in the lower legs maturing first, and the spine last (see diagram, page 44).

Contrary to popular belief, all horses, regardless of breed, mature at a similar rate; no horse or pony will reach skeletal maturity until it is at least 6 years for females, or 6½ years for males. While the breed doesn't have much influence on a horse's growth rate, the size of the horse can — the taller the horse is, and the longer its neck, the later these fusions can occur, with some horses not reaching full maturity until they are 7 or 8 years of age.

Even if a young horse looks like it is mature, its bones are still growing and fusing — which means that excessive ridden work can strain the horse, especially in the neck, wither and back areas. Because horses can appear visually mature before their final growth plates have fused, it is unfortunately common for young horses to be overworked at too early an age, often affecting their long-term soundness. Just because this is common, it doesn't make it right. Good owners will take note of their horse's level of maturity and design a workload, and regular spelling (resting) times, to ensure its ongoing welfare; something that's even more important to consider if the horse is to be worked at speed, on a contact (see page 291), jumped or ridden by a heavy rider (see pages 28–29).

Skeletal issues can also arise through over- or under-feeding young horses. This can cause either rapid or stunted bone growth and increase the risk of contracted tendons, bone chips and angular limb deformities. Growing up, horses should be allowed to move freely in paddocks as their bone density can be compromised if their movement is restricted.

Kelly's first time sitting astride Dauntless, her 4-year-old warmblood.

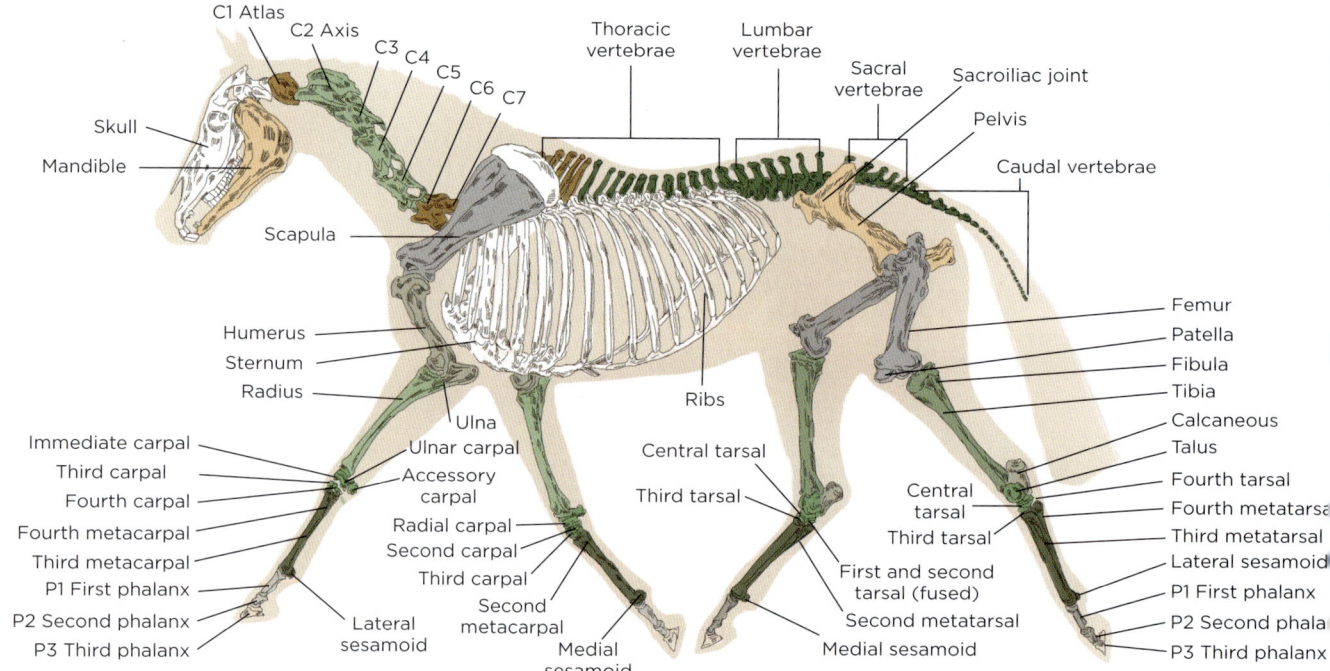

- 🟤 Last ones to fuse
- 🟢 6 years
- 🟡 5 years
- ⚪ 4 years
- ⚫ 3½ years
- 🟢 3 years
- 🟢 2 years
- 🟢 1 year
- ⚪ 6 months
- ⚪ Birth

The musculo-skeletal system of the horse with colour coding to show the order and age that each bone fuses.

OUR PHYSICAL EXPECTATIONS FOR YOUNG HORSES UNDER SADDLE

When our horses are 3 or 4 years old, we begin the backing stage (this includes laying across their backs, and riding them bareback at the walk and trot), which involves one to two weeks of light work before they are turned out to continue growing. Then, as rising 4- or 5-year-olds, they'll be started under saddle and have about six weeks of light work, until they have a basic understanding of body control and are able to confidently walk, trot and canter around the farm.

As 4- or 5-year-olds, they will return to work to learn the basics of both flatwork and jumping. Depending on the horse, they'll be in light work for anywhere from two to six months throughout the year, and spend the rest of the time turned out to continue growing.

At 5 to 6 years of age, their workload will increase to a partial competition season (generally being ridden for four to six months of the year and competing at a limited number of events, depending on their development). It's not until they are 7 years old that we would expect them to campaign for an entire season, and only if they have a strong topline (see pages 275–77) to support the sacroiliac (which fuses from 5 to 7 years of age). Stability of this joint is crucial for the horse to adequately carry the weight of the rider; if the supporting ligaments are not properly strengthened, its long-term longevity can be compromised.

CONFORMATION

Conformation describes a horse's overall shape and bone structure. While conformation may vary from breed to breed, a horse of good conformation will be well proportioned and balanced, with straight legs, a good neck set and correct joint angles. Correct conformation minimises the stresses placed on the body, while enhancing the horse's athletic performance and competition longevity. Meanwhile, horses with poor conformation are at higher risk of injury and lameness due to added stress on their bones, joints and the supporting soft tissues.

While some conformation faults are merely unsightly and may not affect a horse's ridden career, others can significantly affect its ability to perform or may require careful management.

Therefore, when buying a horse, it is important to consider your expectations for it. Do you want a pleasure horse, a Pony Club mount, or a top-level eventer or showjumper? If you aren't used to identifying conformation faults, or which ones might hinder the expectations you have for your next horse, it may be helpful to have an experienced trainer look at the horse with you or have it vet-checked.

When assessing a horse's conformation, it should be viewed from all angles while it is standing still, and also at the walk and the trot.

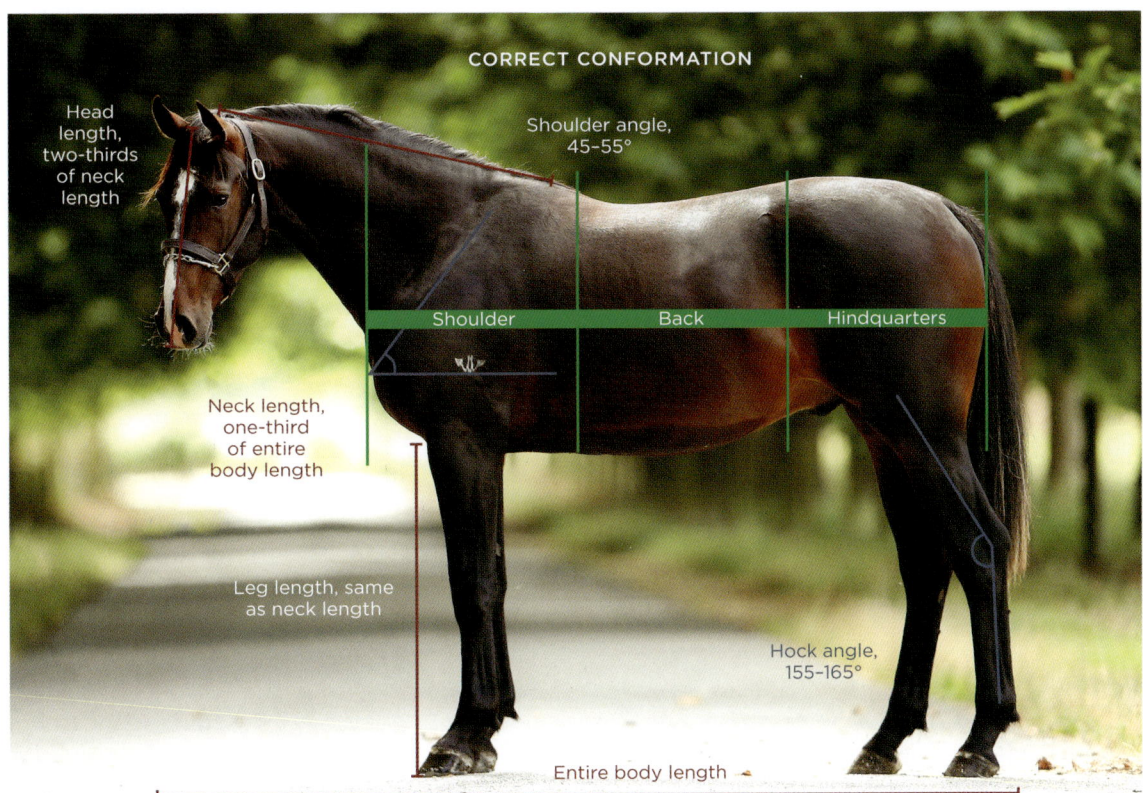

Head

A well-conformed horse will have a head that is approximately two-thirds of the length of its neck, with wide-set eyes, large nostrils, and the upper and lower jaws equal in length so that the horse's front teeth meet evenly. From the side, most horses have a straight profile; others, particularly heavier breeds, show a convex profile (Roman nose), and some have a concave profile (dished face).

Faults

PARROT OR MONKEY MOUTH: If a horse's front teeth don't meet evenly, this prevents it from chewing correctly and the teeth from wearing evenly. A horse with a shorter lower jaw will have an overbite (known as a *parrot mouth*), while those with a shorter upper jaw will have an underbite or *monkey mouth*. The issues caused by either of these faults will require regular, lifelong dental care (see pages 111–13) and good feeding management.

Neck

A horse's neck should be slightly arched from poll to withers, and one-third of the length of its overall body.

Faults

EWE NECK (UPSIDE-DOWN NECK): A concave neck that has more muscling on the underside of the neck than on the top; there may also be a depression just in front of the withers. Some horses are born with a ewe neck, while others may develop one from an injury or incorrect riding (it is often coupled with a hollow back); in these instances good body work, conditioning and training — to encourage the neck to stretch long and low — may correct it.

Shoulders

SHOULDER SLOPE: When a horse is standing square, its shoulders should have a slope of 45 to 55 degrees, measured from the point of the withers to the point of the shoulder (see the blue lines on the Correct Conformation diagram on page 45). A shoulder slope of 45 degrees is often sought after for dressage; horses with a slope of 50 degrees are generally good all-rounders; and a slope of 55 degrees is preferred for jumping.

Faults

UPRIGHT SHOULDERS: A shoulder slope of 60 degrees or more increases the stress-loading on the forelimbs (which can lead to unsoundness) and creates a shorter, choppy stride. These horses are unlikely to cope with high-performance requirements.

OVER-SLOPING SHOULDERS (ALSO KNOWN AS LAID-BACK SHOULDERS): Horses with excessively sloping shoulders (40 degrees or less) may work 'on the forehand', with the majority of its weight bearing down on the shoulders and front legs. This can compromise the horse's performance ability and long-term longevity, as well as make it more difficult to fit a saddle to the horse (see pages 210–11).

Top left: Roman nose. CHRISTIANE SLAWIK

Top right: Dished face. CHRISTIANE SLAWIK

Bottom: Straight profile.

Forelegs

When assessing a horse's forelegs from the front, they should be parallel and form a straight line from the point of the shoulder, down the centre of the horse's forearm, knee, cannon bone, fetlock, pastern and hoof.

From the side, the forelegs should form a straight line from just in front of the withers, down the centre of the knee and fetlock, to the back of the heel.

Any deviations from these lines can cause stress on the horse's bones, tendons, ligaments and muscles, which can increase the risk of lameness or injury.

> **CORRECTIVE TRIMMING FOR FOALS**
>
> If you have a foal, it is important to assess leg conformation within a few weeks of birth so that you can get any corrective work done as early as possible. If a foal is born with incorrect leg conformation, corrective hoof trimming by a qualified farrier, starting as early as 2 to 4 weeks of age and continued every 4 to 6 weeks, can improve or correct the problem. However, the window for corrective trimming is limited — once the growth plates in the legs fuse, the conformation fault will become permanent (see the bone fusion chart on page 44).
>
> Any injury to the foal which causes it to load weight unevenly on one hoof can also alter the growth plates; if this is not corrected early, the foal may develop permanent conformation faults.

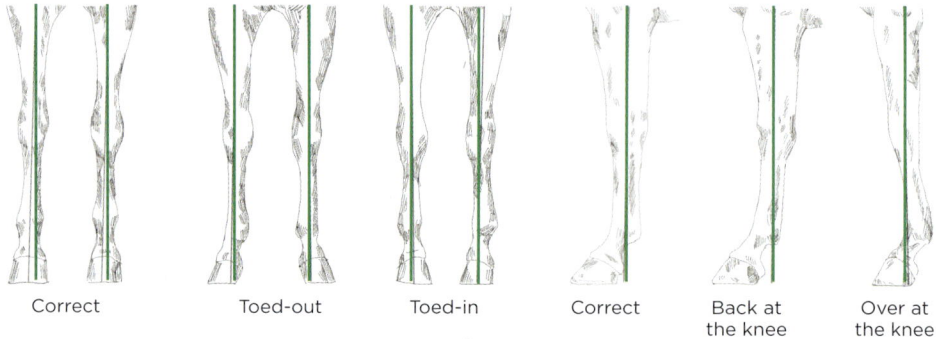

Correct   Toed-out   Toed-in   Correct   Back at the knee   Over at the knee

Faults

TOED-IN OR TOED-OUT: A horse that toes in (also known as pigeon-toed) will have the front hooves angled inward, while a toed-out horse will have the hooves angled outward. The deviation can begin at the shoulder, knee or fetlock and is often present at birth, although it can develop from poor hoof care or an injury that causes the horse to load weight unevenly on its joints. When in motion, a horse that toes in will *paddle* (with the front legs following an outward arc that puts strain on the outside wall of the hoof), while toed-out horses will *plait* (with the front legs following an inward arc that puts strain on the inside wall of the hoof and can risk injury to the horse's legs if they brush each other).

BASE WIDE OR NARROW: A horse that is base narrow stands with its forelegs close together, with the distance between the hooves less than that at the shoulders, while a horse that is base wide stands with its forelegs far apart, with the distance between the hooves greater than at the shoulders. Horses with these faults may have overdeveloped (base narrow) or underdeveloped (base wide) pectoral muscles, which can cause uneven loading on their joints and result in lameness, osteoarthritis or even ringbone (progressive arthritic changes of the pastern or coffin bone, causing new bone growths).

OVER OR BACK AT THE KNEES: Viewed from the side, if a horse's knees are in front of the correct line then they are considered over at the knee, while those behind this line are back at the knee. These deviations are usually present at birth, or can be created by poor hoof care or injury before the knee growth plates have fused. Corrective farrier care is essential to minimise the side effects of these faults, which include excessive strain on the flexor tendons, suspensory ligament and inferior check ligament, as well as stumbling, bone chips and bowed tendons (if a horse is *back at the knee*), or damage to the sesamoid bone, limbs that shake or vibrate, or knees that buckle or collapse (if a horse is *over at the knee*).

OFFSET KNEES: If there is an outward rotation of the knee, this may lead to strain of the bones and ligaments on the medial (inner) part of the knee, eventually causing bone chips or osteoarthritis. Horses with the opposite problem, an inward rotation of the knees, may also have issues.

Hind legs

When assessing a horse's hind legs from behind, they should be parallel and form a straight line from the centre of the horse's buttock, slightly to the inside of the hock and to the centre of the fetlock and hoof.

From the side, the hock should be level with the chestnuts on the front legs (slightly higher than the knee), and the hind legs should form a straight line from the point of the buttocks, to the hock and down the back of the cannon bone to the fetlock. Any deviations from these lines can cause stress on the horse's bones, tendons, ligaments and muscles, which can result in lameness or injury. Soundness issues are less common in the hind legs, however, as they carry only 40% of the horse's body weight. As with the forelegs, many hind-leg faults can be improved or completely resolved with corrective trimming and body realignment.

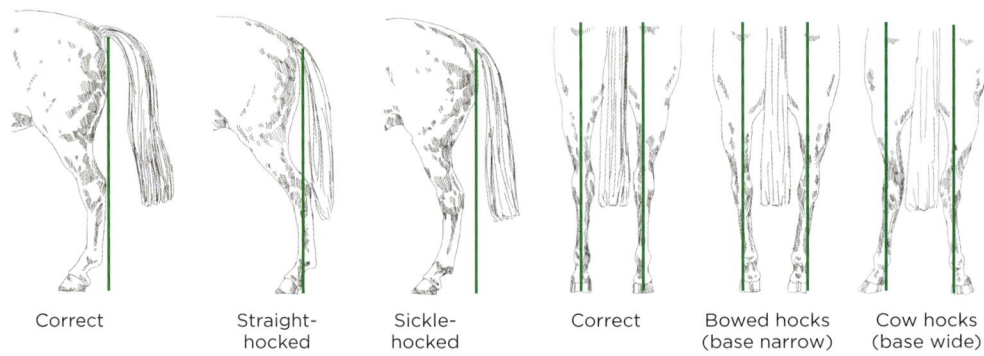

| Correct | Straight-hocked | Sickle-hocked | Correct | Bowed hocks (base narrow) | Cow hocks (base wide) |

Faults

STRAIGHT- OR SICKLE-HOCKED: When assessing a horse from the side, the hind legs should have an angle of 155 to 165 degrees in the hock joint (the angle between the tibia and the cannon bone, at the front of the joint — see the red lines on the Correct Conformation diagram on page 45). A horse with straight hocks (also known as post-legged) will have a larger angle (more than 165 degrees), which can predispose them to suspensory ligament injuries, osteoarthritis, problems with the patella within the stifle joint, and hoof issues related to excessive concussion (impact with the ground). A sickle-hocked horse will have a smaller angle (less than 155 degrees), which can cause osteoarthritis, hock joint issues and curbs (soft-tissue injuries that cause swelling in the tarsal area).

BOWED HOCKS (BASE NARROW) OR COW HOCKS (BASE WIDE): A horse with bowed hocks will stand with its hind legs close, with the distance between the hooves less than that at the hocks. A cow-hocked horse will stand with its hindlegs wide, with the distance between the hooves greater than at the hocks. These faults cause excess strain on the hip, hock and stifle joints and may cause bone spavin, bog spavin, thoroughpin or lameness.

Hooves

There is no truer saying than 'no foot, no horse'. Correct skeletal alignment begins in the hoof, and any imbalances here will be reflected further up the body and in the horse's performance. A good understanding of hoof balance is therefore essential for every owner, to ensure their horse's performance and longevity.

When viewing the horse's hoof from the side, the hoof and pastern should be in alignment (hoof pastern axis) with the hoof wall parallel to the bones. The front hooves should have an angle of 45 to 50 degrees to the ground, with the hind hooves a little more upright, at about 50 to 55 degrees.

 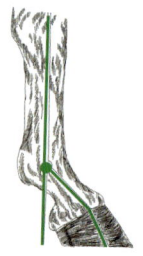 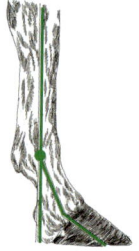

| Correct Pastern axis | Broken-forward Pastern axis | Broken-back Pastern axis |

Opposite page: Back at the knee conformation fault.

Faults

BROKEN-FORWARD PASTERN AXIS (ALSO KNOWN AS A CLUB OR BOXY HOOF): An abnormally upright hoof, with an angle of 60 degrees or more, is known as a club or boxy foot. It is usually seen in the forelegs (often in just one hoof) and can cause contracted heels, suspensory ligament injuries, coffin joint inflammation and rotation, increased heel pressure due to the toe landing first, and stress at the base of the horse's neck and shoulder blades. A club foot can be present at birth or may develop if a foal has long legs or a short neck which causes it to offset its front legs to graze, or after an injury which prevents a horse from bearing weight evenly, causing the hoof to remodel. Early intervention with corrective trimming or shoeing can return some hooves to a normal angle.

BROKEN-BACK PASTERN AXIS: An abnormally long hoof, with a more acute (smaller) angle than the pastern, can be present at birth or develop from poor hoof management if the toes are allowed to grow too long. It causes an increased strain on the coffin joint, deep digital flexor tendons and navicular bone. Good farrier care, with the toes being shortened to return the hooves to 50 to 55 degrees, is essential to reduce navicular changes, heel pain, quarter and heel cracks, and coffin joint inflammation.

Body

The body should be balanced and correctly proportioned. In most breeds, a horse with good conformation can be visually divided into thirds (see the green lines on the Correct Conformation diagram on page 45). It should have equal distances for the shoulder (measured from the front of the chest to the middle of the withers), back (measured from the highest point of the withers to the point of the hip) and hindquarters (measured from the point of the horse's hip to the point of the buttock).

Faults

LONG OR SHORT BACK: A horse's back is considered long if it is greater than one-third of the horse's body length. A long back will need correct fitness and muscle conditioning to strengthen it and minimise the risk of injury, especially in top-level competition. A short-backed horse (with a back less than one-third of its body length) may be prone to forging (overreaching with the hind hooves) and will also need a saddle that does not extend past its 18th rib (see page 210).

SWAY OR ROACH BACK: In a roach back the horse's spine curves upwards in the loin area, while a horse with a sway back will dip excessively where the saddle fits. These issues may be present at birth, develop from an injury, or result from being overworked at a young age. Sway back can develop in horses that are ridden too early, with a poorly fitting saddle, or by heavy riders — pain will cause the horse's back to drop and the ligaments supporting the spinal column to sag, which can increase the risk of kissing spine (see page 137). Once mature, some horses with these faults can go on to perform at the top level, but it is essential that their topline is strengthened and they are ridden in a correctly fitting saddle.

Top: Roached back conformation fault.

Bottom: Ewe neck conformation fault.

EQUINE BODY LANGUAGE

Horses communicate using subtle changes in their body language and movement, which provide important clues to what they are thinking and feeling, allowing you to anticipate what they are about to do and redirect their behaviour if needed, before they react to something. This is achieved by reading your horse's signs of tension, then responding accordingly, before these escalate into a flight, fight, freeze or fawn response. Careful observation is needed, as not all horses communicate the same way — some are very expressive, while others will be staunch or stoic, barely changing their expression when stressed.

To be a successful horse rider you need to understand the horse's unique forms of non-verbal communication. It will take time and attention, but the more time you spend observing your horse, the quicker your horsemanship skills will improve.

SIGNS OF TENSION
- Ears back or swivelling
- Head lowered, raised or snaking
- Forelegs braced, pawing, stomping or striking
- Hind legs raised or kicking
- Lip pinched, teeth clacking or biting
- Nostrils flared or pinched
- Eyes wide, pinched, tense, rapidly darting, or the white of the eye showing
- Clamped tail or rapid swishing
- Body muscles tense
- Trembling
- Swinging hindquarters
- Snorting
- Charging
- Defecating in stud piles
- Sweating

SIGNS OF RELAXATION
- Ears forward or softly turned to the side
- Head lowered in rest
- Hind legs resting
- Lip drooping, chewing or licking
- Laying down or rolling
- Yawning
- Slow blinking
- Exhaling of breath

Head carriage

HEAD LOWERED A lowered head is often a sign that a horse is relaxed or sleeping. This is often accompanied by ears turned softly to the side and resting a back leg. If a lowered head is accompanied by signs of tension, however, it can mean that the horse is overwhelmed by too much stimulus and is trying to hide.

HEAD RAISED If accompanied by other signs of tension, a raised head may indicate the horse has identified something it perceives as dangerous. In this instance it is unlikely the horse will be paying attention to you (unless you are the cause of its distress) and will likely revert to its survival instincts to try to escape the threat. If a horse has a high head carriage under saddle this can be a sign of pain, especially if the horse hollows its back, pins its ears back or swishes its tail.

SNAKING If a horse lowers its head slightly and waves it from side to side while its ears are back or its teeth are bared, it is a threatening act and is often followed by the horse charging at you. In the wild, this behaviour is often used by stallions and mares when they are fighting, or trying to herd an uncooperative horse.

Forelegs

FORELEGS BRACED A horse may spread its front legs a little and rock back when it is scared; this is often followed by a spook or bolt. Injuries, health issues (including laminitis, see page 119) or conformation faults can also cause a horse to stand with braced legs.

PAWING A horse may paw (an arching action with the foreleg) when it's bored or impatient, stressed or confused. Pawing to indicate anger is less common (usually accompanied by ears back), but it is a signal you need to heed well — especially in stallions, as it can be followed by a charge or attack.

STOMPING If your horse raises and lowers its leg forcefully in place, then it is most likely irritated. Usually this will be by something minor like a fly, but stomping can also be a sign of frustration or confusion and can quickly escalate to other signs of tension.

STRIKING Horses can use a forceful, forward kick with their front legs as a defensive or aggressive action. This can be accompanied by a rear, which is dangerous, as a strike can be fatal. Fortunately, horses rarely strike without showing subtler warnings first, such as stomping or pawing, a raised head or pinned-back ears.

RUBBING A FORELEG During training sessions, if a horse rubs its head against a foreleg this can indicate that it's processing information or thinking. It can also just be scratching itself, so also look for other accompanying signs of relaxation like licking lips, chewing, slow blinking or yawning.

Hind legs

COCKED When a horse has a back leg cocked, the toe of the hoof will be in contact with the ground and the hip will be dropped. If the horse's head is also lowered or its ears are hanging to the side, this means that the horse is relaxed or resting.

RAISED If your horse is lifting its hind leg off the ground, it may be trying to dislodge a fly; but if accompanied by other signs of tension, it may mean that the horse is about to kick.

Ears

EARS FORWARD If its ears are forward the horse is alert, paying attention or interested in what is in front of it, or if accompanied by other signs of tension it may mean the horse is worried about something in front of it.

EARS TURNED TO THE SIDE A horse with one ear cocked is likely to be paying attention to something on the side of it; if accompanied by other signs of tension, the horse may spook away from the perceived threat.

EARS BACK If the ears are facing backwards but aren't pinned back, the horse may be listening to, or focusing on, something behind it. But if the ears are pinned back and combined with other signs of tension, like a swishing tail or a hard glint to the eye, the horse may be worried about something behind it.

EARS SWIVELLING When a horse's ears are flicking backwards and forwards it indicates that the horse is highly anxious or alert. It may be overwhelmed by a situation or be attempting to detect the source of a frightening sound or smell.

Muzzle and jaw

DROOPING LIP When a horse's lower lip is drooping and it's standing quietly, the horse is usually relaxed or even sleeping. You shouldn't approach or try to touch a horse when it's sleeping, as it may be easily startled and could react by whirling away from you, spooking or striking out. Instead, talk to the horse or make some noise to gain its attention, and don't approach the horse until it has acknowledged you.

CHEWING When a horse makes chewing motions during training sessions, but isn't eating, this is a good sign — it indicates that the horse is relaxed and thinking, and in a good frame of mind to learn and retain information.

CLACKING TEETH Young horses, especially foals, will sometimes stretch out their neck, curl their lip and click their teeth together when they meet other horses. This is a sign of vulnerability and submission.

YAWNING Yawning can be a positive sign that your horse is starting to positively work through a stressful or confusing situation. It can also be a sign of boredom or tiredness, but with a wild or scared horse it is more likely an indicator that your horse was tense during the training session and is starting to come to a positive place of understanding.

TEETH BARED If your horse swipes its mouth at you, there is a good chance it is scared or angry; this can often be followed by a bite.

BITING If a horse has to resort to biting, it is usually feeling unsafe and trying to protect

---

1. Snaking, ears back and eyes tense.
2. Cocked ear, head raised, eyes tense and nostrils pinched.
3. Flehmen.
4. Whites of eyes showing.
5. Sweating, head raised.
6. Clacking, ear cocked.
7. Flared nostrils, ears pricked.
8. Head raised, ears back, wrinkled nostrils, pursed lips and whites of eyes showing.

itself. Biting is normally a last resort, likely occurring only if you have failed to heed earlier signs of tension, if food is involved, if other horses are nearby or if it is in pain.

LICKING LIPS If your horse licks its lips during training, this usually means that it is recovering from a period of extreme stress, tension or pain and returning to a state of relaxation. This happens because the horse's sympathetic nervous system goes into survival mode when it experiences pain or fear, causing salivation to cease and the mouth and lips to go dry.

FLEHMEN When a horse smells something it is unsure of, it may raise its head, curl its upper lip and breathe in deeply. This behaviour is particularly common with stallions when they come across a mare in heat.

FLARED NOSTRILS Flaring or quivering nostrils are an indication that a horse is nervous or stressed. It is often one of the first signs of tension and can quickly escalate to something more serious if you aren't careful.

PINCHED MUZZLE (INCLUDING NOSTRILS OR LIPS) This is one of the subtler signs of tension and can easily be missed. It is often the first indication that your horse is becoming overwhelmed or stressed. If you notice the horse's muzzle pinching it's important to give it more space, remove it from the stressful situation, or help it work through its anxiety so that it doesn't feel the need to resort to more forceful methods of communication.

Eyes

TENSE EYES When the muscles around a horse's eyes tighten it is the most subtle sign of stress, fear or pain.

RAPID DARTING A horse's eyes flicking from side to side is a sign that it's scared and looking for a way to escape. If the horse has room to flee, it will likely take flight; but if it's in a confined space and can't, then it may resort to a fight or freeze response (see page 60).

WHITES OF THE EYES SHOWING This usually means that the horse is anxious or scared. However, some horses naturally have more white showing around the eye, so it's important to know what is normal for your horse.

SLOW BLINKING During training sessions, slow blinking indicates that a horse is processing information or thinking.

EYE ROLLING Eye rolling often accompanies yawning and is normally a positive sign that your horse is starting to work through a stressful or confusing situation.

Body

TENSION When your horse's muscles are tight and its movements are stiff, this is usually a sign of pain or stress. If it's unlikely that fear is the problem, it's worth having your horse checked for skeletal pain, ulcers, lameness or grass-affected issues.

TREMBLING Shaking is normally caused by prolonged periods of being wet or cold. During training sessions, horses may also tremble if they are exposed to something scary or if they have suffered past abuse; these horses need a lot of time, patience and empathy to help them work through their fear, and you may require the expertise of a professional trainer to help gain their trust.

TOUCHING YOU If a horse reaches forward to initiate contact with its muzzle it may be trying to smell you, or it could be showing curiosity or seeking reassurance.

SWINGING HINDQUARTERS If your horse swings its rump towards you, or from side to side, it can mean that it's feeling threatened and may be a prelude to a kick. A mare in heat may also swing her hindquarters if there is a stallion around, although this is normally accompanied by a raised tail.

HEAD AND NECK ARCHED OR OUTSTRETCHED This can often be a sign that your horse wants to investigate something but is scared to approach it, or is excited. Stallions will also arch their neck and prance (known as posturing) to indicate interest in a mare or as a display of dominance when meeting another stallion.

SWEATING Sweating during training sessions can be a sign of tension, especially if combined with trembling. If your horse breaks out in a sudden sweat, immediately reduce the pressure your horse is under and restore relaxation. Horses can also sweat in extreme temperatures, or if ridden for too long without the appropriate fitness.

LYING DOWN OR ROLLING If your horse lies down or rolls in your presence, it is usually a sign that it feels safe. If signs of tension are present, however, and the horse lies down or tries to roll several times in short succession, it may be showing early signs of colic (see page 131).

PACING A horse that paces back and forward is often displaying stress or fear — which can be caused by pain, boredom or separation anxiety — especially when combined with other signs of tension like tail swishing or sweating.

STUD PILES Stallions will often mark their territory by making manure piles and repeatedly urinating or defecating on them. Proceed with caution if a stallion marks his manure during a training session as this can be a threatening behaviour, especially if combined with other signs of tension.

Vocalising

NEIGH/WHINNY Commonly used to acknowledge the presence of a horse or person.

NICKER This soft, throaty sound is often used by a horse at feed time, or by mares encouraging their foals.

SQUEALS Horses often squeal when meeting another horse, especially stallions. This normally follows sniffing noses and can be sometimes followed by a strike.

SNORT Horses often flare their nostrils and snort as an alarm when they sense a perceived threat. A more rolling, repetitive sound may also be used when horses are very excited or worried.

SIGH Deep fluttery breaths are generally a sign of relaxation or enjoyment. Sometimes a sigh can also communicate boredom, especially if a training session has gone on too long or is repetitive.

GROAN/GRUNT A long, low groan can often be a sign of protest if a horse doesn't want to do something, or can be used to communicate pain or discomfort.

INSTINCTIVE EQUINE BEHAVIOUR: FLIGHT, FIGHT, FREEZE, FAWN

When horses are stressed or scared they respond instinctively to protect themselves — some flee from perceived danger, while others will become aggressive, try to hide or resort to people-pleasing behaviour. While all horses will use flight, fight, freeze or fawn at varying times, most have a dominant instinct and it can be helpful to know which one your horse will default to in a stressful situation.

Flight

Horses are first and foremost a flight animal; they would much rather flee from perceived danger than face it.

Fight

Most horses will only resort to showing aggression if they are under too much pressure and don't have room to take flight. If your horse is confined in a small yard and cannot flee, on a short lead or tied up, or being ridden (especially with a big bit or by a rider with hard hands), it may be forced to bite, kick, rear, buck or exhibit other unwanted and potentially dangerous fight-based behaviours. Horses can also resort to a fight response if they are treated badly or made to work through pain.

There is normally a genuine reason why horses show aggression, so they need to be given the benefit of the doubt. Provide them with a training environment where they can feel safe and have pain-related issues (see page 167) resolved before asking them to work through any behavioural issues.

Freeze

Horses can become shut down and introverted, which can be easily misinterpreted as the horse being quiet, lazy, stubborn or unwilling. They may lower their head, avoid eye contact, hold their breath, hide behind other horses or stand motionless. Horses will usually only freeze if their attempts to take flight, or fight, haven't worked or if they are confused or in pain. Horses in a freeze response need a lot of time and patience to build trust in their handler or rider. They also need to be trained empathetically and given the tools needed to work through their fears so they don't disassociate in times of stress.

Fawn

Horses can resort to people-pleasing and conflict-avoidance behaviours as a coping mechanism if they feel they can't flee or fight their way out of a stressful situation. By fawning, the horse will go along with the demands of the trainer (or another horse), compromising their own happiness to avoid excessive pressure or punishment. *Note:* It is not the same as learned helplessness, in which a horse has given up entirely.

Top: A band of wild Brumbies take flight in the Australian desert.

Bottom: A Mustang mare fights off a young bachelor stallion.

SECTION 2

Caring for your Horse or Pony

One of the most important aspects of owning a horse is understanding how to care for it. This section looks at the special requirements horses need to live a happy and healthy life, including what to feed them, the importance of safe fencing, shelter and paddock companions, and how to maintain your horse's body condition and hoof health.

PADDOCKING YOUR HORSE

In the wild, horses roam freely on large expanses of grasslands, in small bands ranging in size from about two to twenty horses. In domestication, however, the amount of land that horses have access to is often restricted, which limits not only their movement but also their ability to browse for forage and seek out the companionship of other horses. With domesticated horses, it is your responsibility as their human guardian to create an environment that meets their mental, emotional and physical well-being needs.

Ideally, horses should be kept in paddocks large enough to allow them to exercise themselves and with other horses for company. As horses can be prone to paddock injuries and illnesses from poor fencing, poisonous plants and insufficient shelter, it's important to make sure that your grazing, fencing and yarding is safe and suitable for them. Not only will good paddock maintenance ensure the health of your horse, but it will also minimise expensive vet bills.

How much land does my horse need?

In general, 2 acres (0.8 hectares) of grazing land per horse should be sufficient, although this can vary according to climatic conditions, fertiliser history and geographical area. In most seasons, this acreage size should be adequate for a horse at pasture, although additional roughage may be needed during the winter months or in times of drought.

What paddock size is ideal for my horse?

Time spent roaming in a large paddock is important for your horse's emotional and mental state, as well as its physical well-being (as the digestive system, hooves and joints all benefit from movement).

Here are some additional things to consider when paddocking your horse.
- Both young and retired horses need a larger paddock so that they can self-exercise, as do ridden horses when they are turned out.

> Our bands of brood mares and young stock are kept in groups of three to eight horses, in paddocks varying in size from 2 to 10 acres (0.8 to 4 hectares), while our ridden horses generally live in groups of two to five horses, in paddocks ranging in size from half an acre to 3 acres (0.2 to 1.2 hectares).

- If needed, you can use smaller, individual paddocks to separate stallions, dominant or aggressive horses, or horses recovering from injuries, to minimise the risk of injury or further injury. These paddocks should be roomy enough for the horse to self-exercise, with each horse having at least two paddocks to rotate between so the paddocks can be rested to manage the grass growth and worm burden.
- In the winter months, to avoid all your paddocks turning to mud, a 'sacrifice

paddock' or a big yard is worth considering. It can also be used in summer to prevent overgrazing, or if a horse needs to be on a restricted diet. If your horse is off pasture permanently, this area should be no smaller than a quarter of an acre (0.1 hectares), with a non-mud surface — but as large as possible so that the horse can still move about freely. If your horse is still able to go out on grass for half a day, a roomy yard may be sufficient.

- On intensively managed properties (with less than 2 acres (0.8 hectares) per horse), paddocks should be mucked out as often as possible but no less than once a week, to minimise the risk of flies and parasites, and yards should be mucked out at least once or twice daily.
- If your paddocks are prone to deep mud (over the horses' hooves), it is crucial to have a clean, dry area where your horse can stand out of the mud. Having gateways, laneways or yards lined with a rocky base covered with a good layer of sand, limestone, pumice, sawdust or woodchip will give your horse a comfortable and dry place to stand and lie down.

Our 2-year-olds enjoying the freedom of a 4-hectare paddock.

- Having a range of different-sized paddocks can be beneficial to manage your horses' nutritional needs, especially in times of lush grass growth. If this isn't possible, then you can use electric fences to strip-graze paddocks into a more practical size.

Does my horse need shelter?

In the wild, horses can seek out shelter whenever necessary; however, a domestic horse doesn't always have that luxury. It is your responsibility to ensure that your horse has protection from the elements, whether it is extreme temperatures, high winds, torrential rain or snow. If your paddock doesn't have natural shelter from trees or hedges and a cover isn't going to be used, then a man-made shelter should be provided to protect the horse. This is especially important for horses that are intensively managed in small paddocks, or exposed to prevailing winds; in extended bad weather, the wind-chill factor can lead to hypothermia or even death. If it is not possible to build a shelter, then the horse needs to be well covered in extreme weather events.

Types of shelter include:

TREES: Mature trees can provide horses with some degree of shelter, providing shade in the summer and some rain and wind protection in wet weather. Deciduous trees, which lose their leaves, will be ineffective in the winter months, however.

HEDGES: Hedges can provide some relief from wind, but they do little to protect a horse from rain or midday sun.

COVERED YARDS OR FREE-ACCESS SHELTERS: These should be at least 4 x 4 metres for ponies, or 5 x 5 metres for horses, but the bigger the better. A roof and solid walls on at least two sides of the shelter will help protect your horse from rain and prevailing winds. Free-access shelters are generally easy to manage as the horse is able to come in and out as they choose, during the heat of the day or in adverse weather.

STABLES: Stables should never be a horse's sole place to live, unless it is injured or ill, as these restrict the horse's ability to move and behave normally. However, they are useful to have in bad weather, or to keep a horse clean the night before a show. If your horse is stabled, we recommend that it is indoors for no longer than 12 hours a day, with the remaining time spent in a paddock so that it can stretch its legs and graze. While stabled, your horse should have constant access to food and water (see page 69), and be mucked out at least twice a day.

Stables should be at least 4 x 4 metres for ponies, or 5 x 5 metres for horses, with a doorway at least 1.1 metres wide. The layout should be open-plan so that the horse can see and interact with other horses, with the walls and lower door at least 1.25 metres high to ensure that the horse cannot jump out. Obviously, these dimensions will depend on the size and temperament of the horse needing to be accommodated. Stables should have good lighting, a non-slip floor with good drainage, be well ventilated but free from draughts (to minimise the chances of horses developing coughs, colds, allergic reactions and other conditions), and have a deep and dry bedding (like sawdust or straw) so that the horse can lie down comfortably. Having

Top: Rugging horses during severe weather events is important if they have no access to natural or man-made shelters.

Bottom: Wild Kaimanawas during a snowstorm.

an emergency plan in place (escape routes, fire extinguisher, etc.) is also a good idea in case of fire or flooding.

> **EQUIPMENT FOR HORSES KEPT IN STABLES OR YARDS**
> - Water bucket, if the horse doesn't have access to an automatic water bowl.
> - Hay net, if the stable or yard doesn't have a hay manger.
> - Feed bucket, if there is no feed manger to place hard feed in.
> - Mucking-out equipment — including a wheelbarrow, muck rake (for mucking out sawdust or shavings), shovel, broom, pitchfork with blunt prongs (if you are mucking out straw bedding) and hose (for topping up water, or washing down aisles and contaminated stables).

Other key components of a stable yard include:

TACK ROOM: This should be a fully enclosed room to keep your saddlery clean and dry, and able to be locked for security reasons. The space needs to be large enough to store your saddlery, horse covers and equine first aid kits, while also allowing room to clean your gear and air out any wet equipment.

FEED ROOM: This can either be a part of your tack room or a separate space, and should be fully enclosed to ensure that mice, rats and birds can't contaminate your horse's feed. There will ideally be room for a range of hard feeds, as well as shelving for supplements and minerals.

HAY SHED: Ideally your hay shed should be built away from the stable block to minimise the risk of fire. The hay bales should be protected from ground moisture and water runoff by being stacked on top of pallets.

MUCK HEAP: The average 500 kilogram horse will produce about 20 kilograms of manure a day, which is about 7.5 tonnes a year (not allowing for any uneaten hay or soiled stable bedding that is also mucked out). If you're going to stable or yard horses, or manage them intensively in small paddocks, it's important to have somewhere to dump the manure every time you muck out. The muck heap should be within easy reach of your stables and yards, but far enough away (and downwind) to minimise smells, irritation from flies and re-infection from worms, as well as in an area that isn't unsightly either for you or for neighbouring properties. Building a solid, three-sided muck heap, about 3 metres by 3 metres, is ideal; this not only creates a condensed space where the manure can decompose quickly, but is also a tidy and effective use of space.

WASH-DOWN BAY: A wash-down bay should be located near your stables, in a position where you have ready access to water, good drainage and runoff, and away from areas where you tack up or ride so that the spray or runoff doesn't interfere with your daily activities. Ideally it will have a concrete base covered with a non-slip rubber floor; a dirt or grass base will quickly turn to mud and be unsuitable for keeping horses clean, while concrete can become slippery and dangerous.

Leading horses in to be stabled.

How much water does my horse need?

To keep their bodies functioning normally, horses should always have unlimited access to fresh, clean water. Horses normally consume between 25 and 50 litres per day; however, they can drink up to three or four times that amount during extreme heat or humidity, after exercise that results in sweating, if their diet includes large quantities of hay, or if they are pregnant or nursing a foal.

Insufficient water will cause your horse to become dehydrated, which can lead to many health issues. Being left longer than 48 hours without water can cause ulcers, impaction colic, kidney failure or even death.

TOP TIPS FOR WATERING YOUR HORSE

- **MAKE SURE YOUR HORSE HAS ENOUGH WATER:** Regularly check your horse's water to make sure there is a constant supply. Even automatic troughs should be checked in case the water supply fails.
- **IN YARDS OR STABLES:** A large bucket that is secure and cannot be knocked over, or an automatic drinking bowl, is ideal for stabled or yarded horses. Check these regularly to ensure that the horse has a sufficient amount of water at all times. By placing the water bucket close to the gate and away from the feeding area, you can keep an eye on its cleanliness and drinkability.
- **ICY CONDITIONS:** During periods of snow or frost, check water troughs at least twice a day to ensure that the water hasn't frozen over.
- **WHILE RIDING:** During long rides, it's important to allow your horse short drinks from troughs, rivers or ponds whenever an opportunity presents itself. This is especially crucial during hot and humid weather. Too much water at once, however, can cause colic, so frequent short sips — for just a few seconds — is the key.
- **AWAY FROM HOME:** At clinics or competitions, it is important to offer your horse a drink frequently to prevent it becoming dehydrated. Communal water troughs can become a source of infection if other horses have viruses or other diseases, so take your own water to shows or use a bucket filled from a hose. If your horse is prone to knocking its water bucket over, tie the bucket up.
- **AFTER HARD WORK:** Do not offer any water after a strenuous workout (such as jumping or galloping) until the horse's heart rate and temperature have returned to normal; this usually takes between 15 and 30 minutes, and even then no more than 10 litres should be offered. After another 20 minutes, a further 10 litres can be offered, and after another 20 minutes free access is allowed. Allowing your horse to drink too much water too soon after strenuous work can lead to colic.
- **KEEP BUCKETS AND TROUGHS CLEAN:** Dirt can make the water unpalatable and may put the horse off drinking, so clean and refill buckets and troughs regularly. Position them away from trees, hay nets and feed buckets, as rotting leaves or feed will also taint the water.

Opposite page: A horse drinks from a natural water source.

This page: Algae growing in a water trough that is in need of cleaning.

HOW TO TEST FOR DEHYDRATION

If a horse is deprived of water, refuses to drink at a horse show, or is worked to the point of extensive sweating in hot or humid weather, it will lose fluid and electrolytes. As a result, it can become dehydrated and fatigued, which will affect its heart, nerves and muscles, as well as its performance and health. In serious cases, dehydration can lead to colic, kidney failure or even death.

Here are some easy ways to check whether your horse is dehydrated:

PINCH TEST: Use your fingertips to grasp a small piece of the horse's skin on the neck or shoulder area and pull it up into a rough peak-shape, then let the skin go. If the skin remains raised, or takes several seconds to flatten, dehydration is possible.

GUM TEST: Lift the horse's upper lip to check if the gums are moist to touch. If they feel tacky or sticky, dehydration is likely.

CAPILLARY REFILL TIME (CRT): A CRT test can be done by assessing the colour of the gums. The gums should be pink — not pale, nor a dark reddish colour, and definitely not a shade of blue or purple. Push your thumb against the gum above the front teeth for at least three seconds and then remove it. A pale spot should be revealed where your thumb has pressed the blood away from the capillaries — if the horse is healthy and well hydrated, this spot should return to a normal pink colour within a second or two; anything longer is a concern and is usually caused by blood loss, shock or poor oxygen delivery.

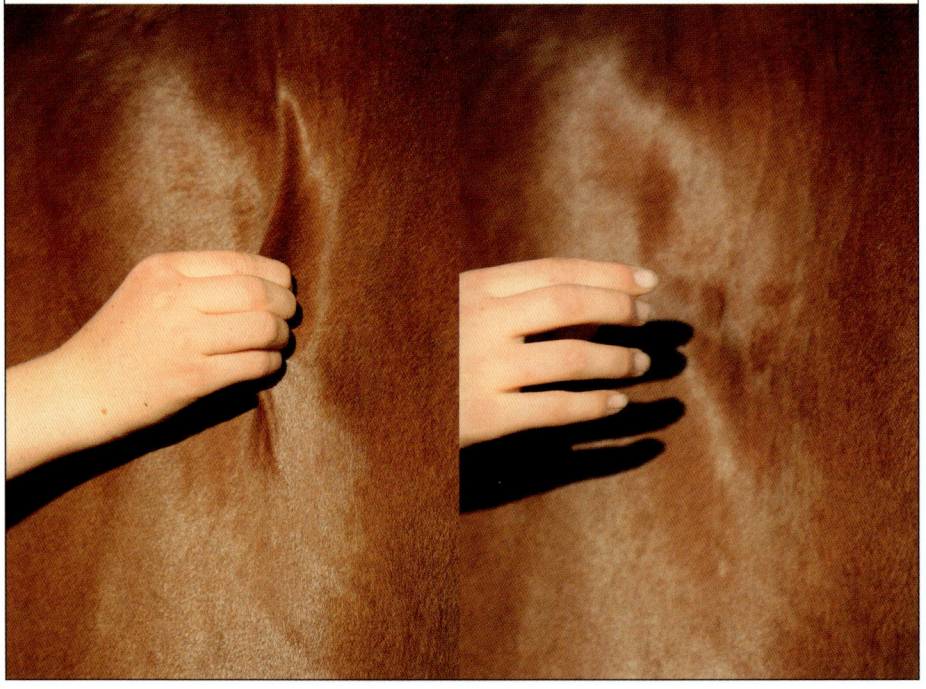

If your horse is dehydrated, or refusing to drink, you can encourage it to drink in the following ways.

FLAVOURED WATER: Some horses may be encouraged to drink if you add a handful of chaff or sweet feed or a few tablespoons of molasses to their water. If you do offer your horse flavoured water, you must also provide a bucket of unflavoured water at the same time in case the horse decides that it doesn't like the taste. If your horse is overweight or has insulin complications, be cautious with the type of flavouring you use.

SUPPLEMENT WITH SALT OR ELECTROLYTES: Dehydrated horses will be more likely to drink if they are supplemented with salt. Start with 1 to 2 teaspoons of salt daily (in their hard feed); if needed, you can increase the amount to 1 to 2 tablespoons, which is the maximum a horse should be given daily. If salt doesn't increase your horse's desire to drink, then electrolyte powder or paste, obtained from a vet, can also be beneficial. While neither will hydrate your horse, both salt and electrolytes should make your horse thirsty enough that it wants to drink.

SOAK HAY AND FEED: Soaking your horse's hay, and adding extra water to hard feed to make a sloppy consistency, can help a horse stay hydrated.

CHECK WATER SOURCES: Some horses may be hesitant to drink from some water sources, such as a trough or an automatic feeder, if it spooks them. If your horse is dehydrated, make sure that it is confident approaching the water source, that there is sufficient water available, and that the water is clean; horses are unlikely to drink from water that is contaminated by rotting plants or animals. It can also be beneficial to provide at least two water sources for a fussy drinker.

TOWN VS RURAL WATER: Some horses find chlorinated water unpalatable, especially if they are used to drinking farm water. If your horse is fussy about what it drinks, it can be helpful to take a tank of water from your property when you go away to clinics or competitions.

Does my horse need a companion?

Horses are herd animals that have evolved to live in family bands and form social hierarchies. To reduce the risk of stress and behavioural issues that can develop from isolation, domestic horses benefit greatly from having companionship.

INTRODUCING YOUR HORSE TO A NEW COMPANION

- **INTRODUCE NEW HORSES ON THE LEAD:** Not all horses will instantly become friends. Before you put them out in a paddock together, introduce them to each other on a lead and allow them to sniff noses. Make sure you're standing beside your horse's shoulder when you do this, or at the end of the lead, so you're out of reach if the horse squeals and strikes out.
- **LET NEW HORSES OUT IN A BIG PADDOCK:** Once you're confident that the horses are good together, let them out in a large paddock with no narrow choke points (with corners greater than 90 degrees), so they can't corner each other. Keep an eye on them until you are sure they are happy together.
- **HERD HIERARCHY:** When new horses are put in together, they quickly sort out a pecking order. Some horses will be more dominant than others, but they usually settle quickly once they have worked out the hierarchy within the herd. However, sometimes two dominant horses may continue to be at odds with each other; in this case, try pairing them up with a milder-tempered horse or paddock them alone.
- **USE ADJACENT PADDOCKS:** If horses need more time to get used to each other they can be separated by a safe fence, preferably with an electric outrigger or laneway between them. This allows the horses time to get to know each other while reducing the risk of injury. Be careful, though — horses can strike or kick through fences if they don't like each other, which can lead to injury.
- **OTHER ANIMALS ARE BETTER THAN NO COMPANION:** Because horses are so social, they need a companion for their mental and emotional well-being. If you aren't able to keep another horse or pony as a companion (due to the cost, or having insufficient land), your horse can bond well with a miniature horse or other animals such as a goat, donkey or alpaca.

Once your horse has a companion, you will need to care for both animals.

- **HORSE COMPATIBILITY:** If horses with different Body Condition Scores are managed together it can make it difficult to maintain an ideal BCS (see page 101) in either horse, as they will have different nutritional needs.
- **MONITOR THEIR BEHAVIOUR:** If you notice that your horse is anxious around the other horses in the paddock, pacing the fence lines, keeping to itself or has bite marks on it, it is likely not feeling safe with its companions.
- **MANAGING A HORSE LEFT ALONE:** If horses are kept in pairs, they can quickly become attached and emotionally dependent on each other, and may become distressed if you remove one from the paddock to go for a ride or attend a show. This can be very unpleasant for both the owner and the horses, so having a third companion animal can help alleviate this.

Top: Two geldings enjoying some mutual grooming.

Bottom: Two young colts playing; although boisterous, they mean no harm to each other.

PADDOCK MAINTENANCE

Horses are very hard on pastures — they are selective grazers that chew close to the ground and leave weeds behind, as well as trampling pasture underfoot when conditions are wet. Regular maintenance will help keep your paddocks in good condition.

AVOID OVERGRAZING: Overgrazing increases the worm burden of the pasture, destroys good plant species and promotes weed growth. To help prevent overgrazing, you can use electric tapes to strip-graze or rotate paddocks as needed to reduce grazing pressure. If land is limited, especially when the ground is wet, use a sacrifice paddock or yards so that your grazing paddocks can be given a rest.

CROSS-GRAZE WITH OTHER SPECIES: Cross-grazing not only helps with worm burden (see pages 106–07) but also with weed management, as other species will eat the weeds that horses leave behind. Horses tend to be selective eaters that chew close to the ground and avoid weeds, while cattle, sheep and goats tend to clean up the pasture by eating older, longer grass as well as weeds that aren't palatable to horses.

MUCK OUT: Horses don't like to eat in areas where they have dropped manure, as it is both unpalatable and infested with parasite larvae. Picking up the manure daily, or at the very least weekly, will help keep the pasture clean and usable.

HARROW LARGE PADDOCKS: If you have large paddocks, harrowing your pastures can be easier than mucking out, and it has the added benefit that the manure acts as a natural fertiliser, returning nutrients to the soil. In hot and dry climates, harrowing can also kill fly and parasite larvae by exposing them to sunlight and heat. After harrowing, leave the paddock for 6 to 12 weeks before grazing it again; this will allow the manure time to break down and the fly and parasite larvae to die.

ROLL YOUR PADDOCKS: After winter, paddocks can dry out very quickly, leaving pugged-up ground that is hazardous to walk over. Rolling a paddock while the earth is still soft will help flatten the uneven ground, reducing the risk of injury to your horse. Be sure to allow the paddocks enough time to dry before driving a vehicle over them, however, so that you don't create muddy tracks.

TEST THE SOIL: Checking the pH balance and nutritional status of your pasture will indicate the amount and type of fertiliser needed. For example, if your soil is low in magnesium you can add this to the fertiliser or supplement it in your horse's feed.

IMPROVE YOUR PASTURE: If your pasture has bare patches, lots of weeds or slow grass growth, you can renovate it by eradicating weeds, fertilising with horse-safe fertiliser (including lime or dolomite), or sowing with horse-friendly grass seed. Paddocks will need to be rested after undergoing any renovation, so you need to have somewhere else to graze your horses over this time. After spraying a paddock, allow it to rest for at least three weeks, including at least one heavy rainfall to wash the chemicals into the soil.

TOPPING: If your grass gets too long, it is a good idea to have the paddock topped before the weeds seed. This cleans out the rank (old) grasses, feeds organic matter into the soil and tidies the paddock, encouraging healthy pasture.

Top four: Mucking out is important in smaller paddocks and yards.

Bottom: Renovating paddocks that are predominantly weeds can improve their grazing capacity.

Poisonous plants

Many pastures, hedgerows and gardens contain plants that are toxic to horses if eaten, potentially leading to serious illness or even death. While some poisonous plants are palatable to horses, others will be eaten only if the horse is short of feed or if they are accidentally consumed in hay or tree prunings, or if leaves are blown in by the wind.

Knowing what plants to avoid will allow you to manage your pasture. If you see your horse eating a toxic plant or suspect poisoning, get immediate advice from a vet — taking a photo of the plant will help them identify the type of poisoning that has occurred and how to treat it.

Some common poisonous plants include:

Weeds
1. Buttercup
2. Ragwort
3. Nightshade family
4. Foxglove
5. Hemlock
6. Mexican devil (also known as crofton weed)
7. Bracken

Trees and shrubs
8. Avocado
9. Privet
10. Yew
11. Oak (including the acorns)
12. Sycamore
13. Rhododendrons and azaleas
14. Oleander
15. Ngaio
16. Tutu

Some plants are more toxic than others, and the effects can be either immediate or accumulative. For example, one leaf of oleander will kill a horse within hours, while Mexican devil is only fatal if it is consumed over several months.

Common symptoms of poisoning include swelling of the facial tissues, excessive salivation, colic, reduced appetite, slow pulse, diarrhoea (which may contain blood), skin twitching, paralysis, convulsions, constipation, depression, loss of coordination, yellow eyes and gums, dark urine, drowsiness, liver failure, sensitivity to sunlight, abnormal behaviours (including compulsive walking and the horse pressing its head against objects), blindness, progressive muscular weakness, dilated pupils, trembling, laboured breathing, increased or irregular heart rate, staggering, collapse, seizures, coughing, and intolerance for exercise.

Safe fencing

Horses are notoriously tough on fences and seem to have an innate ability to injure themselves, so it's crucial to provide a safe place for them to graze. Often, investing money in safe fencing can be cheaper in the long run as it reduces potential vet bills, or even the cost of replacing a horse that might be injured or killed in a fence accident.

Below are some common types of fencing.

WOOD: Wooden post-and-rail fencing is sturdy, highly visible and aesthetically pleasing, and if well-constructed it can be fairly safe. It does, however, require regular maintenance as some horses will chew on the wood, nails can work loose, rails can warp or break, and the fences often require staining or painting. The rails can also splinter and injure a horse; either fine splinters arising from the horse rubbing on the fence, or large splinters which can be driven into the horse during a hard impact and cause a potentially fatal injury. An outrigger (an offset electric wire, 30 to 40 centimetres inside the fence, and ideally made from equiwire) can reduce the chance of impact as well as prevent horses chewing on the rails.

EQUINE WIRE (EQUIWIRE): Made from electric wire and coated in vinyl or plastic, this provides a safe, highly visible and effective fence to keep horses contained. Although it may cost a little more than other wire options, its safety aspects and low maintenance requirements (only requiring an occasional ratcheting to keep it tight) make it well worth the investment.

Left: Horse-friendly netting (with rectangles small enough that even a foal's hoof can't get stuck), with post and rail and an electric outrigger made from equine wire.

Right: A plastic-coated Horserail fence that has the aesthetics of post and rail.

> **PREVENT INJURIES**
>
> Over the past decade we have moved away from traditional wire fencing, due to many fence-related accidents, which resulted in excessive vet bills and even fatalities. Now our preference is equiwire fence, with electrified equiwire outriggers. Since installing this, our vet bills for our horses' fence-related injuries have reduced significantly, which has made us realise the importance of a prevention rather than cure approach to paddocking horses.

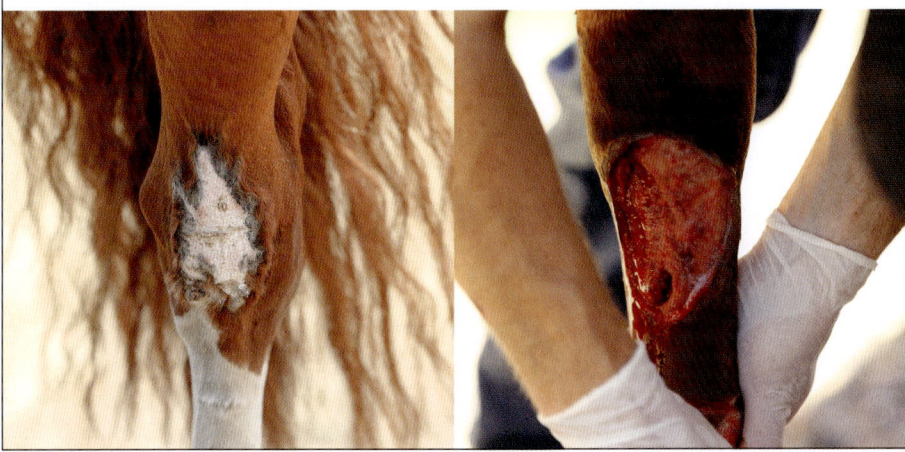

HIGH-TENSILE WIRE: This is one of the most dangerous options for horse fencing. Usually used on cattle and sheep farms, it is a thin (2.5 millimetre) hard wire that easily slices through skin and tendons, and is thin enough that a horse can get a shoe caught in the wire; all of these situations can result in expensive vet bills or even death, including by electrocution. Many of these accidents happen because of poor visibility of the fence, or from wires sagging, especially with two- or three-strand fences that have posts placed far apart. If high-tensile wire must be used, you can increase safety by having a battened 7-wire fence, with an electrified equiwire outrigger.

NO. 8 WIRE: This is a thicker (4 millimetre), low-tensile wire which is more visible than high-tensile wire, and softer, which makes it less likely to cut a horse. If you have a restricted budget and traditional wire must be used, a two- or three-strand electrified No. 8 wire fence, with an electrified equiwire outrigger, and posts placed about 5 to 6 metres apart, can be an affordable choice. Additional wires are recommended for boundary fences.

PVC PLANKS: Similar in appearance to wood but made from a thermoplastic resin, these do not require painting and are resistant to chewing, which reduces the amount of maintenance needed. The PVC does need a solid internal core (made from wood), however, to prevent it shattering on impact and potentially impaling a horse, especially in low temperatures.

ELECTRICAL TAPE: Available in different thicknesses and colours, this offers a highly visible and safe solution for portable fencing. It can, however, sag if standards are not close enough, and can stretch and break if a horse pushes through it. Because of this it should only be used to strip-graze within a fully enclosed paddock.

BARBED WIRE: One of the most dangerous types of wire, as it can cause ragged wounds on horses that become entangled in it or scrape against it. Barbed wire should be avoided at all costs; however, if this is not possible, an electrified outrigger should be used and the bottom barbed wires need to be removed to avoid horses pawing or striking through them.

SHEEP OR DEER NETTING: Another dangerous type of fence for horses — the holes in the netting are large enough for a horse's leg or hoof to get caught in, which can result in horrific injuries or even death. If unavoidable, an electrified equiwire outrigger should be used. If netting is desired, horse-friendly netting is also available and should ideally be capped with a rail.

HEDGES: As long as they don't contain poisonous plants, mature hedges can provide a safe fencing alternative while also acting as a good wind-break. They do, however, require regular maintenance, including trimming, and if bare patches occur it is important that the underlying fence is horse-friendly.

Gates

While most people think about the type of fencing they will use for horses, gate safety is often overlooked. It is, however, a crucial part of creating a safe pasture, as there is a high risk of injury if a horse gets stuck over or in a gate. Horse-friendly gates should be sturdy enough to withstand a horse leaning on them without buckling or warping; have nowhere for a horse's leg to become trapped; have no loose wires or bars; and be high enough to discourage a horse jumping over it. Alternatively, you can use an electrified bungy to keep horses off gateways, which can also prevent injuries from horses socialising over gateways.

Common types of gates include the following.

WOOD: Wooden gates offer a very traditional look, especially for post-and-rail fences.

METAL: Generally made from galvanised steel, these gates come in a variety of styles. Beware of close horizonal or vertical bars, or ones with diagonal support bars which can trap a horse's leg, hoof or head.

Top: Our preferred style of fencing is equine wire with outriggers, to minimise the likelihood of the horses in neighbouring paddocks striking out and getting a leg caught.

Bottom: Our preferred horse-friendly style of gate, with nowhere for the horse to trap a leg, hoof or head.

> Our preference is for strong mesh gates, with small grids to prevent a horse (or even a foal) from getting a hoof or leg caught in them.

ELECTRICAL TAPE OR BUNGY: Two strands of electrical tape or bungy cord can offer a visible and fairly safe gating option, or can keep horses off standard gates if used across the corner of a gateway. While suitable for internal fences, these should never be used for road gates. Beware of gates made from coiled wire — horses can get tangled in them.

CATTLE GUARD: Cattle guards are made from numerous metal bars set over a ditch. They should never be used to contain horses, as they can easily jump over them or break a leg trying to go through them.

TOP TIPS FOR GOOD FENCING

FENCE STYLE AND HEIGHT

- Regardless of the type of fencing chosen, most fences benefit from the addition of an electrified top wire or outrigger, as these teach the horses to respect fences, creating a psychological barrier.
- Fencing should be highly visible, since horses are far-sighted and look to the horizon if they feel they are in danger.
- Fences should be high enough to discourage horses from jumping out; typically, between 1.2 and 1.5 metres is sufficient, but as high as 1.8 metres may be needed for stallions, wild horses or those prone to jumping out.

GATES

- Gates should be correctly hung and swing both ways to prevent a horse from getting its stifle caught while it is being led through.
- Gates should be set at the same height as the fence. The gap between the bottom of the gate and the ground should ideally be less than 10 centimetres so a leg can't get caught if the horse rolls, or over 40 centimetres.
- Gate gudgeons (on which the gate hinges sit) should be flush with the post to prevent a horse impaling itself on them or getting its leg caught between the post and the end of the gudgeon. If a gate has been removed for any reason, removing the gudgeons (or putting a tennis ball over them) can help prevent injury.
- Latches should be secure, so that horses can't open the gates, and gates onto roads should be double-latched or padlocked.
- Most gateways need to be wide enough to allow machinery, such as mowers and fertiliser trucks, through. For horse-only gates, a minimum width of 1.5 metres is recommended.

OTHER IMPORTANT FENCING POINTS

- Most posts are made from wood, or plastic with a wood core, both of which are safe for horses. Metal waratahs, which are often used for temporary fencing, are not suitable for horses, but if they have to be used they should be capped with plastic to avoid horses becoming impaled on them.
- Paddocks should not have any 'choke points' (a corner with an angle of less than 90 degrees) where a horse can be cornered by another horse.
- Roadway and driveway fencing should be more secure than internal fencing, to prevent horses escaping onto the road or onto neighbouring properties.
- Have an emergency plan in the event of a fence accident. This should include having the tools required to cut wire, rails or gates, a twitch to keep a horse still if needed, and knowing the location of a cut-off switch if you have electric fences.

FEEDING YOUR HORSE

Horses are herbivores, evolved to be eating almost continuously on prairie grasslands. Domestication has affected their natural feeding patterns, however, so one of the most crucial elements of horse ownership is to ensure that their nutritional needs are met.

To fully understand how to manage your horse's feed, a basic understanding of the equine digestive system (see pages 40–41) is required, as horses are very sensitive to digestive upsets resulting from an incorrect or inconsistent diet.

Ideally, horses should live in a paddock with access to pasture 24 hours a day; if that is not possible, it is essential to follow good feeding practices to ensure that your horse remains healthy.

FEED OFTEN: If your horse is yarded or stabled, or doesn't have sufficient grass in its paddock, it should have access to roughage at all times; always ensure that your horse has enough hay to last it overnight or during times when you can't check it regularly. As a rule, horses should never be left without food for longer than a couple of hours, to prevent hunger and minimise the risk of gastric ulcers (see page 86).

> **TOP TIP:** For fat or greedy horses, you can regulate the amount they consume, while ensuring constant access to food, by using slow-feeding hay nets.

KEEP TO A ROUTINE: Horses thrive on routine. They have amazing internal clocks, making them much better time-keepers than their human guardians. To reduce stress, keep your horse's feeding schedule as consistent as possible, with meals arriving at the same time each day.

> Our yarded or stabled horses get balage at 7 a.m., then a slice of hay at 10 a.m., 1 p.m. and 4 p.m., then at 7 p.m. they get a hard feed, as well as enough hay and balage to last them through the night (normally the equivalent of 2 to 3 slices of hay).

WHAT TO FEED BEFORE OR AFTER EXERCISE: When horses are exercising, acid in the stomach can splash the stomach walls and create ulcers, unless there is some food to buffer it. If your horse isn't on pasture, and therefore isn't able to eat grass freely, make sure that it eats some form of roughage in the hour before it is ridden; the standard recommendation is 2 kilograms of roughage right before riding or travelling. Hard feed, however, should not be fed within 1 to 2 hours before or after exercise.

Gastric ulcers

> **TOP TIPS TO AVOID GASTRIC ULCERS**
> - Your horse should never be left without food for more than 4 to 5 hours, or without water for more than 6 hours.
> - Never ride your horse on an empty stomach.
> - Minimise stressful situations and changes to your horse's daily routine.

A horse's stomach secretes acid continuously. This is naturally neutralised by bi-carbonate in the saliva, the release of which is stimulated by the horse continuously chewing. Regular access to high-fibre feed is essential in the horse's diet, as it forms a protective 'mat' that reduces acid splashing onto the vulnerable squamous portion of the stomach.

If your horse is not chewing, the accumulating acid is not buffered, which can cause equine gastric ulcer syndrome (EGUS) to develop; a common, painful condition caused by the stomach acid irritating the gastrointestinal lining. Any horse, of any age, can develop ulcers; studies have shown that between 50% and 90% of horses suffer from them at some stage in their lives, and they are most common in racehorses (over 80% of horses in training are affected) and sport horses (about 60% are affected).

Poor management is a leading cause of ulcer development, with a lack of forage increasing the risk of ulcers by 400%, while water deprivation can increase the risk by 300%. The risk of ulcers developing is especially high when horses are in stressful situations, yarded for extended periods of time, taken away from their companions, change routines or are travelling for long distances. A horse rolling or being worked on an empty stomach can also cause ulcers, as can the use of certain drugs such as the painkiller phenylbutazone (also known as 'bute').

Horses with ulcers are likely to exhibit physical, mental or behavioural issues, which can vary depending on the level of pain they are experiencing. However, some horses may show no symptoms at all.

Common signs of ulcers include:
- loss of appetite, weight loss, or poor body condition
- looking tucked up along the stomach meridian

- decrease in performance or a reluctance to train, including a shorter length of stride, fatigue or compromised oxygen uptake
- behavioural issues such as rearing, bucking, napping or biting
- dull coat
- a sudden change in behaviour or personality, including anxiety or stress
- discomfort or aggression when being saddled or girthed
- low-grade colic
- aversion or hyper-sensitivity to being touched, especially around the stomach or flank area.

If your horse is showing any of these symptoms, it is worth considering ulcers as the cause. The only way to get an accurate diagnosis is to have a vet scope them while the horse is sedated. Scoping will reveal the location of the ulcers and their severity. Squamous ulcers (in the upper part of the stomach) are generally caused by acid splash from poor feed or exercise management, while glandular ulcers (in the lower stomach) are often seen in horses with stressful routines or those that have been on anti-inflammatory drugs. Ulcers are graded from 0 to 4, with 4 being the most severe.

The type of treatment required will depend on whether your horse has squamous ulcers and/or glandular ulcers. Once treatment begins, there is generally a noticeable improvement within the first two weeks, although a 42-day course of treatment is usually required. For horses with severe symptoms, it is beneficial to turn them out while they are being treated, so that they are as stress-free as possible and you aren't riding the horse while it is in pain.

You can minimise the risk of ulcers by maintaining a good feeding schedule (or keeping horses on pasture so that they have constant access to grass), avoiding the use of anti-inflammatory drugs, and ensuring stressful situations (such as long travelling times, intensive training or being isolated from other horses) are carefully managed to support the horse's physical, mental and emotional well-being.

What to feed your horse

Roughage
Good-quality grass and hay contain most of the essential nutrients that horses need and should be the basis of any feeding plan. Horses require 1.5% to 2.5% of their body weight in roughage daily, depending on their condition and level of exercise (for example, a 500 kilogram horse would eat between 7.5 and 12.5 kilograms of roughage daily).

HOW TO WEIGH HAY

The average weight of a conventional bale of hay is between 18 and 25 kilograms. Because every cut of hay is different, you can weigh a bale to determine how much you need to feed daily.

To do this, stand on a scale holding a bale of hay, then subtract your weight from the amount. If you weigh 60 kilograms and the scales read 80 kilograms, you will know that the hay bale is 20 kilograms. Therefore, if your horse requires 10 kilograms daily, you will know it needs half a bale of hay fed throughout the day.

During the winter or summer months, when grass growth slows, it may be necessary to provide additional forage for your horse.

PASTURE

Although horses readily consume most grasses, some pastures are more suitable than others.

GRASSES: Horses have evolved to eat low-quality, high-fibre prairie grasses and herbage. Many modern grasses can cause grass-affected behaviours (especially in spring and autumn), so establishing your pasture with horse-friendly grasses — including prairie grass, brome, cocksfoot, Yorkshire fog, timothy and browntop — will ensure the health of your horse.

LEGUMES: These are nitrogen-fixing plants, such as clover and lucerne, that are high in calcium, good for the soil and enjoyed by horses. They typically have a higher protein, energy and mineral content (including calcium) than grasses, but they can cause grass-affected issues in some horses.

IS MY HORSE GRASS-AFFECTED?

Many behavioural issues in horses can result from changes to their pasture throughout the seasons. Grass-affected issues can be caused by any of the following.

SPRING OR AUTUMN GRASS: During times of rapid grass growth, when the leaves are very green and lush and have a high sugar content, horses' behaviour can be dramatically affected (high sugar levels can also cause inflammation and laminitis in horses with metabolic disorders, including those with Cushing's and insulin dysregulation). Even horses that are usually safe and reliable may show erratic changes in behaviour, in hand or under saddle, which can include nervousness or excitement, spookiness, tenseness or even aggressive tendencies. These behaviours are likely to improve if you feed minerals (especially oral magnesium), supplement your horse's diet with hay or remove your horse from the pasture completely. In extreme cases, you may need to source hay from a different region, or hay that was cut during the summer season (rather than spring), so there is a reduced risk of grass-affected behaviours occurring.

STRESSED PASTURES: Paddocks that have been overgrazed, exposed to frost or drought, or have short regrowth generally have higher sugar levels and mycotoxins, which can cause grass-affected issues.

MYCOTOXINS: Some microscopic fungi and moulds that are found in soil, grasses and hay can produce toxins, which are usually concentrated in the seed heads or in the base of the plant. These toxins can cause numerous behavioural issues, such as nervousness or excitement, spookiness, grumpiness, girthiness (a reaction to being girthed), bucking or running the fence line, as well as other anxious or aggressive behaviours. They can also cause a weakened immune system, loss of appetite, loss of topline or weight, gastrointestinal problems (including diarrhoea), lethargy, colic and loss of coordination. These behaviours should improve if you feed a toxin-binder, supplement your horse's diet with hay or remove it from the affected pasture completely. It's important to note that symptoms of mycotoxin ingestion can be similar to mineral imbalances, so both may need to be addressed.

FERTILISERS: Nitrogen, potassium and urea, which are found in many commercial fertilisers, can cause grass-affected behaviours, as well as colic, laminitis, ulcers, abortion or even death. Instead, use horse-friendly fertiliser such as lime, dolomite or seaweed as required. If your property has been fertilised with nitrogen or potassium in the past, you can help counter the effects by supplementing your horse with sodium, calcium and magnesium — which minerals, and how much, can be determined by having a blood sample taken by your vet, who can then advise a treatment plan.

STORED ROUGHAGE

HAY: Hay is the most common type of stored roughage. It is made from cut and dried grasses (meadow hay) or legumes (lucerne or alfalfa hay), with a maximum moisture content of 20%, to prevent the hay going mouldy. Mouldy hay should never be fed, as it contains toxins which can lead to colic or even death. Good hay should be made from horse-friendly grasses, have more leaf than stalk, smell sweet and be green/yellow in colour. Bad hay will have more stalk than leaf, smell musty, may contain poisonous plants and will be yellow/brown in colour.

BALAGE: Balage is slightly softer and damper than hay (with a moisture content of about 40%) and has twice the nutritional content. Note that balage is different from silage, which has a faster and more complete fermentation process and is too rich in protein for horses. Balage is made from cut and dried grasses or legumes, then wrapped in plastic to form bales and fermented for at least 4 to 8 weeks. Good balage should be made from horse-friendly grasses and have more leaf than stalk, smell sweet and be yellow in colour. Important: If the bales have holes in them, the air will cause fermentation to start again and the bale will go off — make sure you cover any holes or tears immediately with good-quality tape. If your balage does go off and mould is present, do not feed the mouldy parts as this can cause respiratory disease, mould toxin poisoning or even death, especially if the mould is coloured.

STRAW: Straw is made from the stalks of cereals (wheat, barley and oats); it is generally used as a comfortable bed in stables, but can also be eaten in moderation. Straw is high in fibre but not very nutritious, so can be good for mixing with good-quality hay for horses that are overweight or for horses with metabolic disorders to help prevent laminitis from insulin spikes from sugar. This allows them to eat more, without gaining additional weight, which will help increase their chewing time and reduce the risk of ulcers.

Hard feed (concentrates)

Although most recreational horses can get enough nutrients from pasture, performance horses and those with increased nutritional requirements may require hard feeding to supply the nutrients and energy needed to maintain condition and performance. There are many choices of hard feed available, most of which are commercially mixed and balanced, and specially designed for horses.

It is, however, important to remember that the horse's digestive system is adapted

From left: Hay, lucerne chaff and CopRice (our preferred choice of hard feed).

for eating roughage and not concentrates — the latter requires less chewing and therefore decreases saliva flow, as well as being unable to mat together to protect the stomach from ulcers (see page 86). Because of the size of the horse's stomach, feeding large volumes of hard feed (more than 2 kilograms or 4 pounds in one serving) can have a negative impact on your horse's health due to the way the horse's digestive system works (see pages 40–41); if your horse needs more than 2 kilograms of hard feed per day, increase its calorie intake by offering the horse several small feeds spaced throughout the day. As a rule, you should not be feeding more than 5.5 kilograms or 11 pounds of concentrates to your horse each day.

Types of hard feed include the following.

COMMERCIAL FEED MIXES: These are carefully formulated feeds, usually made from grains (including rice, oats, corn, barley or maize), which include minerals and vitamins. They are specially designed to offer horses a balanced diet and should be fed with chaff to provide additional roughage. Most brands of feed provide options for horses of different ages and levels of competition (including all-rounders, sport horses, stud horses and veterans) that vary in their carbohydrate, fat and protein levels. Most horse feeds outline a recommended feeding regimen on the packaging, which should be followed to ensure that your horse isn't over- or under-fed.

CHAFF AND CHAFFAGE: Chaff is made from finely chopped hay or straw, while chaffage is made from finely chopped fermented grasses or legumes, and comes wrapped in plastic (similarly to balage). Both can be added to hard feeds to supply fibre, which will increase the chewing time, bulk out feeds and slow down digestion. Ideally the roughage should be cut at least 2.5 centimetres (1 inch) in length so it can mat together inside the horse's stomach, to aid in the prevention of ulcers.

GRAINS: Common grains that can be fed to horses include oats, corn, barley and maize. If you feed grains by themselves, and not within a commercial feed mix, careful consideration should be given to what and how much you feed, as well as how it is fed (some need to be crushed, rolled or boiled to be safe for horses to eat). Grains should be fed together with chaff, and it is important to supplement the horse's diet with additional protein, amino acids, minerals and vitamins since — unlike commercially mixed feeds — they don't provide all of the vital nutrients needed by horses.

SUGAR BEET: This is made from leftover sugar cane, after the sugar is extracted. It is shredded to create a high-fibre, high-energy feed which can help with weight gain. *Important:* Sugar beet *must* be soaked prior to feeding, as it swells in size; if it isn't sufficiently soaked, it will swell in the horse's digestive tract and cause a blockage, often resulting in choke or colic (see pages 131–33).

COPRA: Made from the dried husk of coconuts, this offers a high-fibre, high-protein and high-fat (8%) feed which can be useful if a horse needs to gain weight. It is low in lysine, threonine and methionine, however, which are essential amino acids for growth and immune function, so is not suited as a major feed component for growing horses. *Important:* Copra *must* be soaked prior to feeding as it expands when wet, and should never be fed if it has fermented or gone mouldy.

BRAN: Wheat is the most dangerous grain to feed to horses, except in the form of bran (which is a by-product of milling wheat). When fed dry, bran can cause mild constipation (which can be helpful for a horse with liquid manure). When fed damp, it works as a mild laxative — a warm bran mash is commonly used for sick horses. If fed in excess, however, bran can inhibit calcium absorption, which can affect the horse's growth and health.

Supplements

Minerals and vitamins are vital to ensure that the horse's body can function correctly. They are essential for skeletal development, muscle function, blood formation, hoof and coat growth, and acid–base balance, as well as supporting the internal systems of the horse (see pages 35–42).

If you aren't feeding the recommended rate of a balanced commercial feed (based on your horse's weight, with the feed being weighed for accuracy), you will need to supplement your horse with some additional minerals and vitamins, especially if you live in a nutritionally deficient area, your horse is competing at top level or recovering from an injury, or if you have a pregnant or lactating mare. Supplements can be purchased as commercially formulated mineral mixes, with specific formulations also available to target hoof, coat or joint health.

Signs of mineral or vitamin deficiency include a dull coat, cracked or weak hooves, a poor immune system, spooky behaviour, muscle loss, an inability to gain weight, low energy and poor gut health (including an increased risk of gastric ulcers; see page 86), as well as fragile bones and joints. Unfortunately, many of these symptoms will only become evident once a mineral deficiency has been there for some time, and by this stage the damage can be significant.

Over-supplementing, however, can lead to mineral or vitamin toxicity, so if you have concerns about your horse's dietary requirements, it's recommended that you have a hair analysis or blood work done by your veterinarian to determine what nutritional deficiencies it may have.

ESSENTIAL MINERALS

The minerals that are essential for your horse's health include the following.

CALCIUM AND PHOSPHORUS: These two minerals are the most abundant in the horse's body and work together to support healthy bones and teeth, as well as muscle function. They must be fed at adequate quantities, as well as at the correct ratio. The minimum calcium-to-phosphorus ratio is 1:1, although 2:1 is recommended, as phosphorus intake regulates calcium absorption.

MAGNESIUM: Magnesium is an essential mineral that is vital for nerve function and muscle relaxation, decoding genetic information and protecting the horse's body from free-radical damage and inflammation, as well as for the generation of cellular energy. Deficiencies are more common in spring or autumn, during times of lush grass growth. Symptoms include nervousness, spookiness and excitability (which is why magnesium

A horse licking a multi-mineral block.

is found in commercially mixed calming supplements), as well as muscle tremors, a poor attitude to being ridden, muscle spasms after strenuous exercise (known as 'tying-up'), or in extreme cases may even be life-threatening. Within the muscular system, magnesium (which helps to relax the muscles) works alongside calcium (which helps to contract the muscles). The correct ratio of calcium-to-magnesium is 2.5:1 to 3:1.

ELECTROLYTES: Electrolytes are charged minerals (primarily sodium and chloride, with lower levels of potassium, magnesium, calcium and phosphorous) required by the body for optimum function. If a horse overheats from hot weather, exercise, inappropriate rugging (see pages 184–189), or being stabled or transported with poor ventilation, it may sweat to reduce its core body temperature. This can cause a loss of water and electrolytes, and if they aren't replaced it can cause damage to the nervous and muscular systems, including tight muscles, tying-up and alkalosis.

A correctly formulated electrolyte supplement is advised for horses that sweat often. Sodium and chloride (salt) are vital to support the horse's nervous system and muscle function, as well as regulating its body fluids, while potassium is vital for maintaining acid–base balance and muscle function.

SULPHUR: Sulphur assists in the production of hormones, enzymes and amino acids and is also a vital component of collagen (which makes up connective tissue). Symptoms of a deficiency include weak ligaments and tendons, as well as compromised bone, joint and hoof health. However, over-supplementation can cause mud fever, as well as negatively affect joint and hoof health.

TRACE MINERALS

These are as equally important as the essential minerals described above, but are required in only very small amounts. Important trace minerals include selenium, iron, copper (linked to OCDs — developmental bone chips — in young horses) and iodine. In New Zealand, the most commonly supplemented of these is selenium, as many soils are deficient in it.

SELENIUM: Selenium works alongside vitamin E (see below) to protect the horse's body from free-radical damage, and is also essential for nerve and muscle health. Symptoms of a deficiency include an increased stress response, poor hoof and coat quality, tense muscles, reproductive issues and decreased performance. Because excess selenium causes toxicity, however, a blood test is usually recommended by the vet before supplementing with selenium. Organic forms of selenium (yeasts) are generally safer and more bioavailable than synthetic forms.

VITAMINS

Vitamins, which are important for your horse's growth and well-being, fall into two groups: *fat-soluble,* which are stored in the body fat and include vitamins A, D, E and K; and *water-soluble,* which are produced by bacteria found in the horse's intestines and include the B group and vitamin C.

Top: Delivering midday feed for horses that are yarded on an intensively managed property.

Bottom: In yards or sacrifice paddocks, a bin to keep hay clean is crucial.

TOP TIPS FOR FEEDING HORSES

- Make changes to a horse's diet slowly — over a 1- to 2-week period is ideal as it takes this long for the gut bacteria to adapt to different types of feed. Sudden changes can result in gut disturbances and behavioural changes in your horse and may lead to colic, laminitis or other health issues.
- Never allow your horse to go more than 4 to 5 hours without food, to help prevent gastric ulcers (see page 86).
- Feed on a set schedule, as horses thrive on routine.
- Measure feed by weight, not volume.
- Feed your horse based on its level of exercise and condition, adapting the amount accordingly to maintain an ideal body condition score (BCS; see pages 101–05).
- If multiple horses are in a paddock together, ensure that the feed is placed away from fences and gates (at least 10 metres apart, to ensure they aren't within kicking distance of each other).
- Pay attention to the pecking order of horses — often a bully will eat a greater portion of food, leaving more-submissive horses with insufficient amounts. When feeding hay, always put out one or two extra portions so that any horses that are chased off their food can find an unguarded pile.
- If your horse is stabled or yarded, feed hay in a bin, hay bag or hay net to prevent it being trampled into the ground or defecated or urinated on. For paddocked horses, feed hay into a bin or toss it onto a clean area of grass.

Opposite page: How to safely tie a hay net (see page 100).

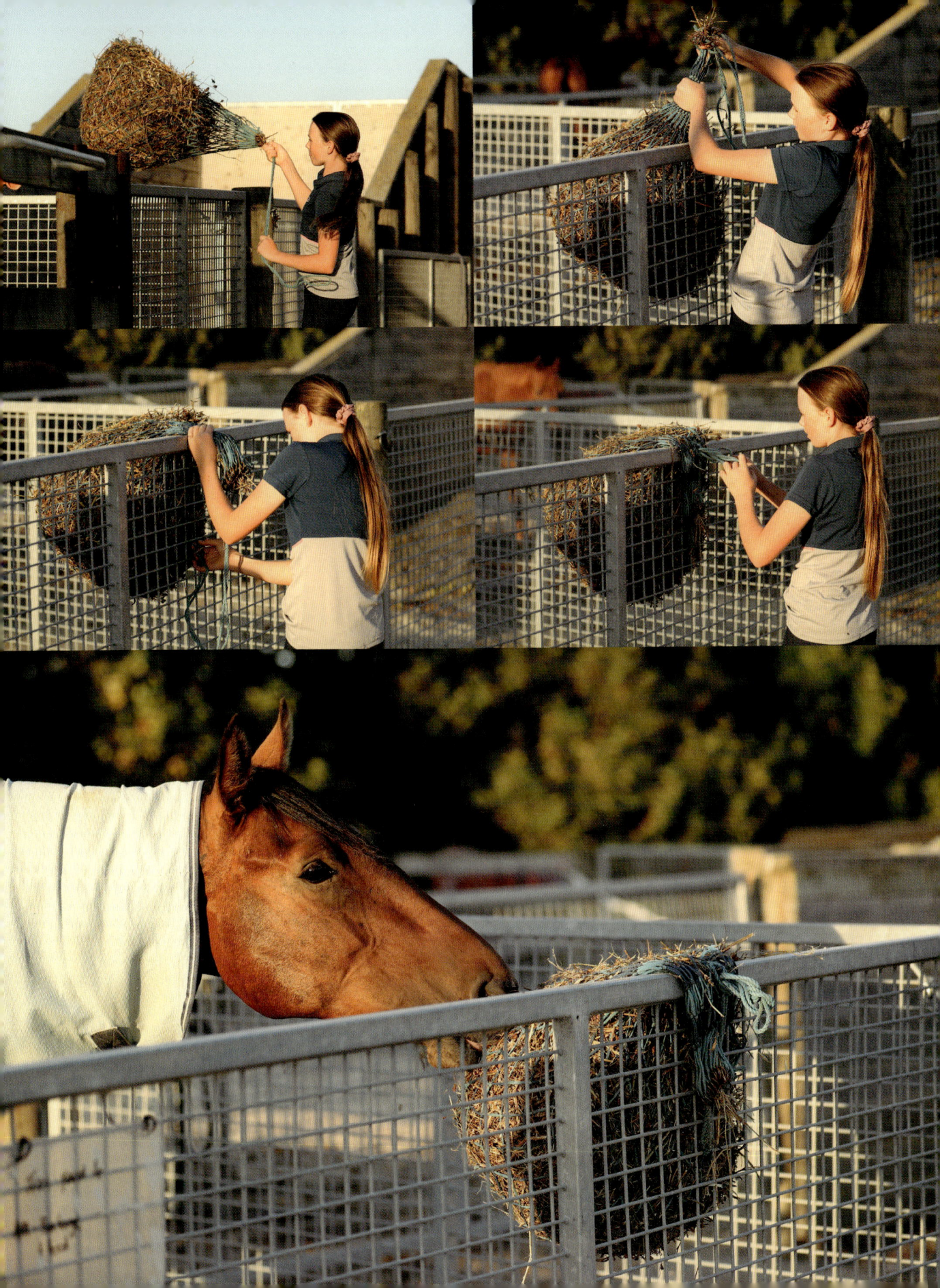

HOW TO SAFELY TIE A HAY NET

Tying a hay net correctly is an essential skill, as horses can sustain nasty injuries if they get a hoof, leg or shoe entangled in one, especially when using a hay net with large holes. Safer alternatives include a horse-friendly manger, feed trough, hay bag or slow-feeder hay net.

If you do use a hay net, follow these steps:

1. Fill the net with hay, then pull the drawstring to close the hole at the top.
2. Loop the top of the hay net over a safe rail or gate (see pages 80–84), or through a ring which is at the horse's head height. It needs to be high enough that the horse cannot paw at the net and get its hoof caught.
3. Pull any empty portion of the hay net, and the drawstring, over the rail or gate so that only the part of the hay net that is filled with hay is accessible to the horse. Wrap any excess hay net around the rail, then take the drawstring and loop it through the bottom of the hay net. Pull upwards so that the top and bottom of the net become as tight and small as possible. This way the hay net will stay folded in half as it empties, rather than lengthening, which could put it within reach of a horse's leg.
4. Pull the drawstring as tight as possible, then tie it with a quick-release knot (on the off-chance that your horse does become entangled in the hay net and needs to be freed quickly).
5. Check your hay net frequently and tie it up again if it begins to sag.

KEEPING YOUR HORSE HEALTHY

Body condition

All horses should look physically healthy, with bright eyes and a gleaming coat as well as a good covering of muscle. A horse that is either underweight or obese will have compromised performance and health, so it's vital as an owner that you keep your horse in optimum condition. If your horse has poverty lines, ribs showing or a ewe neck, then it is too thin; and if it has a crested neck, with fat deposits on its rump and neck, then it's too fat. Horses that are overweight are less athletic and more prone to joint issues and metabolic diseases like laminitis, while horses that are underweight can be more lethargic, have a lower reproductive efficiency, can struggle to carry the weight of a rider or cope with ridden work, or have a weakened immune system.

An experienced horse-owner will be able to assess their horse's condition at a glance, but for those less experienced, a regular assessment of the Body Condition Score (BCS) will tell you if your horse is in a healthy weight range (see the box on pages 104–05). As well as visually assessing your horse to determine its BSC, it's important to also feel over key parts of its body to gauge how much fat cover it has, then score it from 1 (thinnest) to 9 (fattest). The resulting score will help you determine what changes need to be made, if any, to your horse's feeding and exercise regimen to ensure optimum health.

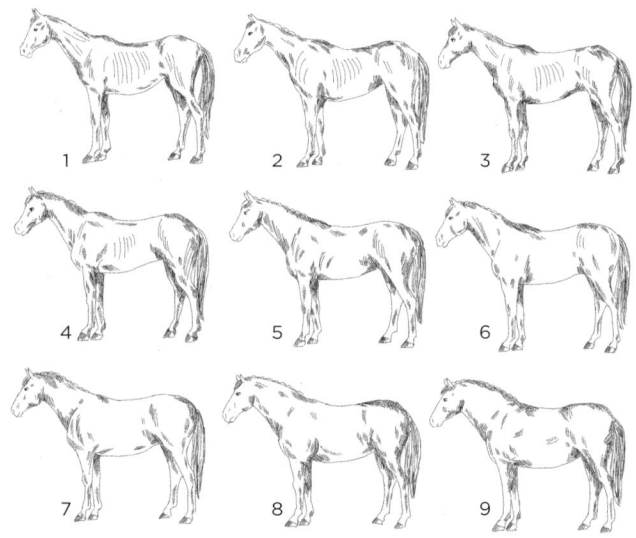

The body condition scores.
1-3: Underweight.
4-6: Good condition, depending on your horse's physical requirements.
7-9: Overweight.

GOOD CONDITION: A horse in optimum condition will have a BCS of 5, which means it is getting the correct amount of energy and calories. A score of 4 to 6 is also considered healthy, depending on the horse's age, breed, competition requirements (a race horse or an eventer might have a BCS of 4, while for showing, a BCS of 6 is often preferred), and the climate it lives in (in cold climates a BCS of 6 or even 7 might be required during the winter months, to have enough fat reserves).

UNDERWEIGHT: If a horse has a BCS of 3 or below, it is in poor condition and very low on fat reserves. When energy is needed, the horse will break down protein from its muscle mass to meet nutritional requirements, so it is crucial to increase the horse's feed rations to provide the energy and calories needed to gain weight.

Common causes of poor condition include feed deprivation, dental issues, ulcers, internal parasites, windsucking or other pain- or health-related issues. If your horse doesn't gain weight with the right increase in good-quality feed, then it is important to determine whether underlying issues are present.

TOP TIPS TO HELP YOUR HORSE GAIN WEIGHT

- **ROUGHAGE:** Getting an underweight horse's digestive system working properly and efficiently requires good-quality roughage; a horse needing to gain weight should have free access to good pasture, with as much good-quality hay or balage as it can eat (the second cut of hay is often more nutrient-rich than the first cut of the season, or you can add lucerne or alfalfa). To gain weight, horses require 2.5% of their body weight in roughage daily, so if a 500 kilogram horse doesn't have access to grass, it will need at least 12.5 kilograms of roughage each day. If your horse doesn't have an appetite for the roughage you offer it, it's crucial to find something that is more palatable.
- **HARD FEED:** Feeds that are high in fat (7% to 14%) are recommended for weight gain, as fat energy is denser than carbohydrate energy. It is possible for a horse to gain one BCS unit every 8 weeks, but to do so it will require an extra 3000 to 4500 calories each day, over and above the horse's maintenance level of hard feed. For example, if you normally feed 2.5 kilograms of hard feed each day, you will need an increase of 1 kilogram daily. To achieve the increase, the feeds should be split into several smaller feeds given throughout the day; gradually increase the ration size over a 1- to 2-week period to avoid gastrointestinal upset. Remember that a horse's stomach is small — so it's important to feed smaller portions often, rather than one large portion.
- **PROBLEM-SOLVE:** Make sure that your horse's teeth have been recently checked by a qualified equine dentist and that no other pain-related issues are present (including gastric ulcers), as these can affect a horse's ability to gain weight.

OVERWEIGHT: A horse above 6 on the BSC is overweight and storing too much fat. Common causes of obesity in horses include over-feeding, lack of exercise, metabolic issues, intestinal parasites or other health-related issues. If your horse doesn't lose weight with the right restrictions of feed, then it is important to determine whether underlying health issues are present.

Top: A horse with a low BCS and a weak topline.

Bottom: An old thoroughbred with a BCS of 1.

TOP TIPS TO HELP YOUR HORSE LOSE WEIGHT

- **ROUGHAGE:** For weight loss, reduce your horse's rations to about 1.5% of its body weight in roughage daily; that's about 7.5 kilograms for a 500 kilogram horse. Because a horse on reduced rations still needs constant access to roughage, to avoid gastric ulcers and other health issues, it's important to limit calorie intake by feeding lower-energy roughages (such as a well-grazed-out paddock, straw or low-nutrient-dense hay) and offering small but regular portions of roughage throughout the day, so that the horse is never left for longer than a few hours without something to eat. Other options include using a slow-feeding hay net, or even a grazing muzzle if the horse is on too much pasture.

- **HARD FEED:** Eliminate or reduce (by at least 50%) any hard feed in your horse's diet. If eliminated completely, a good mineral supplement should be given to ensure that nutritional needs are met, including salt (not iodised) if the horse is on lush grass. This should be fed in a small feed — once a week — made primarily of chaff. Mineral and salt blocks can also be provided, but are often not adequate as a sole source of supplementation.

- **EXERCISE:** If your horse is sound and can be worked, gradually increase their fitness over a 4- to 6-week period by lunging or riding them. Depending on how much, and how rapidly, your horse needs to lose weight, increasing its workload may lessen how much you have to restrict the horse's diet.

- **AVOID STARVATION:** Denying a horse food as a way to help it lose weight is never an acceptable solution and will cause serious health issues, including anxiety, lethargy, secondary liver disease (called Fatty Liver, due to hyperlipemia — high fat levels in the blood that occur when overweight horses are starved), ulcers and colic, as well as behavioral issues.

- **MAINTAIN HYDRATION:** Ensure a constant supply of water is available to the horse, to allow the organs to function correctly.

HOW TO ASSESS YOUR HORSE'S BODY CONDITION

Assessing your horse's body condition every 4 to 6 weeks is ideal, as it can be hard to see a gradual change in condition on a day-to-day basis. In most horses, changes in weight will first appear along the topline, then across the ribcage and at the top of the tail, followed by the withers and shoulders, and finally the crest of the neck.

A visual assessment of your horse's condition, followed by running your hands over the six main areas where body fat is stored, is important, especially during winter, when a hairy coat can disguise poor condition.

- **CREST OF THE NECK:** Very fat horses generally have fat deposits on either side of the neck, which gives the appearance of a 'crest', while thin horses

often have a ewe neck and a pronounced jugular groove.
- **WITHERS:** Very fat horses will have a fat deposit on either side of the wither, while thin horses will have a pronounced wither structure. Note, however, that even fat horses can have a pronounced wither structure if a poorly fitting saddle or an injury has caused the muscle to waste away.
- **BEHIND THE SHOULDER:** Very fat horses will have fat deposits behind the shoulder and elbow area; thin horses will have the point of the shoulder and elbows clearly visible.
- **ACROSS THE RIBCAGE:** Very fat horses will have plenty of covering over the ribs which will make it difficult to feel them, while thin horses will have prominent ribs that can easily be seen and felt.
- **OVER THE TOPLINE (BACK AND LOINS):** Very fat horses will have a depression along the spine, from where fat deposits have developed on either side of the topline, while thin horses will appear to have a bumpy topline due to the spinal columns becoming more prominent.
- **HINDQUARTERS (TOP OF THE TAIL AND HIPBONES):** Very fat horses will have fat deposits above their tail, while thin horses will have prominent vertebrae that can be easily felt, poverty lines on either side of the horse's rump (near the tail), and protruding hipbones.

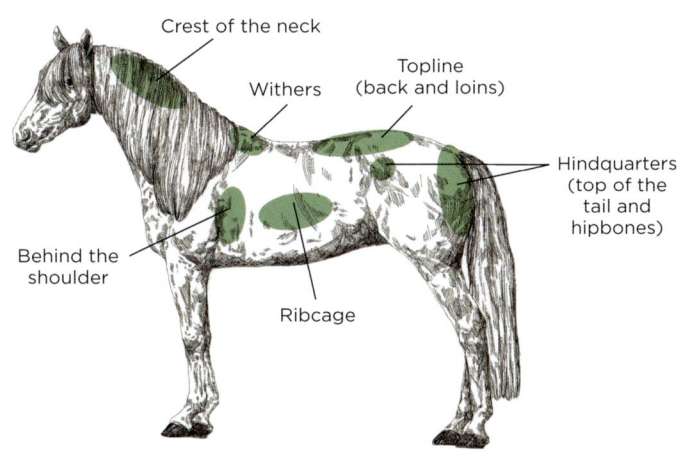

CONSULT TRUSTED PROFESSIONALS

When seeking the aid of an equine dentist, farrier, saddle fitter, skeletal therapist or vet, it is important to enlist the help of well-respected and knowledgeable equine professionals. Not every 'professional' has the same level of training, and some may not have the skills needed to correctly diagnose, treat or work with your horse. If you aren't sure whom you can trust, talk to a leading equine vet clinic or professional horse trainer and ask who they would recommend.

Deworming your horse

All horses have internal parasites, which can pose a threat to their health if the worm burden tips beyond what the horse is able to handle. They pick up internal parasites from contaminated pasture when microscopic eggs and larvae have been passed out with manure, which the horse then ingests when it grazes.

The effects of worm burden can be extensive, especially in young or sick horses, and early signs include poor condition, dull coat, loss of appetite and, in some cases, an itchy tail. If left untreated, worm burden can eventually result in diarrhoea, anaemia, lethargy, increased susceptibility to infection, pneumonia, coughing, organ damage, weight loss, colic and even death. A strategic deworming programme, which includes deworming and careful paddock maintenance, is vital for successful worm control.

Deworming programmes

There are several elements to a successful deworming programme.

CORRECT DOSE: Owners frequently underestimate their horse's weight and as a result under-dose with dewormer. This can cause some worms to survive and become resistant to the active ingredients in the dewormer. Using a weight tape or scales will accurately determine your horse's weight.

USE THE RIGHT DEWORMER: Not all dewormers are effective against all species of internal parasites, so make sure the dewormer you use has the correct active ingredients for the type of worms you need to target. A broad-spectrum dewormer, which has a combination of three different active ingredients that target most worms (including tapeworm and bots), should be used at least once a year.

FAECAL EGG COUNT (FEC): Getting an FEC done is useful for assessing whether your adult horse has a worm burden high enough to require deworming (young horses don't need an FEC and should be routinely dewormed every 4 months). It not only determines the species and the EPG (eggs per gram) in your horse's faeces, but can also indicate what active ingredients need to be used for a successful deworming. However, FECs will only indicate the levels of worms that lay eggs as part of their lifecycle, so will not determine bot, tapeworm, encrusted cyathostomes or pinworm infestation. To collect a sample, take a small handful of fresh manure (less than an hour old) and put it in a small container, then send it to your vet for sampling.

DON'T DEWORM TOO OFTEN: Deworming too often, or rotating quickly between dewormers, has been shown to create resistance; FECs can help determine when and if your horse should be dewormed. With strategic paddock management, adult horses may only need to be dewormed once a year (preferably in late autumn, or spring and autumn if it's a more temperate year) with moxidectin/praziquantel to get encrusted cyathostomes and tapeworm (which cause disease and don't show up on FEC), while 'high shedders' (see below) may need to be dewormed every 2 to 4 months. Therefore, an appropriate deworming programme should be designed by your vet.

EGG SHEDDING LEVELS: 20% of the horses, in any given herd, will shed 80% of the eggs. These horses are known as 'high shedders' and even on healthy pasture will tend to have a high FEC (of more than 500 EPG). Low shedders make up 50–70% of the adult population and on the same pasture will tend to always have a low FEC (of less than 200 EPG).

> ### TOP TIPS TO CONTROL PARASITES
>
> - **PREVENT OVERGRAZING:** When pasture is overgrazed, horses graze close to manure piles, which increases the risk of ingesting parasites.
> - **DON'T FEED ON THE GROUND:** Feeding hay in feed troughs, hay bags or hay nets will help avoid contamination from infected pasture.
> - **PICK UP MANURE:** On intensively managed properties, picking up the manure in your paddock at least twice a week can help keep pastures healthy.
> - **CROSS-GRAZE:** Grazing sheep or cattle on your paddocks (see page 77) will reduce worm burden, as these species are not susceptible to the same worms and will eat the grass close to the manure. Cross-grazing can be achieved by rotating stock through your paddocks once your horse has grazed them, or by grazing different species together at the same time.
> - **REST YOUR PADDOCKS:** Rotate horses between paddocks, allowing 6 to 12 weeks for each pasture to rest before regrazing. This will allow enough time for most worm eggs and larvae to die, although some can be present in the soil for up to a year.
> - **DEWORM NEW ARRIVALS:** All new horses should be dewormed with a broad-spectrum dewormer, and have all bot eggs removed from the coat (see page 110), prior to arriving at your property. This will reduce worm infestation on your pasture and in your existing horses.
> - **HAVE A DEWORMING PROGRAMME:** Establish a good deworming programme, based on advice from your vet, to ensure that your horse's risk of parasites is reduced.

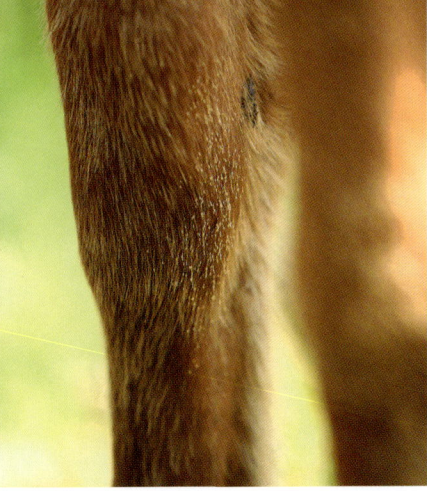

Left: Bot larvae, which have been passed in the horse's manure, will pupate in the soil for 3 to 5 weeks, before hatching into bot flies and starting the life cycle again.

Right: Bot eggs are laid by female bot flies, primarily on the horse's legs.

HOW TO DEWORM YOUR HORSE

For many horses, deworming can be a highly stressful experience. Use this method to train your horse to open its mouth in a relaxed fashion for the paste to be squirted onto its tongue. This method can also be used to prepare your horse for ulcer treatment or oral sedatives.

1. First, get your horse comfortable with having its mouth touched. Slide your hand from the cheekbone down towards its lips until you notice a moment of tension in the horse. As soon as signs of tension become present, pause and wait for your horse to relax, then immediately remove your hand and back away a few steps to reward your horse and give it time to process the experience.
2. Once your horse has shown signs of relaxation (licking and chewing its lips, softening its expression or yawning), repeat the step above, gradually expanding your horse's comfort zone until you are able to run your hand over its lips while it remains relaxed. *Top tip:* Some horses are better to deworm from directly in front, or on the right side, as horses traditionally have their mouths handled from the left and they may have more negative associations with the left side.
3. When you can run your hand down from the cheekbone to the lips on your first attempt (with no signs of tension becoming present), gently insert a finger into the corner of your horse's mouth.
4. Repeat this until your horse is comfortable with you placing a finger into the corner of its mouth, then progress to applying a gentle pressure on the tongue so that the horse opens its mouth. Reward your horse immediately by removing your finger and finishing the session.
5. In future sessions you can move on to introducing whatever you intend to put into your horse's mouth: deworming paste, an oral sedative or ulcer treatment. Build up your horse's confidence in a similar, progressive manner by working through Steps 1–4. Once you can complete these in a relaxed manner on the first attempt, repeat the steps holding the syringe in your hand. Start by running the object from the horse's cheekbone down to its lips, only inserting the object into the corner of the horse's mouth once it is relaxed.
6. Once your horse is comfortable with all of these steps and they can be done in a relaxed manner, in one smooth motion and with no tension present, you can progress to actually squirting the medication in. End each session on a positive note by rewarding your horse.

Top tip: To create positive associations with the syringe, you can initially fill it with molasses, or a similar flavour that your horse likes — only changing to a dewormer or medication once the horse is comfortable about the process.

Top four: The different stages of preparing your horse for deworming.

Bottom: Large strongyles found in a 7-week-old wild foal.

Common species of worm

SMALL STRONGYLES (SMALL REDWORMS): Once ingested from the pasture, small strongyles migrate to the intestinal wall where they reach maturity within 6 to 10 weeks. They can hibernate in the gut while waiting for the right conditions to emerge. If large numbers are present, they can cause loss of condition, colic, dull coat, loss of appetite, diarrhoea (50% mortality), anaemia, depression and death. Moxidectin is required for the successful treatment of small strongles.

LARGE STRONGYLES (LARGE REDWORMS): Once ingested from pasture, large strongyles migrate to the intestinal walls and various organs and arteries where they reach maturity within 6 to 11 months. They are one of the most destructive parasites in horses and can cause blockages in the horse's organs, blood vessels and arteries, resulting in blood clots, colic, lameness, diarrhoea, anaemia, depression and even death.

ASCARIDS (ROUNDWORMS): Adult ascarids can be up to 60 centimetres long and live in the small intestine, where they lay eggs which are passed out in the manure. When ingested, the eggs hatch and migrate to the lungs, where they are coughed up, before returning to the small intestine and maturing into adults. Ascarids can cause damage to the liver and lungs, or even rupture the small intestine, which can be fatal. These are a particular concern in young horses and foals.

TAPEWORMS: Infected horses pass a small number of eggs onto the pasture in their manure; the eggs are then eaten by mites, which become hosts. The horse then ingests the mites, allowing the tapeworm larvae to attach to the horse's intestinal lining, where they cause inflammation of the small intestine, tissue damage and nutritional deficiencies. In large quantities, they can also cause intestinal impaction and colic.

PINWORMS: These white worms grow up to 10 centimetres in length and are found in the horse's large intestine and rectum. They can be passed on to, and picked up from, any surface the horse touches. They cause itchiness, hair loss (from horses rubbing their rumps and tails), digestive issues and poor growth in young horses.

BOTS: Adult bot flies lay their eggs on the horse's coat (typically on the forelegs), which the horse licks off. This motion causes the eggs to hatch, and once in the horse's mouth they burrow through the gums and then migrate and attach to the stomach lining, where they remain for almost a year before being passed out in manure and emerging as adult bot flies. When present in high numbers they can cause colic, or may even rupture the stomach. To help manage bots, it is essential to remove the eggs with a bot knife as soon as they have been laid on your horse. *Top tip:* Never remove bot eggs when the horse is standing on grass or near hay or feed, as they can be ingested; instead, remove them on a driveway, washdown bay or concrete floor.

DENTAL CARE

Horses are designed to eat large volumes of high-fibre feed, which requires their teeth to be correctly aligned to enable their digestive system to work efficiently. When a horse drops its head to eat, or is asked to work on a contact when being ridden (see page 291), the lower jaw must be able to slide under the upper jaw, as well as move from side to side without restriction.

To maintain the correct functioning of the jaw, regular dental care (and the correction of any issues as they arise) is one of the most important and often overlooked aspects of equine management. Abnormalities of the teeth, upper or lower jaw, or the temporomandibular joint (TMJ) can lead to excessive pain when the horse is chewing or being ridden, causing serious health and behavioural issues to develop.

Young horses, from the age of 2½ to 5, should have dental examinations every 6 months, while adult horses between the ages of 6 to 17 years should be checked annually. Older horses, over the age of 18, should be checked every 6 to 12 months, and immediately if they are showing signs of discomfort or struggling to hold their condition.

Dental issues

Numerous dental issues can arise during a horse's lifetime, including the following.

SHARP ENAMEL POINTS: Most horses have sharp points, caused by the horse's teeth constantly erupting throughout its life. Any parts of the tooth that are not worn down by chewing will leave sharp points, which cause painful lacerations on the horse's cheeks and tongue, as well as packing feed in the cheeks.

RETAINED CAPS: Between the ages of 2½ and 5 years old, horses shed their deciduous teeth (also known as milk or baby teeth), and they are replaced by permanent ones. If the caps don't shed at the correct times, it can cause infections or eruption cysts (also known as teeth bumps), as well as misalignment or deformities to the permanent molars beneath. Because of this, horses within this age range should have their teeth checked every 6 months.

WOLF TEETH: Small tooth remnants that sit just in front of the first cheek tooth, most commonly on the upper jaw. Horses may have two, one or none, and some do not erupt through the gum (known as blind wolf teeth). Their presence interferes with bit placement and can cause pain-related issues to develop, including rearing, head tossing or bolting. Wolf teeth should always be removed prior to riding a horse in a bit, and can be done by an equine dental technician or equine veterinary dentist under sedation.

RAMPS: Because horses' teeth continuously erupt throughout their lifetime, they rely on the opposing tooth to wear them evenly. When a tooth is not in alignment, or is fractured, missing or damaged, the tooth above or below will grow into the gap, causing ramps to develop. This will affect the lateral (side to side) and anterior/posterior (back and forth) movement of the jaw, which will cause difficulty chewing.

TEMPROMANDIBULAR JOINT (TMJ) CONDITIONS: The TMJ is found where the lower jaw (manibular) connects with the upper jaw (maxilla), about halfway between the base of the horse's ear and the outside corner of its eye. Its function is primarily for chewing, as well as allowing the rider to communicate with the horse using a bit (through hand aids, see page 281). TMJ issues can include inflammation, arthritis, subluxation (partial dislocation), fractures, breaks and infection, as well as damage to the soft tissue or muscles that support the joint.

HOOKS: Hooks generally develop on the first upper premolars and last lower molars. If misalignment results and there is no opposing tooth to wear them down, they can become very sharp over time and inhibit the anterior/posterior movement of the jaw, as well as cause TMJ issues.

EXCESSIVE TRANSVERSE RIDGES (ETR): Excessive ridging of the grinding surfaces of the teeth can cause restricted movement in the jaw and difficulty chewing.

WAVES: If there is uneven wear of the molar arcades, from a lack of dental care, retained caps or impacted molars, it can cause difficulty chewing.

INTERPROXIMAL SPACES: Gaps between the teeth, which can trap feed and lead to painful tooth decay, gum infections and bad breath.

ABSCESSES: If a tooth is fractured or damaged, an abscess may develop, draining from the root canal to the outside of the jaw.

MISPLACED TEETH: Developmental abnormalities can cause teeth to grow in the wrong place, including on the neck.

PARROT OR MONKEY MOUTH: If the top and bottom jaws do not align correctly, often due to birth abnormalities, it can cause the teeth to wear unevenly, resulting in hooks and ramps.

CHALKY TEETH: Insufficient mineralisation due to nutritional deficiencies during development.

SHEAR MOUTH: This is a serious dental issue that happens if the table angle of one side of the arcades is steeper than the opposite, due to uneven wear. A shear mouth will often be accompanied by slanted incisors.

PERIDONTAL DISEASE: Inflammation of the gums, tooth ligaments and underlying bone affects up to 30% of horses at some stage of their lives. The precursor to periodontal disease is gingivitis and if left untreated, it can result in the loss of the tooth.

Signs your horse may be suffering from dental or TMJ issues
- Bad smelling breath
- Quidding (dropping partially chewed feed)
- Difficulty chewing or eating
- Packing feed inside the cheeks (often seen as hampster-like swellings on the cheek)
- Decreased appetite
- Weight loss
- Presence of undigested food in the manure
- Hard or soft swelling above or below teeth
- Pus discharging from the jaw
- Lacerations of the cheeks or tongue

Top left: Retained caps and wolf teeth, after being removed by an equine dentist.

Top right: Bloody clumps of grass packed between the teeth of a 2-year-old.

Bottom left: A horse wearing a speculum during a routine equine examination.

Bottom right: Misaligned, displaced and broken teeth in a 17-year-old wild stallion; most likely from impacts during stallion fights, malnutrition and lack of dental care.

- Bumps under the jaw (can be a symptom of eruption cysts)
- Draining tracts on face
- Nasal discharge (particularly on one side)
- Lolling the tongue or opening the mouth excessively, including when ridden
- Colic and choke (caused by insufficient grinding of feed)
- Food pocketing between the teeth
- Excessive salivation
- Bleeding from the mouth

The chronic effects of dental or TMJ abnormalities can also cause serious behavioural issues which, if left untreated, can lead to bad habits that are hard to break. These include the following:
- avoidance of being haltered or bridled, including being difficult to catch
- head shyness
- head shaking, head tossing or head tilting, especially when being ridden
- ridden vices including rearing, bucking, spooking or a high head carriage
- performance issues including inability to pick up the correct canter lead (see page 285), refusing jumps, difficulty turning or stopping, or resistance to working on a contact (see page 291)
- chewing the bit excessively.

HOOF CARE

Care of the hoof

Good hoof knowledge and care is one of the most important requirements of horse ownership, and the saying 'no hoof, no horse' sums up just how important hoof care is. If a horse's hooves are not balanced, its joints, tendons and ligaments will be placed under stress, which has a cumulative effect throughout the body. Because so many soundness issues start in the hooves, every owner and rider should know what a healthy hoof looks like so they can determine whether their horse requires professional care to correct problems before these develop into major issues.

> Like a human fingernail, a horse's hoof grows continuously. In the wild, they are usually worn down naturally by travelling long distances, often over rocky or sandy terrain. In domestication, however, horses don't cover as much distance and the hooves are not able to wear down as they would naturally. Because of this, regular trimming and care is required to maintain good hoof balance and function.

A balanced hoof can be determined visually and should show the following.
- A good hoof–pastern axis (see diagram on page 50).
- From the side, the coronet band should be a smooth, straight line. If it is bowed, then the hoof is unbalanced.
- From the front, the coronet band should be parallel to the ground, indicating correct heel height. If it is sloping, the heels will be uneven and placing stress on the hoof structure.
- On the front legs, the heels should be placed directly below the supporting bones of the leg. If a line was drawn through the centre of the knees and fetlock, to the back of the heels, it should fall in a straight line.

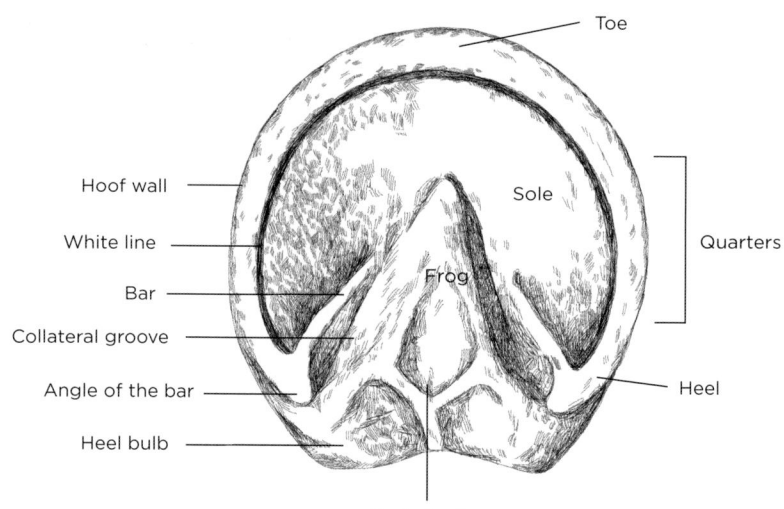

The points of the horse's hoof.

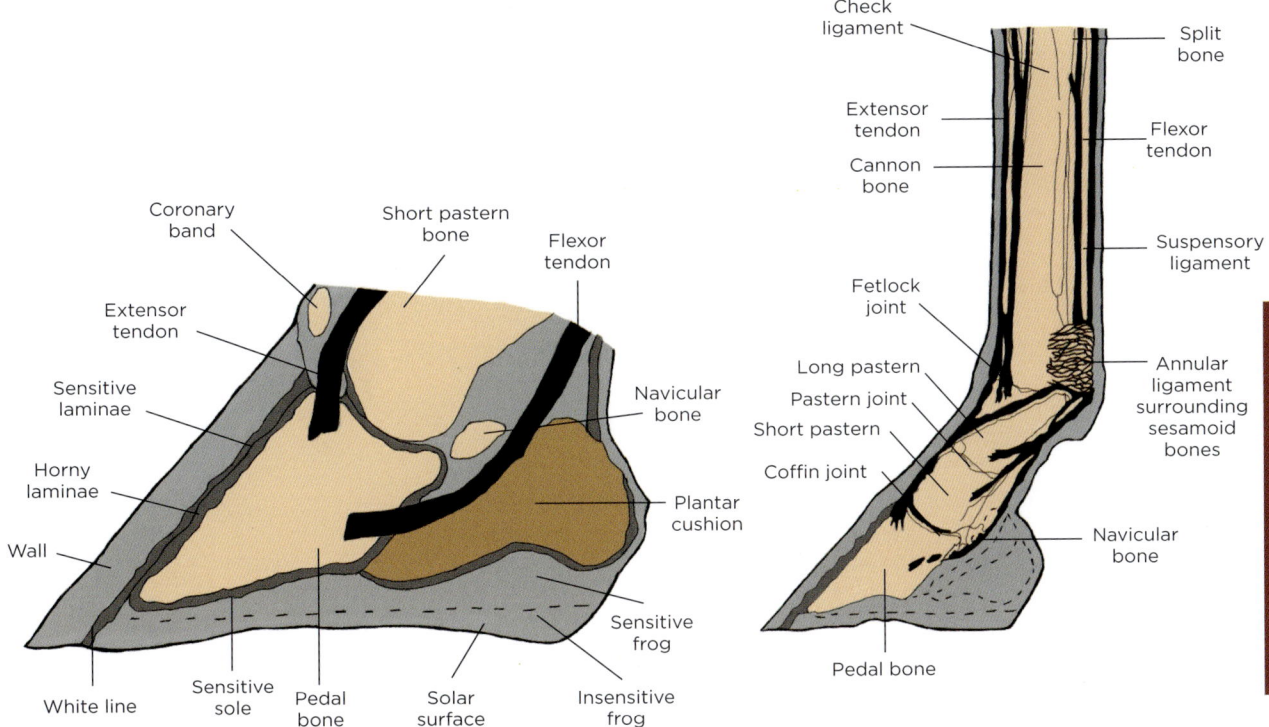

TOP TIPS TO CARE FOR YOUR HORSE'S HOOVES

- **PICK OUT THE HOOVES:** Your horse's feet should be picked out before and after they are ridden, to remove dirt and any stones lodged in them. While doing this, keep an eye out for any issues such as thrush, contracted heels, seedy toe or cracks (see page 117), any foreign objects — such as a nail — embedded in the hoof or a sprung shoe.
- **HAVE REGULAR HOOF TRIMMING DONE:** All horses, no matter their age, should have regular farrier care to maintain or correct their hoof balance. Foals should have their first trim at about 2 to 4 weeks, then be trimmed every 4 to 6 weeks for the rest of their life.
- **OIL YOUR HORSE'S HOOVES:** Applying a good-quality hoof oil to your horse's hooves after they have been trimmed or shod, and before every ride, will help them retain moisture. In hot, dry conditions, it is recommended to soak your horse's hooves in water before oiling.
- **FEED FOR GOOD HOOVES:** In most cases, good-quality grass provides all the nutrients needed for a healthy hoof, but if your horse has poor-quality hooves then it may be nutritionally deficient; if so, a hoof supplement will be beneficial.
- **REGULAR EXERCISE:** Movement increases blood flow to the hoof, so regular exercise is essential for good health. A horse that is confined to a stable or yard, or with limited ability to move around, will likely have compromised hoof quality, including an increased risk of boxy feet or contracted heels.

The internal structure of the hoof.

- **PROTECT THE BOTTOM OF YOUR HORSE'S HOOVES:** If your horse has sensitive hooves, you can apply a 'toughening' product to the soles to harden these tissues, or if it is shod, you can have a plastic or rubber pad placed under its shoes to provide extra protection. Hoof boots are also an option for barefoot horses.

Common hoof issues

SEEDY TOE: The white line between the hoof wall and the sole is relatively fragile and can be easily compromised if small rocks become embedded in it (especially if the laminae has been stretched, which indicates past inflammation of the laminae), allowing fungi and bacteria to track up the hoof wall. Often a crack in the hoof wall will develop, indicating that the white line has been compromised. The white line can also weaken and separate if horses have long toes (which can cause inflammation of the laminae), uneven hooves or have laminitis, which can increase the risk of seedy toe. Regular trimming, good hoof care and frequently picking out the hooves will help prevent seedy toe, but once it is established it will need to be treated by a farrier or vet to prevent it from worsening.

CONTRACTED HOOVES: When viewing the hoof from underneath, the bulbs of the heels should not be inside the line of the collateral groove. If they are, then the hoof is contracted, which will cause reduced blood flow and limit the hoof's ability to expand and contract correctly. Contracted hooves can be caused by poor hoof care or injury, are often associated with deep cleft and thrush, and corrective trimming will be needed.

ABSCESSES: Hoof abscesses occur when bacteria get into the internal hoof structure, often through a damaged white line, crack or nail hole, and cause pus or an infection to build up. This creates extremely painful pressure under the hoof wall or sole, which can cause severe lameness (even to the point you may think your horse has a broken leg). Farrier or vet attention may be needed to drain the abscess. Left unattended, the pus will usually rupture at the horse's coronary band, through the sole of the hoof, or further up the horse's leg, which can cause extended suffering and can compromise the hoof structure.

GRASS OR SAND CRACKS: Grass cracks in the hoof wall usually begin as small fissure lines starting from the toe and moving upwards, while sand cracks start at the coronary band and move downwards. Grass cracks are usually caused by a sudden change in ground conditions from very wet to very dry, overgrown hooves, poor nutrition, a lack of exercise, uneven hoof balance, poor conformation or seedy toe. Sand cracks usually occur as a result of trauma to the coronary band caused by unbalanced hooves or concussion stress. To prevent cracks worsening, it is important to have them stabilised by your farrier or vet; with severe cracks, the horse may even require corrective shoeing, including having the crack glued or wired together.

THRUSH: This is a common fungal condition of the frog, which can be caused by prolonged exposure to wet and muddy ground, as well as infrequent trimming or poor

Top left: A sand crack on the right side of the hoof from a fence injury, and a grass crack at the toe.

Top right: An unstable hoof crack, which required veterinary intervention.

Middle left: Long toes.

Middle right: Grass cracks forming from overgrown hooves that are overdue for re-shoeing.

Bottom: A severe case of laminitis in a wild horse, showing long toes and separation of the laminae, bruised and cracked soles (from pedal bone rotation) and overgrown heels.

hoof balance (which can prevent the frog from touching the ground, restricting its ability to function correctly). Thrush has a strong and unpleasant smell, and causes the affected areas to become sensitive and black in colour. In extreme cases, the thrush can eat down into the frog cleft, between the bulbs, affecting the internal structures — this can take months to correct and in extreme cases can be very painful to the horse and result in behavioural issues or lameness. Once the hoof has been correctly trimmed, thrush can be combatted with hydrogen peroxide, Thrush Buster or a copper sulphate solution to kill the fungus; this can take several days, or even weeks, and requires constant care until the frog and bulbs return to a healthy state.

LAMINITIS (ALSO KNOWN AS FOUNDER): The hoof wall is attached to the coffin bone by interlocked structures called laminae. When these are compromised, the coffin bone can rotate and tip down towards the sole of the hoof, triggering laminitis (usually seen in the front hooves). It is usually caused by over-feeding, a sudden intake of high-sugar feeds (including fast-growing grass in spring and autumn), or a trauma or injury that alters the internal structures of the hoof. It can also be caused by retained placenta in mares that have recently foaled, from a horse bearing weight on one leg unevenly (due to an injury) or by excessive concussion on hard ground. In the early stages the hooves will become hot and the digital pulse (which is caused by blood pumping through an artery, and can be felt by pressing your fingers against your horse's fetlock and pastern area) will increase; when this happens, the horse will not want to move forwards and instead may rock back on its forelegs to relieve the pressure and pain. As soon as these symptoms are present, the horse should be placed on soft bedding and be given immediate vet attention, as laminitis can quickly cause irreversible damage. Corrective trimming may also be needed to restore foot balance. Once a horse has had laminitis, it can become prone to laminitic episodes, which may require careful management in the future.

SHEARED HEELS: When a horse develops sheared heels, the symmetry of the horse's heel becomes unbalanced, resulting in one heel bearing most of the weight and distorting upwards from the other. This can be caused by injury, poor limb conformation or incorrect hoof balance, and requires good-quality radiographs and an experienced farrier to correct it; the earlier the better.

The function of the barefoot and shod hoof

A bare hoof is designed to expand as the horse places weight on it, then spring back into shape when it is lifted off the ground. In the wild, the horse's constant movement allows this natural contraction and expansion cycle to maintain blood flow to the hoof, with the bulbs and frogs absorbing concussion on the horse's lower limbs.

However, in domestication, reduced exercise and unnatural workloads and expectations can compromise the correct function of the hoof, as well as the horse's performance and willingness to work. The decision to keep a horse barefoot or shod is one that should be made for each individual horse, depending on its hoof quality and conformation, the terrain it is ridden over, and its competition needs.

Top left: Hooves being trimmed in preparation for shoeing.

Top right: For horses with tender hooves, shoes can provide protection when walking on abrasive surfaces.

Bottom: Farrier tools.
1. Shoeing hammer.
2. Hoof tester.
3. Nail clencher.
4. Nail puller.
5. Shoe puller.
6. Hoof nipper.
7. Hoof knife.
8. Hind shoe.
9. Front shoe.
10. Rasp.

> **BAREFOOT VS SHOD IN COMPETITION**
>
> Barefoot = lower levels, or on arena surfaces
>
> Shod = higher levels, or on grass
>
> While we will often leave our horses and ponies barefoot when they are being started under saddle, or jumping at lower heights, they usually benefit from being shod, so they can wear studs, when they are performing at the higher heights. Because many events in New Zealand are held on grass arenas, with less than ideal surfaces, we have found that many horses that are showjumped barefoot (and especially by amateur riders) often have to guard their bodies to prevent themselves from slipping around corners or on take-off. This can result in the horse developing stilted movement, which can limit its ability to perform correctly, often leading to muscular and skeletal issues. This not only compromises the horse's long-term soundness, but also risks a loss of confidence; once a horse has lost its footing a few times, it can quickly learn to chip in or start refusing at the jumps. Some horse and rider combinations, however, are naturally balanced and may perform barefoot at high levels for many years, with no soundness issues; as always, it depends on the individual horse, and how they are ridden and managed.

Reasons for shoeing include the following.

PROTECTION: If the hoof wears away faster than it grows then it can become tender, resulting in bruising, abscesses and lameness. Horses with poor hoof quality or thin soles, or those working on abrasive arena surfaces, roads or rocky surfaces are more likely to need some form of protection. Hoof boots or glue-on shoes may be sufficient for pleasure or trekking riders wanting their horse to have some protection in certain situations.

TRACTION: Many performance horses, especially at the higher levels of competitions, need extra traction for the manoeuvres required of them. Jumpers that have to twist and turn on grass or slippery surfaces usually benefit from studs screwed into the shoe (see below); meanwhile, reining horses need less traction for sliding stops, which can be provided by using sliding plates.

CORRECTIVE SHOEING: Some horses require shoeing to correct conformational faults or help a weak hoof maintain proper balance and shape, while others may need it for remedial reasons like laminitis or ringbone.

Studding

Studs are blunt metal spikes that are screwed into a horse's shoes to provide extra grip on slick grass surfaces, or in muddy conditions. They are most often used in eventing, showjumping or games, where horses have to jump at speed or turn on tight corners, and in top-level dressage, to help the horse stay balanced. Even in other disciplines, or at lower levels, studs can be necessary to ensure that your horse doesn't lose its confidence from slipping on corners or at the base of a jump.

Top: Shoes being removed by the farrier.

Bottom: A horse with grass studs, which allow for extra traction.

Left: A well-balanced hoof, showing a good hoof-pastern axis and appropriate heel support.

Right: Oiling your horse's hooves will help them retain moisture, reducing the chances of cracks and other hoof issues developing.

Opposite page: A basic stud kit, with an array of studs and tools.

TOP TIPS FOR STUDDING

- **USE THE RIGHT TYPE OF STUDS:** The studs used must be appropriate for the surface: bigger, squarer studs are needed for wet or muddy conditions, while smaller, pointed studs are better for hard ground. If you aren't sure what studs to use, ask an experienced rider or trainer what studs they would recommend to suit your horse or pony's size, the ground conditions and the class height you are entered in, as these will all factor in to which studs to select.

- **HAVE YOUR HORSE STUDDED FOR THE SHORTEST TIME POSSIBLE:** Stud just before you tack up your horse to ride, then unstud as soon as you've finished. This is important to prevent strain on your horse's tendons and suspensory ligaments (if the ground is hard, being studded is much like a person wearing high heels) and to reduce the risk of injury if your horse kicks another horse, itself or a person. Never keep your horse studded while travelling or overnight.

- **DON'T OVERSTUD:** While studs do provide important traction for horses, it's crucial that they aren't overstudded; on landing, the hoof is supposed to slide a little to prevent concussion to the lower limbs, which can be restricted by using studs that are too big for the conditions. For this reason, you should use the smallest studs possible for the conditions; it's much better to understud (or use no studs and ride more cautiously) than overstud and risk injury.

- **KEEP THE HOOF BALANCED:** Generally, your horse should have one stud on both the inside and the outside heel of every hoof, with blunter and slightly smaller studs on the inside (to prevent damage to the opposite leg and hoof if the horse were to slip or stand on itself). Using only one stud in each hoof can cause uneven strain on the horse's leg.

- **CLEAN THE STUD HOLES IN ADVANCE:** Small rocks and dirt can become impacted in the stud hole in between competitions, so it's beneficial to use screw-in stud keepers, rubber stud plugs or cotton wool to keep the holes free from debris. If you use plugs or cotton wool, some dirt can still get imbedded in the stud hole, so it's beneficial to clean out the stud holes the day before a competition, then put the plug or cotton wool back so that it's easier and quicker on the day of the show.
- **ALWAYS USE BOOTS:** A horse should always wear jumping boots (see page 230) while studded, for protection against puncture wounds if it accidentally strikes its own leg. Overreach boots may also be beneficial if your horse is prone to puncturing its coronet band.
- **WEAR A STUD GUARD WHILE JUMPING:** It's important to use a stud guard (see page 214) when you are jumping to prevent the studs puncturing your horse's belly.
- **PRACTICE MAKES PERFECT:** Practise putting studs in at home, when you're not in a rush and at risk of missing your class, in case it takes longer than expected.

ILLNESS AND INJURY

If you take on the responsibility of owning a horse, it is essential that you are willing and able to meet the costs associated with any medical treatment it may need. Horses can fall prey to illnesses and injuries that can seriously affect their health, so knowing when to call a vet is important.

If you are knowledgeable and capable, you may be able to manage some basic health care yourself, but in many cases calling a vet will be imperative to your horse's well-being. In emergency situations, the sooner you call a vet, the more likely it is that your horse will have a positive outcome; especially in the event of colic, poisoning or a life-threatening injury.

Vet bills can be substantial at times, especially if the vet needs to be called after hours, you live rurally, or your horse needs surgery or special treatment. When it comes to deciding whether to call a vet, however, the health of your horse should always be put first; if you are concerned about the cost of unexpected vet bills, insuring your horse can provide peace of mind.

> If your horse is insured, be sure to immediately notify your insurance company in the event of any injury or illness, so they are able to be involved with the costs of treatment.

Recognising illness or injury

An understanding of your horse's vital signs is important to determine when your horse is unwell, allowing you to differentiate between what is 'normal' and what is 'abnormal'.

Vital signs

- **TEMPERATURE**: Using a digital thermometer, grease the end with petroleum jelly and gently insert it into the rectum, holding the tail up with your other hand. Make sure you stand to the side of your horse's rump, out of kicking range, in case it objects to the procedure. When the thermometer beeps, remove it; it should read between 37.5 and 38.5 degrees Celsius. Anything over or under this means your horse's temperature is not normal and you should call your vet.
  Note: Make sure you wash the thermometer after you have used it, before placing it back in your first aid kit.
- **PULSE**: Place your fingers (not your thumb) on the digital artery on the pastern, or the facial artery (where it crosses the jaw bone), and count the number of beats over a 15-second period, then multiply this number by four to get the number of beats per minute. This should be between 25 and 45 beats per minute (although new-born foals will be between 80 and 120, and yearlings can range from 40 to 60 beats per minute). If it is higher than this while your horse is resting, a vet should be called.

- **RESPIRATION**: A horse will normally take about 10 to 20 breaths per minute while it is at rest. Watch its chest move in and out and count the breaths. Call a vet if your horse's respiration rate is above or below normal.
- **GUMS**: These should be pink and take less than 2 seconds to return to the normal colour if pressed during a CRT test (see page 72). It is worth taking note of your horse's normal gum colour so you are able to determine if the gums are lighter or darker than they would normally appear.
- **SKIN**: This should quickly spring back when it is pinched. If the skin doesn't rapidly retract, it is a sign of dehydration (see page 72).
- **GUT MOBILITY**: The horse's gut should produce consistent and active rumbling sounds on both sides of its body. Evaluate each side for at least one minute by resting your ear against the back of the stomach or using a stethoscope; between one and three rumbles (known as borborygmi) a minute is normal. If you can't hear any rumbling, or more than three per minute, your horse is likely in distress, and may even be colicing (see page 131).

Other signs your horse might have an illness or injury
- Standing with its head down, not moving, in a depressed stance, or alone
- Starey coat (a dry, brittle coat that isn't shedding or is dull in colour)
- Dull eyes
- Drooling
- Shivering or sweating
- Diarrhoea
- Weight loss or inability to gain weight
- Glands enlarged
- Snotty nose, cough or difficulty breathing
- Unable or unwilling to eat
- Drinking more or less than normal
- Urinating more or less than normal
- Herring gut (tucked up along the stomach meridian)
- Lameness
- Changes to behaviour, including when ridden
- Choke (see page 133)
- Not passing manure

First aid kit

It is advisable to have a range of basic veterinary products available in your equine first aid kit, so you can treat minor injuries and illnesses. We suggest the following.
- Thermometer
- Blunt-ended scissors and clippers to remove hair
- Antiseptic wash or an iodine scrub
- Antibiotic powder, for dressing wounds

- Active mānuka honey
- Cotton wool to pack into holes in the hoof wall
- Disposable nappies, for poulticing hooves, as absorbent pads for wounds, or as hock dressings
- Gamgee, for wound protection
- Animalintex poultice dressings, for hot or cold poulticing
- Vetwrap or cohesive bandages
- Elastoplast (sticky 10- to 15-centimetre bandages), for wound dressings
- Stable bandages and leg wraps
- Electrical tape, to secure bandage ends
- Scalpel blades, to remove Elastoplast bandages
- Epsom salts, for poulticing
- TuffRock GI, for colic
- 60 millilitre syringe, to administer TuffRock GI
- Wire cutters, in case of fencing emergencies

Basic first aid care

Every owner should have a basic understanding of how to care for their horse. Attending an equine first aid course can be beneficial, to give you the skills needed to deal with minor injuries or illnesses, or to keep your horse stable in an emergency until the vet is able to arrive.

Common first aid practices for injuries include the following.

POULTICES: Hot poulticing (using a product like Animalintex) is used to draw infection or inflammation out of an area; cold poulticing (e.g. with clay) is used for bruised, swollen or raw tissues.

LINIMENT: A liquid or gel, with medicinal herbs, which can be applied directly to the skin to create either a cooling or heating effect. They help remove toxins, reduce swelling and relieve stiffness or soreness.

> We often use a deep-heat liniment on horses with back muscle pain to help reduce inflammation and draw out toxins. Add liniment to hot water, then soak a towel in it before wringing it out. Once the towel is cool enough to touch, place it on the horse before covering it with plastic and then a wool rug to prolong the benefits of the added heat.
>
> For a cold poultice, we use the volcanic-rock-based TuffRock, which is very effective at reducing inflammation and drawing out excess heat.

TUBBING: Used to soften the hoof wall and draw out infection in the hoof (usually caused by an abscess or a puncture wound). Add Epsom salts to hot water in a bucket; once it is cool enough to touch, place the horse's clean hoof in it and leave for up to 20 minutes, twice a day. Some horses can be difficult to tub, so use a shallower basin if needed and stay with the horse, or use a hoof boot. Dry the hoof and pastern thoroughly afterwards.

COLD HOSING: Used to reduce heat and inflammation in swollen or bruised tissue, and to relieve pain. Hold a hose with a steady stream of cold water on the affected area for 15 to 20 minutes, two or three times a day. *Note:* If your horse is not used to being hosed, untie and hold it, then quietly start hosing from the hoof, before gradually moving up the leg to the injured area.

COLD COMPRESSES: Cooling packs or ice boots (which are kept in the freezer) can be used as an alternative to cold hosing. They are useful at home and at shows, for injuries or to help with recovery after strenuous exercise (especially on hard ground). *Note:* Ice can burn the leg, so dampen the boot after it is removed from the freezer and then leave it on for no more than 15 minutes.

ALTERNATIVE THERAPIES: There are numerous therapies available to aid healing in a horse, all with their own benefits. Just like vets, practitioners have varying degrees of experience and ability so find what feels right for you and remember to stay open-minded to all practices, as each horse requires different, individualised care.

- CHIROPRACTIC OR PHYSIOTHERAPY: Helps to restore full range of movement to the horse, to reduce pain and increase performance by focusing on the whole make-up of the equine skeleton including bone, muscle, fascia, ligaments, joints, tissue, etc.
- CONTACT C.A.R.E.: Works to release skeletal sensory shock, which is caused by the bone contracting under impact.
- HEAT LAMPS/VIBRATING FLOORS: Increase blood flow to the tissues. These are usually quite expensive to purchase, and are usually seen in rehabilitation facilities to reduce recovery time.
- LASER THERAPY: High-power laser light aids healing and reduces inflammation by promoting tissue, ligament, muscle and bone repair. It is especially beneficial for splints, wounds and tendon injuries and substantially reduces the recovery time.
- MASSAGE THERAPY: Massage (including massage units and pulse machines) increases blood flow to the tissues, promoting quicker recovery.
- ENERGY HEALING: Works to clear, balance and restore the horse's energy system, as well as reducing pain and enhancing recovery.
- EMOTIONAL RELEASE THERAPY: Works to clear negative emotions that become trapped in the body, which can be caused by the horse switching into a survival instinct (see page 60) rather than processing stress as it happens. Trapped emotions can cause irrational fears, aggression, weakened immune system, depression, anxiety and PTSD.

> ## ALTERNATIVE COMPLEMENTARY THERAPIES
>
> Alternative complementary therapies can be beneficial to restore health following injuries and illness (even in times that aggressive veterinary treatments are also required). We have had great success using alternative complementary therapies (see page 127) to help restore the full range of movement to horses, increasing recovery times from illnesses and injuries, as well as drastically improving behavioural issues.

COMMON INJURIES AND AILMENTS

Outlined below are some of the most common injuries and ailments your horse may experience, to help you gain an understanding of basic health care and when to call a vet.

Injuries/wounds

Horses are prone to injuries; while some can be treated satisfactorily at home, others will require veterinary attention to promote healing, minimise scarring or long-term damage, or prevent death.

Emergencies include the following.

CUT ARTERY: Blood spurting uncontrollably from a wound indicates that an artery has been cut. Apply firm pressure by pressing a wad of gamgee or a nappy to the wound (if possible, bandage it in place; if not, hold the pressure until a vet arrives). Horses can lose up to 10 litres of blood without showing signs of shock, so don't panic; even if the horse appears to have lost a lot of blood, a full recovery is often possible.

PUNCTURE WOUNDS: Deep puncture wounds can cause internal damage and allow tetanus and other bacterial infections to develop. If a puncture happens near a joint or tendon, it is even more serious. Giving a tetanus shot and antibiotics is normal procedure for any puncture wound, unless the horse is already vaccinated.

In the event of a hoof puncture, keep the hoof off the ground if there is still a protruding object in it. If you have pulled the object out, or if the object has come out on its own, mark the entry point so that the vet knows where to treat.

TETANUS: Tetanus is a soil-borne bacteria that can enter a wound and cause severe muscle contractions (tetany), leading to a very painful death. Vaccination, from as young as 5 to 6 months of age, should be considered as a preventative so the horse is able to create its own immunity. In the event of a puncture or open wound, a tetanus-antitoxin (TAT) is 99% effective at preventing tetanus and should be given if the vaccination status is unknown; the sooner the better. Vaccination should also be given following an injury; particularly a puncture wound (including hoof abscesses, wolf teeth extractions, castration and other surgeries).

INJURIES THAT INVOLVE JOINTS AND TENDONS: Because these are such delicate structures, any infections in or around these areas can cause serious damage. If a pale-yellow fluid (synovial fluid) leaks from the wound, it's a sign that the bone or tendon sheath may be damaged; this can have serious consequences, so vet care is imperative.

INJURIES TO THE EYE: If your horse's eyelid is closed or weeping, or you notice a blue or white spot, or haze on the eye, immediately seek vet attention to help prevent permanent eye damage.

Lameness

Lameness refers to an abnormality of the horse's gait and is usually caused by pain in the muscles, ligaments, tendons, joints or bones. It can occur at any time, for any number of reasons; while most episodes of lameness don't require emergency treatment, it is important to call a vet if the lameness is severe or sudden.

Common causes of lameness include the following.

FRACTURES: Stress fractures, if picked up early enough, can heal quickly with appropriate rest. However, working a horse with a fracture can result in a break, so an X-ray and appropriate care are crucial.

SPLINTS: The splint bone is a long, thin bone that runs down the side of the cannon bone. It is susceptible to fracture, breaks and ligament strain that can cause varying degrees of lameness. It usually takes about 3 weeks after an impact before visual swelling and bone growth appear on the splint bone (known as a splint). Splints caused by damage to the bone usually take about 6 weeks to heal if they are rested and given correct care, while ligament damage can take longer.

HOOF ABSCESSES: See page 117.

NAVICULAR SYNDROME: The navicular bone is a small bone situated below the coffin bone, over which the flexor tendon runs. Any inflammation or degeneration of the navicular bone is known as navicular disease and will usually result in lameness. A vet will need to take X-rays to assess the degree of damage; navicular disease is not curable and in severe cases the horse may need to be put down. Flat-footed horses, with low heels and long toes, tend to be more prone to developing navicular disease due to the extra stress placed on the navicular bone, as are jumping horses due to the surfaces they are ridden on. Corrective shoeing can help to alleviate pressure and promote a healthy hoof balance, which can halt or slow the progression of the disease.

A lame horse shuffles from one leg to the other to alleviate the pain.

PRICKED HOOF: If a farrier places a shoeing nail too close to the white line of the hoof, inflammation and pain can develop within days of the horse being shod. If your horse goes lame after shoeing, any high nails may need to be removed; the hole will need to be filled with an antibacterial product like hydrogen peroxide to combat any potential infection.

TENDON AND LIGAMENT INJURIES: Any swelling over the tendons or ligaments should be looked at immediately by an equine vet to determine the cause and the required treatment. Horses are not always lame following these types of injuries, but if they are worked while injured (no matter how small the injury) more damage can be caused; in some cases it can result in a complete rupture of the ligament or tendon. Some injuries can end a horse's career; other horses, with careful management, can make a full recovery.

ARTHRITIS: Arthritis can affect any joint in the body, especially if an old injury is present. If your horse is starting to show stiffness, is lame or pulls away from you when its legs are flexed, it is well worth getting X-rays to find the source of its discomfort. If arthritic changes are present, the vet will advise a treatment plan and your horse's future outlook, taking into consideration its current level of pain from this location, as well as any behavioural issues that are present. *Note:* The degree of changes does not always correlate to the amount of pain an individual horse will feel (some small changes can be very painful).

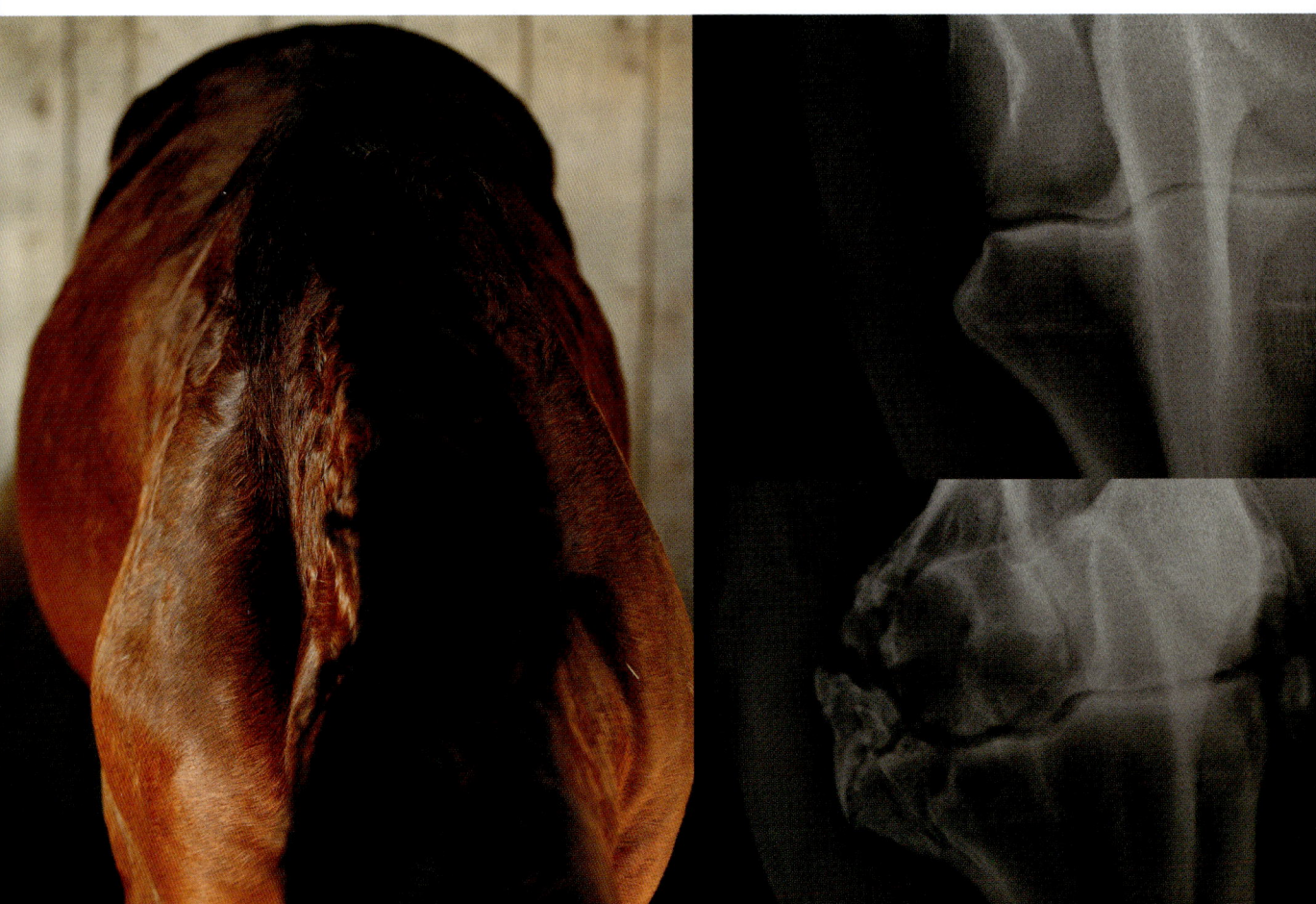

Left: Muscle atrophy from an injured shoulder.

Top right: A clean X-ray of a horse's elbow.

Bottom right: An X-ray of a horse's elbow (from the same angle as the one above), showing old fractures and extensive arthritis, which was causing the horse intermittent lameness.

BRIDLE LAMENESS: Bridle lameness occurs when a horse is sound on the ground but lame when ridden under saddle. It is usually caused by a horse that is experiencing pain from the weight of the rider, a rider with an uneven position, an ill-fitting saddle, dental issues, or the horse being ridden in Rollkur (see page 291).

LAMINITIS: A painful condition caused by inflammation within the sensitive laminae of the hoof wall (see page 119).

Illnesses and ailments

Colic

Colic is a collective term that covers any abdominal or thoracic (chest) pain experienced by horses, and is one of the leading causes of death in horses. Even mild colic should be taken seriously, as it can quickly become life-threatening. Call a vet as soon as any of the following symptoms are seen.

- Excessive restlessness, discomfort, pawing or sweating
- Kicking at the belly
- Turning the head to look at the belly
- Lying down more than normal or in a restless manner, or rolling and thrashing excessively
- Increased heart rate, breathing rate or temperature
- Decreased manure production
- No gut rumbling sounds
- No appetite

POSSIBLE CAUSES OF COLIC

- Impaction colic, resulting from undigested food or foreign objects (including worms) blocking the intestines.
- A twist or strangulation in the horse's digestive system, which can cause a loss of blood supply and possible death to parts of the digestive tract or blood vessels. This is incredibly painful and can progress quickly, often resulting in death; usually surgery is required to give the horse any chance of recovery.
- Stress colic, from horses being exposed to stressful situations.
- Heavy worm burdens (which is why regular deworming is important, especially in young stock — see page 106).
- Poor dental health, which causes an inability to chew and break down food correctly (see pages 111–12).
- Rapid diet changes, including too much grain, or insufficient forage.
- Sand colic, from eating sand (which is why it's important to use a hay net or manger if your yards have a sand surface).
- Poisoning, which can come about from ingesting poisonous plants (see page 79) or chemicals.
- Infections such as colitis or enteritis.

- Gastric ulcers (see page 86).
- Excess gas.

> **WHAT TO DO IN THE EVENT OF COLIC**
> 1. Call the vet immediately.
> 2. Remove any hay or feed from the horse.
> 3. Keep your horse warm, if it is cold.
> 4. While waiting for the vet, drench your horse with 50 millilitres of TuffRock GI (using a plastic syringe).
> 5. Ensure that your horse doesn't roll, as this can further twist the horse's gut. Don't exhaust your horse by walking it continuously, however; allow it to rest (including lying down) as much as possible and only walk it enough to prevent rolling.
> 6. Watch for any manure being passed — your vet will need to know this.
>
> Once the vet arrives they will assess your horse and administer drugs, which may include pain relief, sedatives, laxatives and IV fluids. In most cases this will remedy the colic, but if the symptoms return after the drugs wear off, it may require colic surgery or even end in death.

Tying-up (azoturia)

Tying-up (also known as azoturia) is a condition in which the muscles contract and become hard. It can happen following exercise, especially after a day off, or from a sudden change in feed. If you see any of the following symptoms, call a vet — the condition is very painful and the resulting muscle damage can be long term.

- Reluctance to move
- Stiff throughout the body
- Tight, cramped muscles, especially in the hindquarters
- Sweating
- Increased breathing/pulse rate (see pages 124–25)
- Red or brown urine (indicating muscle damage)

CAUSES OF TYING-UP (AZOTURIA)
- Lactic acid build-up in the muscles after heavy exercise
- Exercising above the horse's fitness level
- Excess carbohydrates in the diet — if your horse is prone to tying-up, feed grain-free feeds
- Electrolyte imbalances (which can be determined by getting a blood test)
- Genetic predisposition; certain breeds are more susceptible than others
- Continuing to feed a high-energy diet on days the horse is being rested

WHAT TO DO
- Stop all exercise immediately.
- Call a vet.
- Keep your horse warm, especially over the rump, and don't try to move it.

Choke

Choke happens when the oesophagus is blocked; it is often caused by a horse eating dry sugar beet or copra (feeds that swell when wet), or too much hay or hard feed. The blockage prevents food entering the horse's stomach, which causes it immense distress. During choke, excessive saliva and partially digested food may spill from the horse's mouth or nostrils and the horse will often extend its neck and cough, have difficulty breathing or stagger backwards.

All feed and water should be removed immediately until the choke has resolved. It often self-resolves within 30 minutes and can be aided by gently massaging the food mass to help break down the blockage. If the choking doesn't resolve itself, or worsens, immediate vet care will be needed.

Poisoning

If a horse eats any poisonous plant (see page 79), it will need urgent vet care. Some plants will cause death, while others can cause serious and sometimes long-term health issues. If you know what your horse ate, keep a sample for the vet so that they can determine the best sort of treatment.

Staggers

Staggers is a neurological condition resulting in ataxia, a loss of coordination (including wobbling, staggering and hind-end weakness), erratic behaviour and trembling. Because the horse will be unable to walk in a straight line or coordinate its legs, it may be in danger of staggering uncontrollably through fences or into waterways, or even become unsafe to handle; if you can, get the horse to a safe yard or paddock while waiting for a vet.

Staggers can arise from mycotoxins (usually in rye grass, tall fescue and paspalum seed heads), fungus overgrowth during humid conditions, rapid grass growth (usually spring and autumn) or mineral imbalances.

WHAT TO DO
- Do not stimulate your horse in any way — keep them quiet and safe in a contained, flat area.
- Call a vet if symptoms are severe.
- Avoid pastures with rye grass, lucerne, clover or paspalum, as these may exacerbate the problem; in extreme cases, remove your horse from the pasture and feed it hay that wasn't grown on the property.
- Add salt to your horse's feed, as well as suitable supplements (such as magnesium or toxin binders).

Cellulitis
Excessive swelling, heat and stiffness of a limb can indicate that a horse has cellulitis, a low-grade infection under the skin which is usually caused by a small laceration. It can be severe and will require veterinary attention and antibiotics.

Cushing's
Cushing's is often found in older horses, and is caused by the pituitary gland (which is responsible for hair growth and sugar digestion) becoming overactive, affecting the horse's ability to shed its winter coat, while increasing the risk of infection and laminitis. A diagnosis can be made through blood tests, which will enable the vet to offer advice on how to manage your horse's needs.

Ringworm
Contrary to its name, ringworm is actually a fungus that causes a horse's hair to fall out in circular patches. It is common in younger animals and can be caught from infected pasture, or from cattle or other horses. It is very infectious to both horses and humans, so if your horse contracts it you will need to isolate it (as well as your gear and yourself) from other horses until it is no longer contagious (usually 3 to 4 weeks). Ringworm can be treated with suitable antifungals from your vet, or if left untreated will eventually resolve itself. Once a horse has ringworm it will gain a natural immunity, making it less likely to get it again.

Rainscald
Rainscald is very common in prolonged humid and/or wet conditions when the skin becomes wet and cracks, exposing it to bacteria; it results in scaly, scabby skin lesions, especially on the poll, neck and back. Some horses appear to be more prone to it, particularly if they have a weakened immune system, thin coats, are in poor condition or have nutritional deficiencies.

WHAT TO DO
- Keep your horse dry while it recovers (in wet weather keep it in a stable, shelter or waterproof rug).
- Wash your horse with an antibacterial product.
- Soften the scabs with oil and gently rub them off, if the horse allows you to. Clipping, under sedation, can also help remove scabs and speed up the healing process. *Note:* If you leave the scabs on, bacteria will live underneath them and the rainscald will worsen.
- Once the scabs are gone, you can aid your horse's skin and hair recovery using active mānuka honey or products containing vitamins E and A.

Mud fever/cracked heels

A very painful bacterial and/or fungal infection that is similar to rainscald, but found on horses with white legs. It usually occurs in wet or muddy conditions, although it can also be caused by photosensitivity (see below). The skin will become crusty and scabby and may ooze a yellowy fluid and swell.

WHAT TO DO

- Soften the scabs with coconut oil or a high-vitamin-E oil and then rub gently until all scabs are removed, if the horse allows you to. If not, a vet will be required to sedate the horse.
- Apply an antifungal/antibacterial agent such as mud gel, Kwillow Powder or mānuka honey sprays for several days until the scabs begin to heal; if no improvement is seen, call a vet, as a steroid-based product and a course of antibiotics may be needed.
- Keep the legs dry and apply a moisture barrier, such as coconut oil, emu oil or zinc to the legs until they are totally healed.
- In extreme cases that continue to worsen with treatment, we have found Silver Whinny's Sox to be the most effective option. They are designed to be worn by your horse 24 hours a day (hold them in place with insulation tape, as it stretches with movement and is less likely to cause pressure sores) and results are usually seen in 2 to 3 weeks.

Sun photosensitivity

Horses with white markings and pink skin can become sensitive to the sun and develop crusty, painful skin lesions; these should be treated the same way as mud fever (see above). Sun photosensitivity can also be caused by excessive phyto-oestrogens consumed in clover or other plants (including St John's wort). Reduce exposure to these plants and apply sunscreen to susceptible areas, have the horse wear a nose guard or mask to protect it from the sun, or add a UV-based product (like Hippo Health) to the water trough.

Left: Mud fever showing no improvement after 8 weeks of vet treatments.

Middle: To stop Silver Whinny's Sox slipping, hold them in place with a strip of insulation tape below the knee and above the fetlock.

Right: 2 weeks after using Silver Whinny's Sox, the scabs have gone and the skin has started healing.

Lice

Horses are susceptible to lice infestation, especially if they are malnourished or immune-compromised. The lice usually settle in the mane and tail regions but can eventually cover much of the body. They are extremely infectious and the horse should be kept away from other horses (and all gear) until it has been successfully treated.

SYMPTOMS OF LICE
- Poor Body Condition Score (see pages 104–05)
- Itching constantly
- Depressed
- Lethargic

WHAT TO DO
- Wash with a lice treatment, repeating every few days as new eggs hatch.
- Recheck the horse weekly and re-treat if needed.
- In the event of a serious infestation that isn't easily resolved with treatment, it can be beneficial to clip the horse before treatment.

Respiratory issues

Coughing, abnormal breathing or nasal discharge may indicate a respiratory issue, which can be caused by the following.
- Broken wind (chronic obstructive pulmonary disease) — caused by an allergy to dust or fungal spores, which requires long-term management to prevent the development of potentially severe allergic reactions.
- Allergies to pollens or certain grasses.
- Upper respiratory infections caused by viral infections, which can result in an elevated temperature, nasal discharge or cough. This will be contagious to other horses, so the infected horse should be isolated and given time to recuperate. Natural supplements like garlic powder, vitamin C and cider vinegar can be helpful to improve recovery times.
- Bacterial infections will result in a high temperature, pus-like nasal discharge and swelling beneath the jaw. If severe, a vet should be called so the horse can be treated with antibiotics, and it should also be isolated.
- Travel sickness can occur following long-distance travel. It causes pneumonia, which will require prompt veterinary attention.
- A breathing issue in which the horse makes a noise while it is being exercised is known as roaring. A horse that roars will struggle to get enough oxygen in times of exertion. It is often caused by partial or full paralysis of the vocal cords and is especially common in big horses with long necks. The vet can use a scope to grade the horse's air-flow restriction. While those with a lower-level roar can continue ridden work, grades 4 and 5 will restrict the performance of horses that gallop or jump. Tie-back surgery can be effective in these instances, but results are not guaranteed.

Cancer

The symptoms of cancer are often vague but include weight loss, failure to gain weight, apathy and behavioural issues. Early detection is beneficial, but often cancer can be quite well established before it is evident that there is a problem.

MELANOMA

A skin cancer that occurs predominantly in grey horses. Nodules are often found on the dock, head or neck but can also occur internally. If these start growing vigorously or become ulcerated, veterinary advice should be sought.

SARCOIDS

Sarcoids are a type of tumour that in some cases can become quite aggressive and may grow rapidly. There are different types including flat, scaly sarcoids and knobbly, wart-like ones; these are common around the eyes, muzzle and lower limbs, although can also be found elsewhere on the body. In some cases, sarcoids will disappear over time, but usually veterinary treatment is required.

Diarrhoea

Mild diarrhoea can be caused by too much fresh grass or balage that is too rich. If this isn't the issue, it is usually a symptom of something serious — if not addressed, it can lead to dehydration and may even become life-threatening. A vet should always be called to ascertain the cause (which may include heavy worm burden, stress, cancer, poisoning or infections such as salmonella and leptospirosis).

Kissing spine

The vertebral processes, which rise up from the thoracic vertebrae, should have a gap between them for the spine to correctly function. If a horse becomes sore from an injury, a rider that is too heavy for its structure or an ill-fitting saddle, it may start compensating by hollowing its back. As it does this, the processes can close and start rubbing on each other, creating an area of inflammation; with time, this will damage the bones and can cause them to fuse together, which can be career ending.

Horses with kissing spine will stand hollow (with a sunken back), are often sore to touch along the spine, and can develop extensive behavioural issues when ridden. An X-ray will show if kissing spine is present and how far it has progressed; if caught early enough, a steroid injection, followed by rehabilitation, can settle the inflammation. Depending on the degree of changes to the vertebral processes, the vet will advise a treatment plan and your horse's future outlook, taking into consideration its current level of pain from this location, as well as any behavioural issues that are present. *Note:* The degree of changes does not always correlate to the amount of pain an individual horse will feel (some small changes can be very painful).

Stringhalt
Sometimes, especially in large horses, the flexion in one or both hind limbs is exaggerated, appearing as an awkward, jerky movement up towards the abdomen or out from the hock. It is an uncontrollable neurological response that happens when the horse is asked to step forward, turn or back up and is mostly seen at the walk, although some horses also show it at the trot. Stringhalt is not a reaction to pain, so affected horses can go on to perform at high levels.

Stifle lock
Stifle lock is caused by the medial patella ligament (attached to the femur) locking, which causes the hind leg to briefly collapse or to be held rigidly in extension behind the horse. It can be hereditary and can also affected by a lack of muscular fitness, poor body condition, trauma to the area or conformation faults within the joint or limb itself. Stifle lock can lead to inflammation and arthritis of the joint over time.

Shivers
A neurological and progressive disease that is diagnosed by gait abnormalities when the horse is backing up. Other signs include trembling of thigh muscles, hind legs or the tail. Shivers can have a genetic component and is often found in warmbloods and draught horses. Although horses with shivers can have difficulty picking up their hind legs, many go on to perform at high levels.

Wobblers (also known as ECVM)
Wobblers is caused by a damaged spinal cord, from a fall, damage to or malfunction of the cervical vertebra, or herpes or protozoa infections. A horse with mild wobblers may have difficulty changing canter leads or halting, while more severe cases can cause gait abnormalities and wobbling (where the horse staggers or stumbles as if it were sedated). The long-term prognosis for wobblers is often poor and a diagnosis and treatment plan will need to be determined by a vet.

Vices

Horses may develop abnormal behaviours, usually arising from stress, boredom or pain. These include the following.
- **WINDSUCKING**: The horse finds relief by arching its neck and gulping in air.
- **CRIB BITING**: The horse grasps an object such as a post or rail with its teeth (often drawing in air), and may also chew wood. Mineral deficiencies, boredom or stress, particularly in young stock, are usually contributing factors.
- **WEAVING**: The horse swings its neck from side to side, swaying from one front leg to the other in a rhythmical fashion. It is usually caused by stress or boredom and is less likely to occur if the horse is turned out to pasture or kept with other horses for company.

Cold poulticing a horse's legs after jumping will help reduce inflammation by cooling the tendons, ligaments and muscles.

SECTION 3

Handling your Horse

In this section you'll gain an understanding of safe and sensible handling practices, what equipment you'll need for groundwork, and why establishing a partnership with your horse and teaching it key skills on the ground — long before you think of riding it — is vital.

HANDLING BASICS

Safely handling horses

Due to their unpredictable nature and sheer size, working with horses can be hazardous. Even the calmest horse can hurt someone if it is startled or scared, and handling one that is inexperienced can greatly increase the risk of accidents. Here are some top tips to keep yourself safe when working with horses.

- When possible, always have another person around. If this isn't possible, keep a phone on you and make sure you tell someone where and when you'll be working your horse and what time you expect to be back.
- Wear covered footwear at all times when working with horses (see page 243).
- Always wear a helmet when riding, to minimise the risk of a head injury.
- Avoid wearing clothing that rustles, especially around young or spooky horses.
- Keep yard and paddock gates shut at all times — this is especially important if your property borders a road.
- Avoid wearing jewellery when handling and riding horses, as rings, earrings and necklaces can get caught and cause injury.
- Make sure you have your horse's attention before you approach it, and always approach the horse from the head, neck or shoulder (never from behind).
- Ensure your body language and movements are quiet and steady, with no sudden or unpredictable movement.
- Never loop a lead rope or lunge line around your hands or arms; if your horse pulls away, you will be at risk of being tangled or dragged.
- Speak calmly and quietly to avoid stressing your horse, as horses can sense our energy and emotions.
- When tying up your horse, use a well-fitting halter and a lead rope (never a bridle), and use a quick-release knot (see page 148).
- Avoid standing or walking directly behind a horse, even when brushing its tail.
- Stay in close proximity to your horse: being kicked at close range will do less damage than if you're standing further back and the horse hits you with a fully extended leg.
- When handling your horse's hooves, don't squat or kneel. Instead, bend over facing towards the horse's tail so that you can get out of the way quickly if your horse moves suddenly. When picking up the hind hooves, make sure you let the horse know you are coming by sliding your hand along its back to the hind end — if you suddenly reach for a hind hoof without warning, you may cause the horse to spook or kick out in response.
- Never encourage a horse to nibble or bite by playing with its muzzle, or teasing it with food.
- When holding a horse for the vet or the farrier, always stand on the same side of the horse as the person, to ensure you're able to safely manoeuvre the horse away from them if the horse panics or kicks out.

Appropriate attire for riding at home or at a lesson.

- Have an equine and a human medical kit close by at all times.
- Horses can sense your energy and moods, and will get worried or stressed if you hold your breath, or are anxious, scared, angry or upset. If you are nervous or anxious around horses but want to pursue your love of them, it is worth having professional handling or riding instruction or seeing a sports psychologist.

Equipment

Being able to safely handle your horse, and develop a partnership built on mutual trust and respect, is aided by having correct, well-fitting equipment.

Choosing a halter

Choosing the right halter is important for your horse's comfort and safety, and for effective handling and training. While all halters will allow some control of the horse, some are more mild (wider straps or padding) and others are more severe (thin, stiff rope). Here are the most common types of halter and their pros and cons.

LEATHER HALTERS: These offer a traditional look and can be used for daily use or showing. They are fairly safe in most situations, since leather will break under extreme pressure. They come in a variety of styles and shapes, with options of decorative stitching, engraved nameplates, or padding for extra comfort. Like all leather items, they require regular cleaning and conditioning to maintain the integrity of the leather, but with correct care can last a lifetime.

WEB HALTERS: Usually made from nylon, these are popular for everyday use because they are cheap, easy to maintain and durable. Because web halters are difficult to break or cut through in an emergency, they should not be left on the horse in the paddock.

BREAKAWAY HALTERS: Made from leather or web, these are designed with safety in mind. They can feature a leather crownpiece, a snapped leather strap connecting the crownpiece to the cheekpiece, or Velcro straps; all of which are designed to release under pressure. They are ideal for horses turned out to pasture (in case the horse becomes snagged on something), for travelling or for tying up a difficult horse.

ROPE HALTERS: Ideally made from a soft rope, with various knots placed on pressure points on the horse's head, these halters are a valuable training tool as they enhance communication between horse and handler.

Professional trainers usually prefer rope halters for groundwork and starting horses under saddle (before the horse is ready to wear a bridle), and they are also commonly used for pleasure-riding as a bitless option. Because rope halters are virtually indestructible they should never be left on the horse in the paddock or be used to tie up a horse, unless they are secured to baling twine or breakable ties.

PLASTIC (PVC) HALTERS: Available in varying colours, these are designed to be strong and durable. They do, however, cause horses to sweat under the halter in summer, which can burn their skin and cause their hair to fall out, and in winter the halters can rub and cause rain rot. Because of this, they are never suitable to leave on in the paddock.

Top: A full fly mask is beneficial for horses with pink skin around their eyes.

Bottom: A nose guard, fitted onto a halter, can be good for horses prone to sunburn.

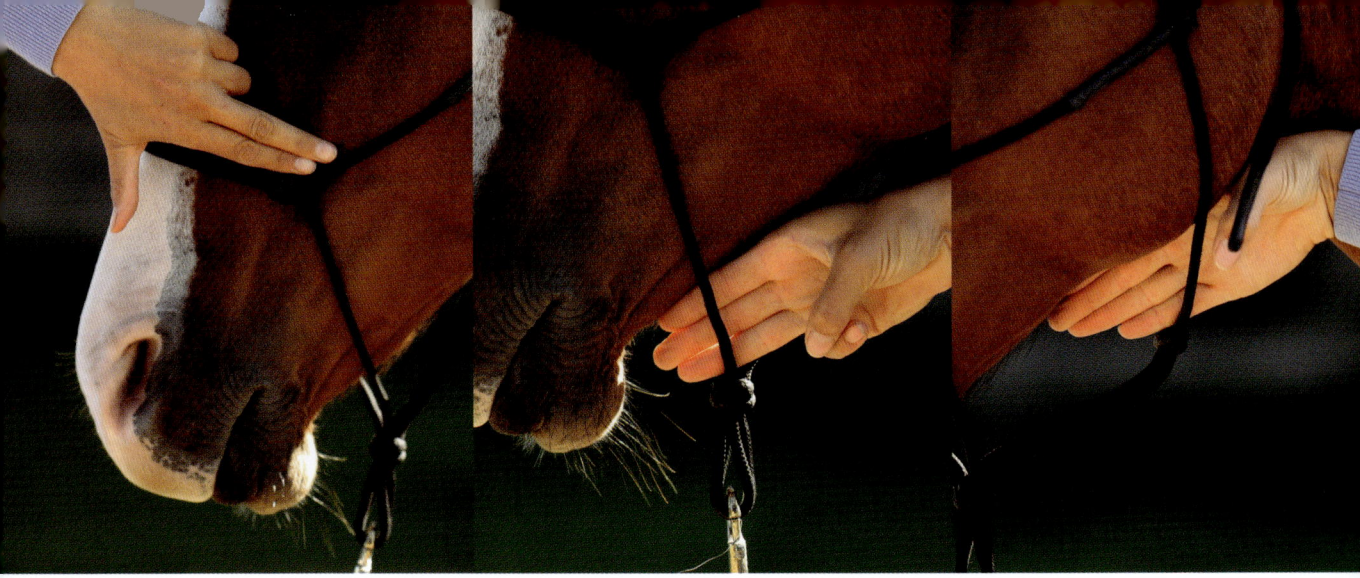

Halter accessories

LEAD ROPES: With a well-trained horse, a standard 8-foot (2-metre) lead rope is a popular choice for most of your on-the-ground handling. When training a young or inexperienced horse, however — whether it be teaching it to go over obstacles, load on a truck or trailer, or to move backwards or laterally — a horsemanship lead rope ranging from 12 to 18 feet (4 to 6 metres) will be beneficial.

LUNGE LINE: When exercising your horse on the lunge, a specially designed lunge line ranging from 25 to 32 feet (8 to 10 metres) should be used. The added length is important as it will allow the horse to work on a 15- to 20-metre circle around you; any smaller and the horse will struggle to maintain a trot or canter.

NOSE GUARD: In sunny conditions, horses with pink noses can blister and burn. Nose guards are usually made from mesh, with UV protection. They are generally attached to the noseband of a halter (ideally breakaway or leather), although there are also halter-free options available.

FULL FACE MASK: For horses with sensitive eyes, or pink skin around their eyes or muzzle, a face mask with UV protection (of at least 90%) is ideal to prevent squamous cell carcinoma (a skin tumor found in horses). These can either cover the eyes or come with a built-in nose guard to offer protection for the whole face. They also double as a fly mask, offering protection from insects.

Use the width of your fingers to check the fit of your horse's halter; from left: 2 fingers beneath the cheekbones, 3 fingers under the noseband and 4 fingers under the throatlatch.

SAFETY CONCERNS WITH HALTERS

- A hoof getting caught in the halter.
- Rubs and wounds from the halter being left on.
- Damage to the horse's nasal bone from a halter sitting too low.
- The halter not breaking if the horse gets into a bad situation.
- Permanent damage to the skull plates if the halter is too small and left too long on a growing horse.
- Excessive sweating under the halter, which can cause burns and hair loss.

Fitting a halter

Fitting the halter correctly is important for your horse's safety and to help provide optimum control. If you don't know your horse's halter size, use the standard sizes as a guide — these are foal, weanling, pony, cob, full and draft sizes. The correct halter size will vary depending on the breed and bone structure of your horse, so the standard sizes are designed to be further customised by adjusting the straps.

> *Top tip:* When buying a new halter, it can be useful to take in your horse's old halter to replicate the fit.

When fitting a halter, consider the following.

CROWNPIECE: The crownpiece sits across the horse's poll, and should be positioned close behind the ears without pushing into them.

NOSEBAND: The noseband should lie 2 fingers' width beneath the cheekbones, with the knots or hardware on the side of the noseband positioned directly below the cheekbones. If the noseband is lower than this, it can impair your horse's breathing, damage the nasal bone if they were to pull back or step on their lead rope, or the halter may even slip over the nose and risk a hoof or the horse's lower jaw getting stuck in the dangling halter.

THROATLATCH: The throatlatch should sit in the groove where your horse's neck meets its jaw. It should be loose enough that the horse can comfortably breathe and swallow, but not so loose it allows a hoof to get caught; a gap of 3 to 4 fingers' width between the throatlatch and the horse's jaw is ideal.

CHEEK PIECES: The cheek pieces should run below the horse's cheekbones and almost parallel to them, to avoid them rubbing against the facial bones. If the cheek-piece angle is incorrect, it can be altered by adjusting the crownpiece or noseband.

FITTING A ROPE HALTER: It is crucial that rope halters are also the correct size for each horse — contrary to popular belief, they are not 'one size fits all', although they are often sold as such. Like all halters, getting the right fit is important to ensure that the halter doesn't slip off, gape and risk a leg being caught, or damage the horse's nasal bone if it sits too low on the nose. Use the guidelines above to ensure a correct fit.

Tying up a horse correctly

This is a basic yet essential skill that anyone handling horses should know how to do correctly. Incorrectly tying up a horse will increase the risk of injury if things go wrong, including the horse getting its legs caught over the rope, its head caught under the rope, or pulling back and becoming tangled in the rope.

To minimise the risk of accidents, here are important tips on how to tie up a horse safely, and what to avoid.

HOW TO TIE UP YOUR HORSE CORRECTLY

- **FIND A SAFE PLACE TO TIE:** Make sure you tie your horse somewhere it can't become tangled in things around it and that there are no wire fences or hay nets that your horse could get a leg caught in.
- **ALWAYS USE A QUICK-RELEASE KNOT:** A quick-release knot (see caption) is essential so you can untie the horse quickly in emergency situations.
- **TIE WITH BREAKABLE TIES:** Tie your horse to a piece of twine or with breakable ties. This way, if your horse pulls back, only the twine is broken, reducing the chance of injury.
- **ONLY TIE TO SOMETHING SOLID:** Only tie your horse to objects that it cannot move or pull over, like a tree, hitching rail, strong post, horse truck or a trailer that is secured to an attached vehicle (horses are strong enough to drag an unhitched trailer).
- **TIE YOUR HORSE AT A SAFE HEIGHT:** The rope should be tied at about the same height as your horse's wither. If you tie your horse too low, it can get a leg over the rope or get its head stuck underneath the rope; both can cause the horse to panic and pull back.
- **TIE YOUR HORSE AT THE CORRECT LENGTH:** The rope should be long enough for your horse to stand comfortably and move its head, but not so long that the horse can get a leg caught over the rope, or its head stuck underneath the rope. Ideally, about 2 to 3 feet (60 to 90 centimetres) in length should be sufficient, but this will depend on the size of your horse and the height it is tied.
- **NEVER TIE UP WITH A BRIDLE:** Using a bridle to tie your horse up can damage its mouth if it pulls back, as well as risk breaking the bridle. If you want to tie your horse up while it's bridled, wrap the reins around the horse's neck so that it can't get a leg tangled in them, then put a halter over the bridle to tie it up with.
- **PROVIDE FOOD AND WATER:** If your horse is going to be tied up for longer than an hour, like at a horse show, offer it hay and water regularly.
- **PLAN FOR AN EMERGENCY:** In the event of an emergency, have scissors in your grooming box so you can cut your horse's rope or halter, if it isn't able to break itself free. If a horse is pulling back violently, do not approach it until it has settled.

Below: To tie a quick-release knot: (1) Loop the end of the rope and pass it through the baling twine. (2) Twist it so the end of the rope is underneath. (3) Create a loop with the end of the rope, then (4) pass this through the twist and push down towards the baling twine. To undo the knot, simply pull the free end and it will fall apart — if it doesn't, you have tied the knot incorrectly and will need to keep practising until it does.

Opposite top four: How to tie a rope halter.

Opposite bottom: A correctly fitted rope halter.

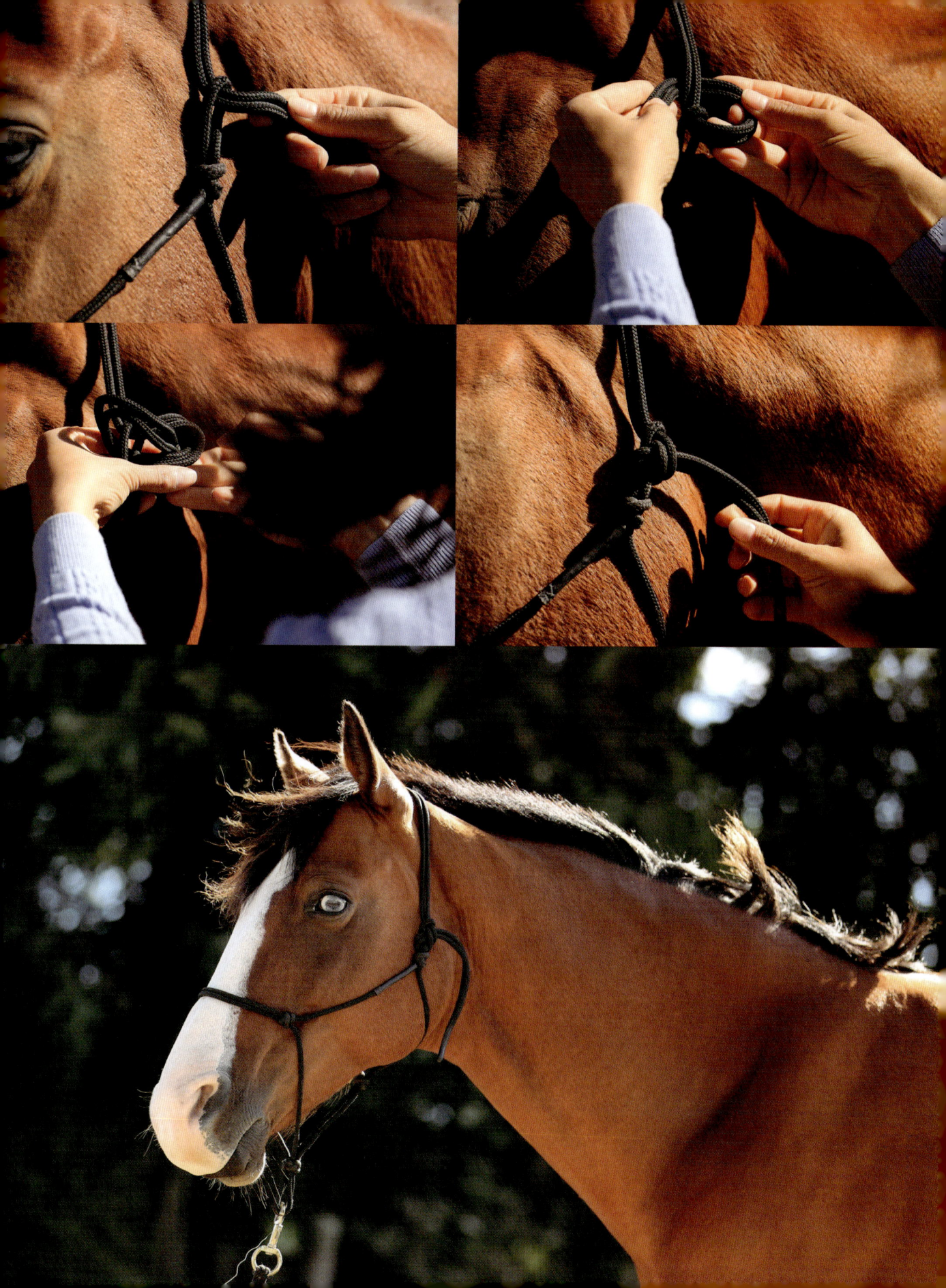

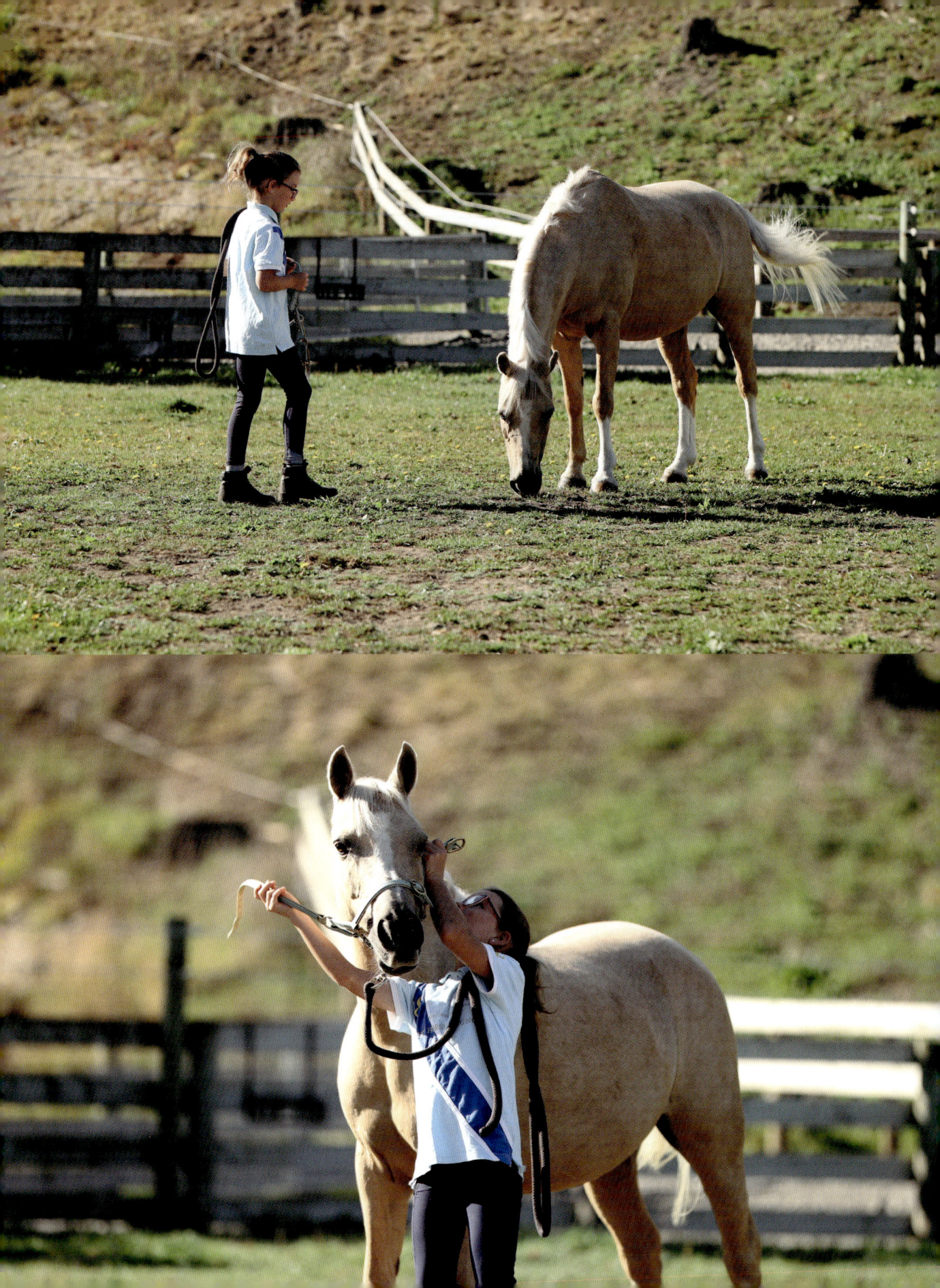

Catching a difficult horse

Having a horse that is difficult to catch can be both frustrating and time-consuming. In some instances, there may be underling issues that are causing the horse to mistrust humans or avoid being haltered. These can include fear, poor training, bad associations with being handled or ridden, or skeletal issues (especially in the head or neck area).

For these horses, it's important to find the root cause of the problem, then work to gain their trust and teach them positive associations when being caught going forward. With horsemanship techniques, and correct timing and feel (see page 168), you should be able to retrain the horse to approach you when you enter the paddock and stand quietly to be haltered. If, however, you allow it to continue evading you, it's likely that the horse will always be difficult to catch.

Set yourself up for success

- If your horse is paddocked with another horse for company, make sure that the other horse is easy to catch — your horse is likely to mimic the behaviour of its companion.
- If your horse is in a yard or paddock with several horses, always catch the easiest horse first. This will prevent the horses running off together or your horse from hiding behind its companions.
- Be prepared before you approach your horse, by placing the halter and lead rope tidily over your shoulder instead of holding it in your hand. Once you're able to get close to the horse, it may be helpful to quietly put the lead rope around its neck before haltering it.
- Ideally, you shouldn't leave a halter on when your horse is turned out in the paddock. However, while you're retraining a hard-to-catch horse, it may be beneficial to leave a leather or breakaway halter on to minimise the stress of haltering. This is only a short-term solution, however, as leaving a halter on for an extended period of time can be a safety concern.

Create positive associations

You can help improve your horse's association with being caught by going into the paddock and having neutral or positive experiences with it, rather than always having expectations of it.

- Don't try to catch your horse every time you enter the paddock. Instead, take the time to just go in and offer your horse a rub, or a handful of grass or a treat, or muck out around it without trying to engage with it.
- Once your horse is caught, make sure you do something fun straight away. If your horse associates you with discomfort, pain or hard work, there is little chance that it will want to spend time with you.

Be mindful of your body language

- When approaching your horse, do so slowly and calmly, and be alert to its body

If your horse is difficult to catch, prepare your halter and lead rope before you approach, with the rope slung over your shoulder.

language. Never march up to your horse full of purpose and intent, as your speed and body language is likely to overwhelm it.
- Make sure you're in a neutral or positive frame of mind before you begin working with your horse — if you are stressed, frustrated, impatient, angry or in a hurry, your horse will be able to pick up on your tension and may be harder to catch.
- Avoid direct eye contact — this can be intimidating for your horse.
- With sensitive horses it can be helpful to approach from a slight angle towards the shoulder, rather than directly towards the head.
- Make the first contact where your horse is most comfortable being touched. If this is on the right side of the neck, then approach from the right and make that your first point of contact, even though you would then move to the left side to halter it.
- Once your horse allows you to approach, give it time to relax before attempting to halter it — often a scratch or a rub can be a good reward for the horse standing still. When your horse is relaxed you can progress to quietly and efficiently haltering it, being careful not to either scare or bore your horse to the point where it leaves you.
- When you're ready to let your horse go, wait until it's relaxed, then unhalter it and give it a rub or a scratch so that it learns to stand and wait until you walk away.
- As much as possible, try to avoid using food to bribe a horse that is difficult to catch; instead, take the time to retrain it. Food is only a short-term solution — horses are smart and will soon learn to let you catch them only if you offer a treat.

GROUND MANNERS

Horses that are obedient and willing to handle are not only a pleasure to be around, but they're also generally safer to work with. A horse with good ground manners will respect your space, listen to your subtle body language and aids, and have a good understanding of body control (how to use their head, shoulders, ribs and hindquarters independently when cued).

Improving your horse's body control on the ground is the first step to improving most handling and ridden issues. Good ground manners start with a horse that understands how to walk by your shoulder; yield its head, forehand, ribs and hindquarters; back up; and lunge in both directions. Once your horse has learned the cue for each of these movements, it will have more respect for you on the ground and any previous undesirable behaviours will start to be replaced by positive ones.

If you are struggling to teach your horse good ground manners, it can be worthwhile investing in horsemanship lessons to further your education.

Top: Conquistador side-passing at liberty, just four months after he was mustered from the wild.

Bottom: Conquistador was the winner of the Horsemanship and Obstacle Classes in the 2021 Stallion Challenges, with a perfect score of 50/50 in each, due to his flawless ground manners.

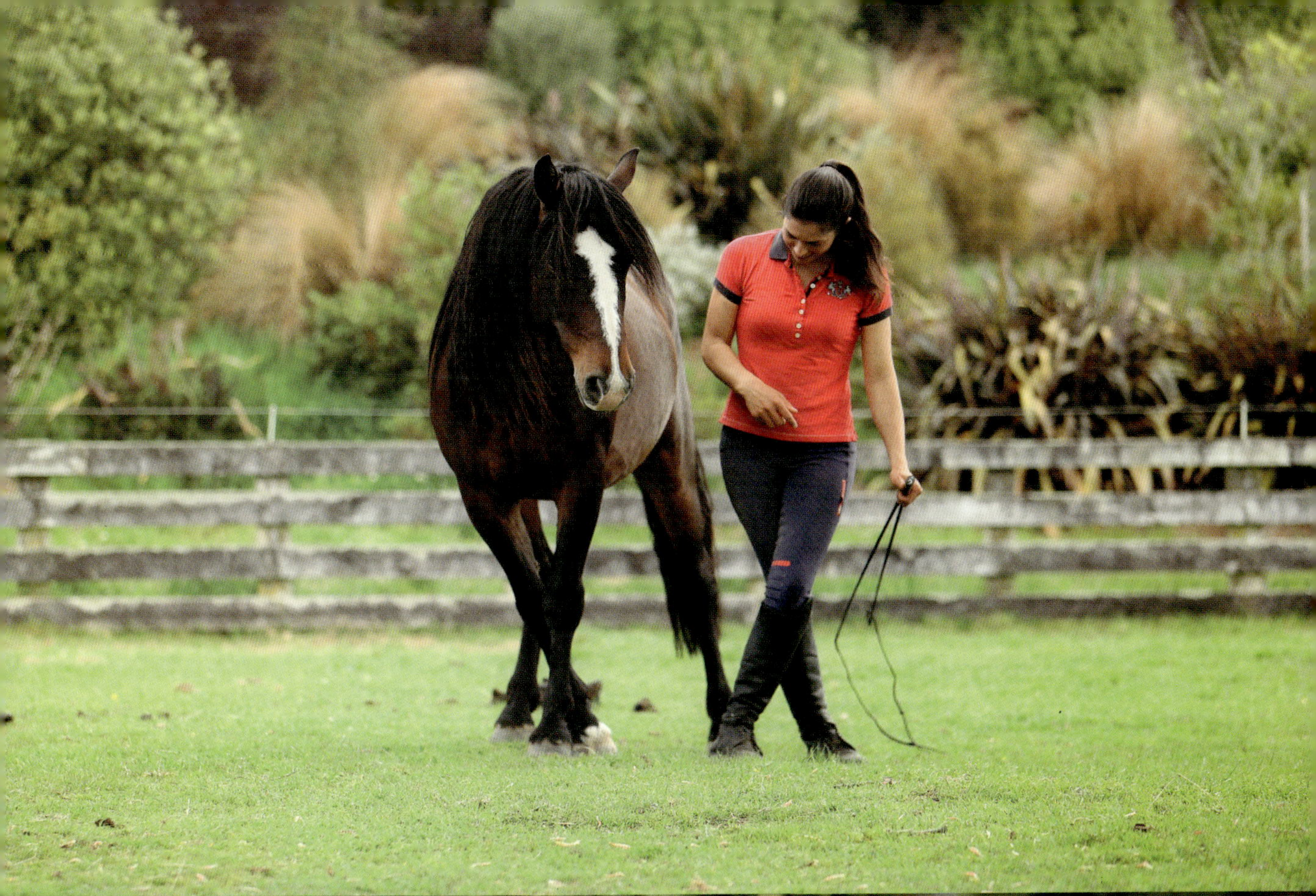

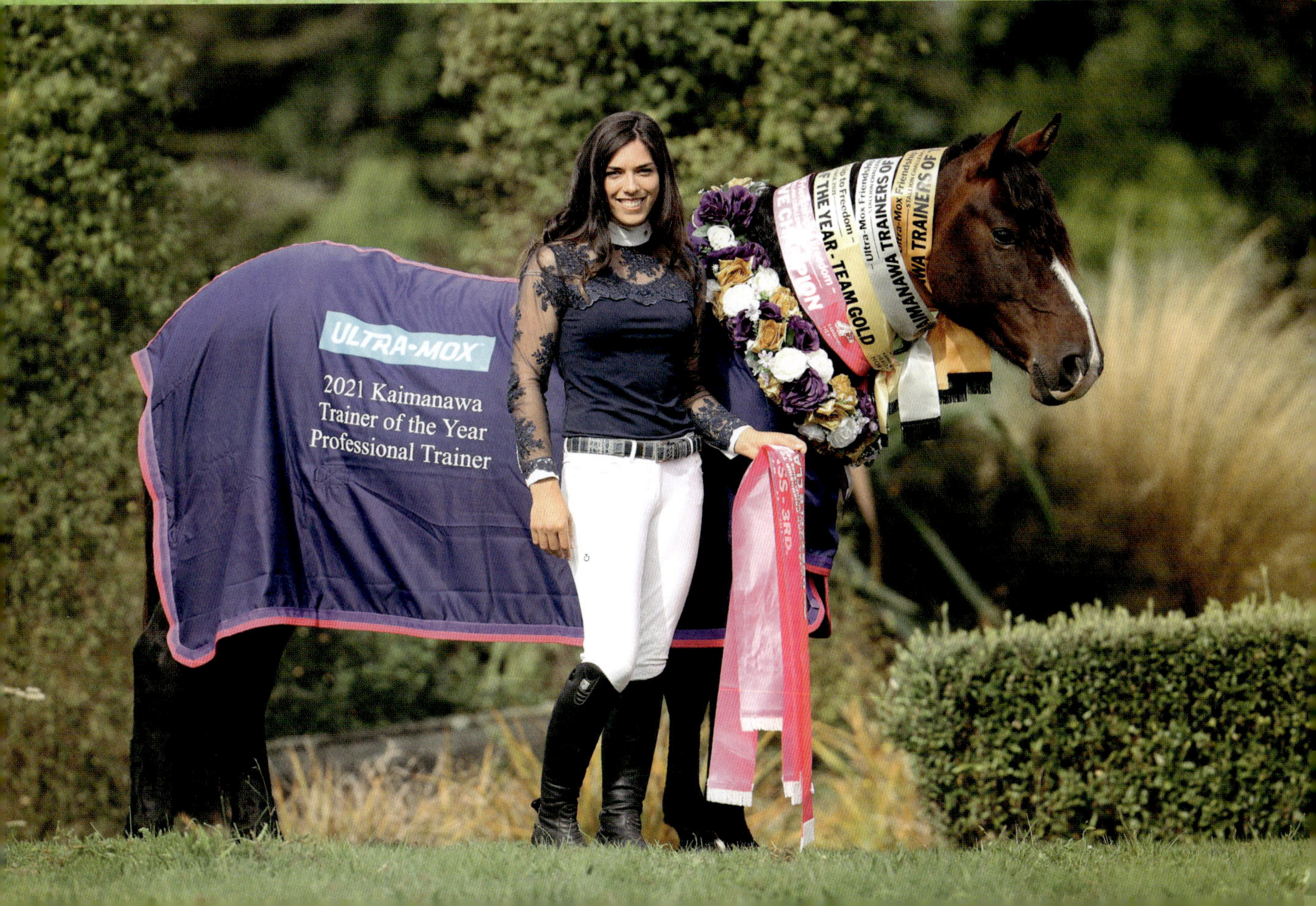
ULTRA-MOX
2021 Kaimanawa
Trainer of the Year
Professional Trainer

Leading your horse

Leading is the basis of most of your on-the-ground training. The more responsively and willingly you can get your horse to lead, the easier it will be through every other stage of its training. A horse that drags on the lead will often be stubborn when approaching things that it's scared of or confused by, difficult to load onto a horse truck or trailer, and may even be heavy to your aids when ridden.

When you're leading your horse, it should ideally shadow your movements; if you step forward, your horse should step forward; if you speed up, your horse should increase its stride to keep pace; when you stop, it should stop; when you turn, it should turn too without bumping into you or crowding into your space.

Every horse can be taught to lead well, but it's a skill that comes from patient education. If your horse crowds into your space, drags you around or has to be dragged, this is normally the result of insufficient or incorrect training. Poor ground manners have the potential to put both your horse and yourself in dangerous situations, and make handling your horse very unenjoyable.

> **TOP TIPS FOR LEADING**
> - When leading your horse from the side, be careful you don't fall behind your horse's shoulder, as you may be at risk of being kicked if your horse gets too far ahead of you.
> - Don't micro-manage your horse or hold the lead rope too short — this encourages the horse to be heavy and unresponsive to pressure or overly anxious.
> - When asking your horse to change pace or stop, use the Pressure Scale of 1 to 10 (see pages 160–62).

Improving your horse's leading skills

Some horses can struggle with forward motion when being led, especially if you're standing in front of them and trying to pull them forward. They can often get stuck and refuse to move, or may drag on the rope. Having a person behind the horse to encourage it forward can be helpful, but if you're by yourself and your horse refuses to budge then there's not much you can do. In this situation it can be useful to have an alternative means of establishing forward momentum, such as teaching your horse to lead while you're standing by its shoulder, or to lunge around you.

LEADING BY THE SHOULDER: Horses are traditionally led from the left side, with the person facing forward and looking in the direction they want to go. Stand with your shoulder aligned about 20 to 30 centimetres behind the horse's poll, holding the lead in your right hand about half a metre from the buckle; this length will allow the rope to be slack when the horse is doing the right thing, and only become tighter if you apply pressure to correct or direct the horse. Use your left hand to hold the end of the

Horses are traditionally led from the left side of their shoulder.

lead in a tidy coil (without wrapping it around your hand), so that the horse can't step on the rope.

LUNGING: When you lunge a horse, it should move in a circle around you while maintaining a constant rhythm, changing pace only when cued. Lunging is usually done on an 8 to 10 metre (25 to 30 foot) lunge line and is a good technique for improving your horse's flexibility, balance and fitness, settling an exuberant horse before being ridden, bringing a horse back into work or rehabilitating it after an injury. With a horse that has poor ground manners, lunging can also be useful for improving basic leading and impulsion; once a horse understands how to lunge, it can be lunged over obstacles, jumps or even into a float.

> Lunging is hard work for a horse, since it's expected to work on a small circle about 15 to 20 metres in diameter. As a general rule, we lunge our horses for only 5 to 10 minutes in each direction, including no more than 1 to 3 minutes at canter, and ideally on an arena surface. If a grass surface is used, we would only expect our horses to walk and trot, unless they are very balanced (or wearing studs), as cantering or jumping on small circles on grass can cause them to slip and jar their bodies.

Top: A horse with a weak topline will benefit more from being lunged in a lunging system (see page 275) to encourage it to drop its head, engage its core, push from its hindquarters and lift the muscles over its back.

Bottom: A horse being lunged in a soft lunge training aid, which encourages it to use its body correctly.

BODY CONTROL: Having a horse that knows how to move sideways and backwards off pressure is important for maintaining straightness and control during every stage of its handling. The foundations of good body control include lateral movements like hindquarter and shoulder yields and the side-pass, as well as the rein-back. All of these movements are taught at the halt, and when done correctly the horse will be soft and supple throughout its body and have a relaxed and engaged mindset. Ideally your horse should establish body control on the ground, before you expect it to perform these movements under saddle.

- **REIN-BACK:** When you ask a horse to rein-back, it should step backwards in a straight line. If you have a horse that pushes into your personal space, or is impatient to handle, teaching it to rein-back can be an important way to teach it patience and respect. It is also an important skill for your horse to learn if you plan to travel it in a straight-loading horse trailer.
- **HINDQUARTER YIELD (TURN ON THE FOREHAND):** During the hindquarter yield, the horse's forelegs should remain relatively still while the hind legs step around them in a circle. As the horse's hindquarters step sideways, the inside hind leg will cross over, and in front of, the outside hind leg.
- **SHOULDER OR FOREHAND YIELD (TURN ON THE HAUNCHES/HINDQUARTERS):** During the shoulder yield, the horse's hind legs should remain relatively still while the forelegs step around them in a circle. As the horse's forehand moves sideways the inside foreleg will cross over, and in front of, the outside foreleg.

The shoulder yield is one of the most basic lateral movements, teaching your horse how to be respectful of your space and balanced through its hindquarters.

- **SIDE-PASS**: During the side-pass, the horse should move sideways, with no forward motion, while keeping its head and neck straight. Like all lateral movements it can be performed on the ground or ridden, but the horse should have an established hindquarter and shoulder yield before progressing to the side-pass. As the horse moves sideways it will alternate between the inside foreleg crossing over and in front of the outside foreleg, and the inside hind leg crossing over and in front of the outside hind leg. Teaching a horse how to side-pass is beneficial for opening gates and for safely navigating trails and obstacles, and is the foundation for more advanced lateral movements — like the leg yield — that are seen in dressage and working equitation competitions.

Using the 1 to 10 Pressure Scale to shape behaviour

When we ask our horses a question, we want to teach them to respond to the most subtle cues possible by training them using a Pressure Scale of 1 to 10 (see pages 160–62 for details). In any given situation the trainer should begin by using Pressure 1, and then continue to gently, but firmly, add more pressure until the horse shows a response. This progression of energy is important because it creates horses that start seeking to answer the question off a light pressure.

If the horse doesn't give you a positive attempt off the lightest pressure, it's important to move through the pressure scales until your horse offers a positive attempt. If instead you keep nagging your horse with an insufficient amount of pressure (sometimes referred to as micro-managing), the horse can become confused, heavy to the aids, or desensitised to pressure. Through poor feel and timing on the handler's behalf, these horses often develop a lazy work ethic and may require constant nagging to do even the simplest of tasks. If your horse doesn't respond off a light pressure, it's important to retrain it; a horse that learns to respond to lighter aids will benefit in every aspect of its daily life.

At the other extreme, if a handler uses too much pressure, or doesn't recognise or reward a horse when it is attempting to answer the question asked of it (by immediately softening the amount of pressure applied), the horse can quickly become hypersensitive, worried and erratic, and it may start over-anticipating future cues.

This is why it's important to use the Pressure Scale of 1 to 10 correctly; not only to know when and how much pressure to use, but also to know when and how much reward is needed for any positive attempt the horse offers. The moment the horse gives you a positive attempt, it's important to offer them a suitable reward for their effort (see pages 164–66); this may include vocal praise, a gentle pat, backing away to give the horse time and space to process what it's just learned, or finishing the session.

When training a horse, it's important that you ask it only simple questions, breaking down more complicated concepts into several lessons, to gradually shape your horse's behaviour. If a training session is not going well, or the horse is getting

Side-passing over a pole can be beneficial to encourage accuracy and straightness.

confused, it is very likely that you are asking the horse a question it doesn't know the answer to, or you may be asking the question in a confusing way (through poor posture or confusing body language, inconsistent or incorrect aids, or by using too much — or too little — pressure for the situation). If you get to this stage in a handling session, it is important you ask the question in a less confusing way or find a good place to finish, then seek the aid of a professional to further educate both you and your horse.

Top four: Example of the Pressure Scale when teaching a horse to lunge.

Top left: Pressure 1 — raise your energy.

Top right: Pressure 2 — point in the direction you want the horse to go.

Middle left: Pressure 4 — Position your second hand in preparation for adding a swing to the rope.

Middle right: The horse moves off, into a circle from pressure 4, so no additional pressure is needed.

Bottom: A shoulder yield.

THE PRESSURE SCALE

The success of the Pressure Scale is based on being able to accurately read the horse's body language (see pages 54–59). This will help you determine when to ask your horse a question, how much pressure to apply and when to reward it.

It's important not to expect perfect answers and instead reward any positive attempt. It's a bit like playing the 'hot and cold' game: if the horse gets closer to 'hot' (or the correct answer), reward it, but if it stays the same or moves towards 'cold' (the wrong answer), increase the pressure. Once your horse's body language changes to indicate it is thinking of responding to your question, remain at that level of pressure until the horse starts to move. If the answer is correct, reward it, and if not, ask the question again. If you miss the moment when your horse is thinking and keep adding pressure, it may become very worried, confused or over-reactive.

As a horse's understanding grows, it should need less and less pressure for any given question, resulting in a horse that is light, responsive and eager to work with, and able to respond to questions off the lightest pressure.

- **PRESSURE 1** — First suggest to the horse that you're about to ask it a question, by changing your body weight and energy.
- **PRESSURE 2** — Next ask the horse the question, by giving it a clear physical or verbal cue (without applying any pressure to your horse).

COMMON CUES: Cues can be whatever you like, and will be something your horse learns through association and repetition. With good training a horse will be able to learn to answer all questions off Pressure 2. Some of our basic cues for groundwork include the following.

- Rein-back — stand in front of your horse and walk on the spot, or if you are asking your horse to rein-back while standing beside its shoulder, walk backwards by your horse's shoulder, with your elbow closest to the horse moving in and out at the same tempo of the horse's stride.
- Side-pass — cross your legs, then step sideways (continuing to cross your legs with every step) in time with the horse as it moves

> sideways; this cue can be used while standing in front of your horse, or beside it.
> - Walk to trot — when asking your horse to transition into a trot, while leading it from the shoulder, change your own speed from a walk to a run. This change in your gait will cue the horse to trot.

- **PRESSURE 3** — If the horse makes no attempt to respond within a couple of seconds, add a vocal cue (such as a click or a cluck).
- **PRESSURE 4** — If the horse continues to make no positive attempt, position your body in preparation for applying a gentle hand, leg or seat aid.
- **PRESSURE 5** — If the horse still doesn't respond, apply a hand, leg or seat aid, using the lightest pressure.
- **PRESSURE 6-10** — If the horse continues to ignore the question, gradually increase the pressure of the aid every few seconds to match the resistance the horse is offering.

When training horses it's important to clearly communicate to the horse when it's doing the right or the wrong thing, by rewarding or correcting the horse as needed (see following page). If you're moving up the Pressure Scale and the horse continues to ignore you, or gives the wrong answer, it can quickly form a bad habit. Behavioural issues (both on the ground and ridden) generally come about if you continuously allow incorrect or half-hearted answers — even three repetitive attempts are enough to start forming a new behaviour, whether good or bad.

Note, however, that even at Pressure 10 the increased pressure should be a *correction* and not a punishment — you should not need to use physical harm to inspire a good work ethic or correct behaviour. Your horse should be giving you the right answer through an understanding of your expectations and wanting to please you, rather than through fear of being punished (see page 282).

Using reward and correction effectively

Horses learn very quickly through the use of well-timed rewards and repetition, especially if relaxation is fostered throughout the training session; a relaxed horse is more likely to give you the correct answer *and* will usually retain what it has learnt, while a tense horse is more likely to give you the wrong answer and may struggle to retain the information it has been taught. Understanding how and when to reward your horse is important for teaching it new behaviours, or to refine existing behaviours.

Top: A firm, consistent pressure applied to the rope, to ask the horse to step up onto the bridge.

Bottom: As the horse takes a step, the pressure is immediately softened to let it know it has given the right answer.

The best ways to reward your horse

Rewards can be classified as negative reinforcement (removing discomfort) or positive reinforcement (adding comfort).

NEGATIVE REINFORCEMENT

Negative reinforcement is often used to motivate a horse to learn something new, or to do something it is confused by or scared of. When you ask your horse for a specific behaviour, work through the Pressure Scale of 1 to 10 (see pages 160–62) until the horse responds in a positive way. Good trainers will reward the horse, by releasing the pressure and then giving them time to process, for even the slightest positive attempt. This will shape the horse's behaviour, helping it to understand and positively respond to what is being asked of it.

Correct timing is essential. Releasing the pressure too early, before the horse has given a positive response, can be counterproductive — if you reward the horse while it is still offering resistance or doing the wrong thing you will confuse it, slow down the learning process or may even accidentally teach it bad habits.

Negative reinforcement can be applied in a number of ways:

RELEASE OF PRESSURE: This reward is an important training tool when working with horses. For it to be effective, the release of pressure must be done immediately, within 1 to 3 seconds of the desired behaviour, otherwise your horse will not associate the reward with the correct action. Examples include pressure applied to a rope or reins to guide the horse's speed or direction, or pressure applied from your hands or legs when asking your horse to go forward, backwards or laterally when it is under saddle.

SHORT BREAK: If your horse has done something well, especially if it is something that it has previously struggled to understand, back away to give the horse space and time to reflect on what has just happened. If you are riding, halt the horse and stand on a long rein for a few minutes, or take it for a walk on a loose rein. This short break will allow your horse time to process what it's learned; the next time you ask the question, it will be more likely to repeat the answer you are looking for.

FINISH THE SESSION: If your horse has responded with a few positive attempts in a row, or has just grasped a difficult concept, this is a good time to finish the training session. Make sure you finish on a good note, rather than repeating a question until the horse is bored or confused (if you ask your horse to repeat a question that it has just answered correctly, without rewarding it, it may assume it got the question wrong and not offer that answer again). Allowing your horse to return to its paddock is one of the best forms of reward you can give it.

POSITIVE REINFORCEMENT

Positive reinforcement is used to complement negative reinforcement, and should be used when the horse offers the correct answer. It allows you to clearly communicate to your horse that it has done the right thing, encouraging the horse to repeat the desired behaviour during future training sessions.

When offering your horse a treat, make sure your hand is flat, with your thumb and fingers pressed closely together.

Ways to apply positive reinforcement include the following.

VOCAL PRAISE: Use a low, encouraging or reassuring tone to reward your horse verbally. The pitch and volume you use is more important than what you say.

PHYSICAL CONTACT: If your horse is confident being touched, then rubbing, stroking or scratching it on the head or neck, or allowing it to reach forward and sniff or bump you with its muzzle are ways you can use physical contact to reassure your horse and let it know it's done the right thing. Most horses prefer a good scratch, rub or massage to patting or hugging — spend some time learning what gives your horse the most comfort; its body language will show you which reward it likes best.

FOOD: Food is the most controversial reward and should only ever be used with caution. If food is going to be given, then a handful of grass or hay can cause fewer negative side effects than hard feed or treats. Food may be helpful when teaching your horse a rare and much-desired behaviour that has been especially challenging for it to learn; the rest of the time, train with non-edible rewards. If used incorrectly, food can lead to negative behaviours such as the horse pushing into your space, nipping and biting, or becoming resentful if you don't offer the food in the future.

> **HOW TO FEED YOUR HORSE A TREAT**
>
> When offering your horse food, make sure that your hand is flat, with your fingers and thumb pressed closely together, with the food on your palm. Doing this will lessen the chance of a finger being bitten when the horse takes food from your hand.

Correcting undesirable behaviour

Sometimes, it may be necessary to correct undesirable behaviours before they can become bad habits. Although horses respond better to reward-based training (see above), occasionally they need to understand that dangerous or naughty actions won't be tolerated. As with rewards, the timing of the correction is crucial — it must be done immediately when the undesirable behaviour is exhibited.

If the behaviour continues, it is important to ask yourself *why* your horse is behaving this way. Horses aren't generally difficult on purpose, and there is usually an underlying reason for poor behaviour. You may be offering the horse confusing signals or asking it a question it doesn't know the answer to, or it could be in pain. In these instances, horses often become overwhelmed and react from their survival brain rather than their thinking brain (see page 60). If pain or stress is not the issue, find a clearer way to communicate with your horse so that it can understand what you want. Also consider whether you are expecting too much of your horse — if your requests aren't reasonable for its level of experience, you need to simplify your questions and expectations so that your horse can progress in a positive way.

PAIN IS OFTEN THE PROBLEM

If there is a sudden change in your horse's behaviour, or if it starts showing poor behaviour as you increase your physical demands, there is usually a reason behind this. Horses don't just wake up one morning and decide to be naughty — most often, pain or stress is the root cause.

It can, however, be challenging at times to pinpoint the problem, and even vets can struggle to diagnose why a horse's behaviour has suddenly regressed (you may not even notice a regression if your horse was already in pain when you purchased it). There are so many variables that can cause pain-related issues, and since your horse can't tell you what's wrong, it's your job to go through a process of elimination until you find the root cause of its discomfort.

Here are some common pain-related issues that can cause handling and ridden vices:

- ulcers (see page 86)
- teeth issues (see page 111)
- saddle fit (see page 204)
- skeletal issues
- nutritional deficiencies or being grass-affected (see page 89).

How to hold your hand when feeding your horse a treat.

TIMING AND FEEL: THE FOUNDATION OF GREAT HORSEMANSHIP

One of the most significant differences between good horsemanship and great horsemanship is the ability to demonstrate feel and timing when working with horses. 'Feel' is an intuitive awareness of both the horse and yourself, allowing you to make observations at a glance, to sense your horse's emotions, tension or pain, as well as being able to anticipate what the horse is about to do before it does it.

Equally important, 'timing' is the ability to know when to ask your horse a question and when to reward it. If your timing hasn't been developed and is either too early or too late, this will lead to confusion, fear or frustration in your horse.

With good feel and timing, you can have a continuous conversation with your horse — albeit silently — by giving subtle cues that appear almost invisible to observers. This ability to converse with your horse is crucial if you want to develop a true partnership with your equine companion. It allows your horse to understand your intentions, both during ground work and while being ridden, and encourages it to work with you, rather than against you.

Like learning to read or write, or drive a car, good timing and feel will become second nature, allowing you to instinctively work with any horse and anticipate what it is about to do. This includes knowing exactly how much hand or leg pressure is required to get the horse to go in the direction or at the speed you want, picking up on subtle tension in the horse before it escalates into a flight, fight or freeze response, and even understanding whether a horse is in pain or merely being naughty. Once you develop feel, you will be able to sense these things and respond intuitively without conscious effort.

While it does take time to develop feel and timing in every facet of handling and riding horses, every rider will have moments when they experience it. The first time you find your balance while rising to the trot, or are able to maintain a balanced position while jumping, is actually due to your subconscious mind starting to do its work and instinctively anticipate what is needed in any given situation.

Top: Showtym Spotlight performing bridleless at the 2016 Riding with the Stars show.
LIBBY LAW

Bottom: Working a horse at liberty is the ultimate test of feel and timing on the ground. Here, Kelly performs with Showtym Moonlight at Equidays in 2018.

GROOMING AND OTHER CARE

Grooming

Grooming should be a pleasurable experience for both you and your horse, giving you an opportunity to enjoy your horse's company with no other expectations. Done well, it not only results in a polished level of presentation and improved coat condition, but also allows you to keep an eye on your horse's overall health and well-being. While grooming, take time to run your hands over your horse to check for any injuries, illnesses or abnormalities, see whether its hooves are due for the farrier, and remove any bot eggs (see page 110) or ticks.

If you are only riding at home, brushing your horse (especially under the saddle, girth and bridle areas) and picking out its hooves may be sufficient, but if you are attending a lesson or a training day, your horse should be spotless from head to hoof. For a horse show, your presentation should be taken to the next level, including washing your horse before giving it a thorough groom, followed by trimming and clipping excess hair (see page 183).

Top: Time spent grooming should strengthen the relationship you have with your horse.

Bottom: Grooming equipment for home use.
1. Hole punch.
2. Bot knife.
3. Mane comb.
4. Rubber curry comb.
5. Hoof pick.
6. Sweat scraper.
7. Mane and tail brush.
8. Body brush.
9. Rubber groomer.
10. Dandy brush.
11. Sponge.

> **WHAT TO INCLUDE IN YOUR GROOMING KIT**
>
> Here are the most common brushes and accessories to include in your grooming kit:
>
> - Rubber curry comb or rubber groomer (to remove loose hair and dirt)
> - Dandy brush (medium bristles for use on the body)
> - Body brush (soft bristles for use on the head and legs)
> - Finishing brush or grooming mitt (extra soft to shine the coat)
> - Mane and tail brush
> - Hoof pick
> - Hoof oil
> - Sweat scraper
> - Washcloth or rag
> - Sponge
> - Metal mane comb (for fake-pulling manes, see page 180, or plaiting)
> - Mane and tail detangler
> - Shampoo and conditioner (horses have sensitive skin, which can be irritated by the ingredients in human products, so use a horse-friendly product)
> - Scissors (for trimming hair, or emergencies)
> - Clippers (optional)

BODY: Begin at your horse's neck and move down the body towards the tail, paying extra attention to the area under the saddle, including where the girth sits. Some horses can be ticklish, especially around their flank areas — if your horse's skin is quivering or it becomes grumpy, the brush you are using might be too hard.

1. **RUBBER CURRY COMB OR RUBBER GROOMER:** Start with a rubber curry comb (brushing in a circular motion) or a rubber groomer (running in the direction of the hair), to remove dirt and shedding hair from your horse's coat. A light stroke can feel ticklish to your horse, so use a firm pressure to make the grooming session feel more like a massage. When using a curry comb, avoid the bony areas of the horse, such as the head, legs, withers, spine and points of the hips. To clean your curry comb, bang it against a hard surface such as a wall or wooden rail.

2. **DANDY BRUSH OR BODY BRUSH:** Next, use a brush to whisk away any grime that has been brought to the surface by the curry comb. Use short and firm brush strokes in a flicking motion, in the direction of your horse's hair growth. Horses with sensitive skin can be reactive to a dandy brush, so if your horse appears ticklish and agitated, a body brush may be better suited.

3. **FINISHING BRUSH OR GROOMING MITT:** On show days it is good to finish with a soft finishing brush. Use long, smooth brush strokes, in the direction of your horse's hair growth, to give the coat a shiny, glossy look.

HEAD: Using a body brush, groom in the direction of your horse's hair growth, paying particular attention to the area under the bridle, including behind the ears. Be particularly gentle on the bony and sensitive areas such as around the eyes and the ears.

If you are grooming before a lesson or a show, finish with a soft finishing brush or grooming mitt to give your horse's head a shiny, glossy look, then pay particular attention to the following areas.

- **EYES:** Clean out any dirt build-up in the corners of your horse's eyes with a soft, damp washcloth.
- **NOSTRILS:** Clean out your horse's nostrils with a soft, damp washcloth or sponge.

MANE AND TAIL

- **TAIL:** Excessive or rough brushing of your horse's tail can pull out hairs or cause breakage, which will eventually result in a thin tail. To prevent this, it should be brushed as little as possible. Ideally you should only brush your horse's tail (or a long mane) the night before a lesson or show, and even then, only after it has been shampooed, conditioned and sprayed with a mane and tail detangler or baby oil. Hold the tail just below the horse's dock with one hand, to prevent pressure being applied directly to the roots of the hair. Then use a tail brush in your other hand to work through small sections of the tail at a time, brushing the knots from the bottom before moving gradually up the length of the tail.

> It takes up to four years for a horse's tail to grow to full length, so be careful not to pull out strands when you are brushing it.

- **MANE:** If your horse has a pulled mane and forelock (page 180) it can be brushed at any time, using a mane and tail brush or comb. However, maintaining a long mane will require the same care as the tail to prevent shortening or thinning it.

HOOVES: Your horse's hooves should be picked out before every ride. This not only improves your horse's grip, especially on grass surfaces, but it also gives you the opportunity to remove any rocks and debris that may have got wedged in the hooves or shoes, and also check their condition.

Using a hoof pick, start picking out the hoof at the heel (in the groove on either side of the frog) and pull the hoof pick down towards the toe, until the hoof is clean. Use this time to check the hooves for any issues, like thrush, seedy toe (stones in the white line, see page 115) or cracks, or whether they are due for a trim or shoe (see page 114). If your horse's hooves are dry or brittle, or you are about to ride in a lesson or at a show, make sure to oil them.

A full-body grooming includes picking out the hooves.

SHEATH: Geldings (and occasionally stallions) build up dirt and dead skin cells in their sheath and urethra; in its waxy form this grime is known as smegma and in its hardened form it is called a bean. Either can cause severe discomfort, swelling or infection, as well as interfere with urine flow, so it's important to get your horse's sheath cleaned at least once or twice a year by a professional, to ensure that he is comfortable and able to perform at his best (to a horse, smegma or bean can feel like walking with a pebble in your shoe). Cleaning the sheath correctly does require skill, so enlisting your veterinarian is recommended.

Bathing your horse

Having a clean, well-groomed horse at a lesson or show is not only a sign of respect but also the very first impression you'll make on the instructor, judge and spectators. If your horse is particularly dirty, or has manure or grass stains on its coat, grooming may be insufficient — even if your horse looks clean from a distance, a layer of dust against its skin may be evident on closer inspection or if someone were to run their hands over your horse. This is where bathing your horse comes in handy. Because shampoo can strip the natural oils from your horse's coat, however, it is important not to wash your horse too often (especially if it is uncovered) — save this for an important lesson or show day!

Here are some of the top reasons why you should bath your horse.

- You are preparing for a show — shampoo your horse the night before, then rug it to keep it clean, using a tail bag and hood if needed.
- You are preparing for a lesson and you have a light-coloured horse whose coat is stained — if the weather is warm, shampoo your horse all over; if the weather is wet or cold, use a sponge to wash only the parts of your horse that are dirty, to avoid it catching a chill.
- You need to clip your horse — shampoo your horse beforehand to avoid dirt blunting the clipper blades. After clipping, give your horse a hot oil wash (see page 177) to help restore the coat's natural oils and prevent skin irritation.
- Your horse is caked with wet mud and you want to ride it — a rinse-off with a hose can sometimes be sufficient, rather than a full shampoo.
- Your horse is sweaty from a workout — a rinse-off with a hose or sponge, followed by a sweat scrape, will be sufficient to remove sweat from the skin.

Full body wash

LEGS: Start by wetting your horse's legs with a hose or sponge, then shampoo them using a body brush or sponge to work the shampoo into the coat and remove any grime or stains. By starting with the legs, you not only allow your horse to gradually get used to the temperature of the water, but also ensure its body is wet for the shortest amount of time possible (this is especially important in cold or wet weather).

BODY: Next move on to the neck and mane, before working your way towards the hindquarters on one side. It's important to wet, shampoo and then rinse each side of the horse's body as you go — otherwise, the coat can dry too much to allow you to work up a lather. Apply the shampoo to the coat using a rubber curry comb, body brush or sponge. The deepest layer of grime builds up against the horse's skin, so it's important to lather the shampoo deep into the coat. You'll also need a sponge for the more sensitive areas, such as around the horse's sheath or udder and under the tail.

Before moving on to the other side of your horse, rinse off the soap from your horse's coat on the side you have just washed. Start with the upper neck and mane, then work your way back to the hindquarters, using your hand or a rubber curry comb to work the water deep into the coat to help rinse the dirt and soap suds from the roots. Finish with a sweat scraper to remove excess water from the coat, running it in the direction of the hair and being careful to avoid any bony areas.

If your horse is particularly dirty, it may be necessary to shampoo it twice; you'll know your horse is clean when the water runs clear off the horse and no dirt is visible if you part the hairs of the coat, especially at the base of the mane and tail or along the topline.

Once both sides of your horse have been shampooed, rinsed and sweat-scraped, rub the coat dry with a towel. If there's a cool breeze, put a show rug on your horse to keep it warm while you move on to the tail and head.

TAIL: For the tail, use your hands to lather the shampoo into the hairs, especially at the base of the dock. It may be necessary to shampoo the tail two or even three times (especially with a white tail), until the water runs off clear. Once it does, work conditioner into the tail, then rinse again. Brush the tail only once it has dried and a tail detangler has been applied.

HEAD: Lastly, wash your horse's head using a clean sponge. Take special care with this step, making sure that no water or shampoo gets into your horse's ears or eyes. Rather than wetting the horse's head with a hose, you can use the sponge to dampen the head and forelock, then wash with shampoo before rinsing out the sponge and using it to rinse the suds from your horse's head.

HOT OIL WASH: After your horse has been shampooed, rinsed and sweat-scraped, it can be beneficial to rinse your horse with an oil-based coat conditioner while the coat is still damp. A hot oil treatment, made from a small amount of horse-friendly oils, diluted with warm water, is sponged onto the horse and left to dry (no rinsing needed). It is ideal for restoring the natural oils that are lost during shampooing, improving hair and skin quality, reviving dull or dry coats, and restoring colour after clipping. For a basic conditioning treatment use 20 millilitres of hot oil in 2 litres of warm water. *Top tip:* Make sure that the water is warm enough to break up the oil particles, but not too hot that it burns your horse — if it is too hot for your hand to comfortably rest in it for 5 to 10 seconds, then it is too hot to sponge onto your horse. Stir the oil/water mixture thoroughly before dipping the sponge in each time — this ensures that the oil is spread evenly over the horse's coat rather than leaving it with oily streaks.

POST-BATH CARE: Once your horse is clean, make sure you leave it tied up, or in a clean stable or yard, to dry. A freshly washed horse will usually roll if it is let out into

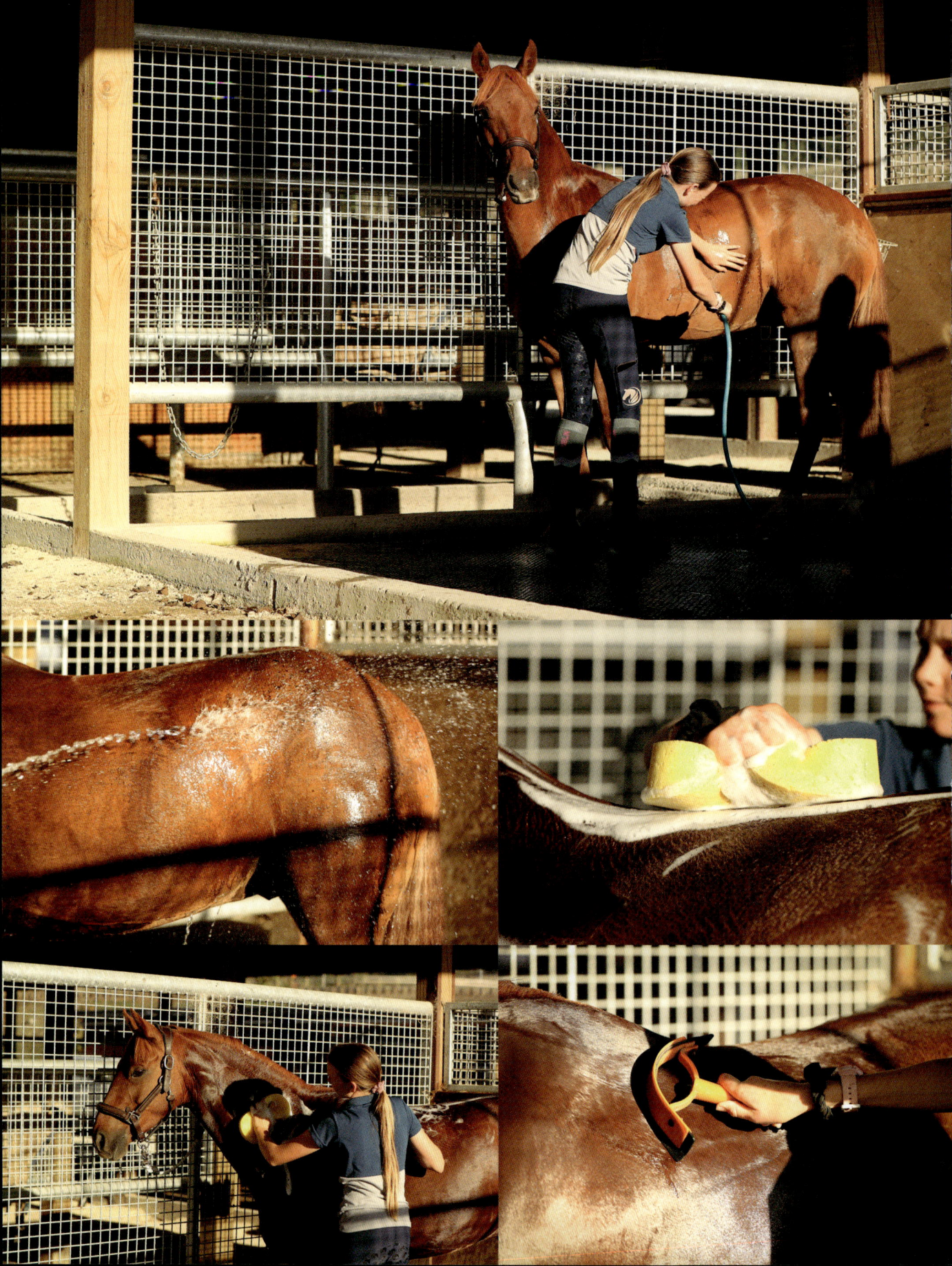

a paddock or yard, defeating the purpose of bathing it in the first place! Rugging your horse with a freshly washed summer sheet (either on its own, or underneath a turnout rug — depending on the weather) will keep your horse clean overnight, and for light-coloured horses a hood and tail bag may be needed (see page 189).

Trimming and clipping

Trimming or clipping involves the removal of hair from the horse's coat. Clipping is usually done in the winter months, to make a horse easier to groom and less likely to sweat while it is being worked, while trimming is usually done year-round to improve a horse's appearance, especially for competition.

> While it was once common practice to trim or clip hair from inside the horses' ears and remove their whiskers, this is now illegal due to welfare issues. If you need to clean out the waxy grime at the base of your horse's ears, gently bring the edges of each ear together and run clippers or scissors down the edges. This will give your horse's ears a tidy appearance while still leaving the hair inside the ears to protect them from insects and rain.

Trimming

Here are the most common places to trim:

BRIDLE PATH: Trimming a bridle path behind your horse's ears allows the bridle and halter to sit comfortably without the bulk of excess mane. Using scissors or cordless clippers, trim a strip about 2 to 4 centimetres long, using the position of where the halter or bridle naturally sits to guide you.

TAIL: In English disciplines, horses' tails are usually 'banged' at the bottom, with a horizontal blunt cut, to give them a tidy appearance. Your horse's tail needs to be clean, dry and brushed first; then, gather the top of the tail in one hand and run your other hand down the tail to the desired length. The length comes down to personal preference, but usually the tail should hang halfway down the cannon bone when the horse is moving. While standing safely to the side of your horse (never behind), keep a tight grip on the tail and use scissors or cordless clippers to cut straight across so that the end of the tail hangs parallel to the ground.

- *Top tip:* Horses hold their tails higher when they are moving, so make sure you allow for this when determining the correct length of tail for your horse. If in doubt, it's better to cut a tail too long than too short; only take off a few centimetres at a time, until you reach a length that flatters your horse's conformation.

A washdown bay, with non-slip matting, is a tidy and safe place to wash your horse.

> In some disciplines pulling or trimming the top of the tail is common practice, but this should only be done by a professional — a badly pulled tail can be unsightly and score lower than leaving the tail natural.

LEGS: Most horses have extra hair at the back of their legs, known as feathers, which grows longer than the normal coat. With heavier draught horses these feathers can be impressive and a highly desired character of the breed so are usually left intact, but for most other horses — especially those competing in English disciplines — feathers are usually trimmed to show the definition in the horse's legs.

In the lead-up to a competition, trim your horse at least four days out to allow any clip lines to fade. Be careful when clipping white hair, if the underlying skin is pink, as removing the hair can cause the sun to burn the skin.

Following the direction of the horse's hair growth, use cordless clippers for a tidy, quick trim down the back of the horse's legs; if your horse is ticklish, or worried about the noise or feel of clippers, use scissors, followed by a razor. When trimming the feathers, it's important to make it look natural, with no obvious clip line.

MANES: Horses' manes are generally pulled, not trimmed, as cutting the mane with scissors can cause a messy finish if it isn't done well and can make the horse's mane difficult to plait. Instead you can fake-pull the mane to give it a tidy appearance and maintain the ideal length (about 10 to 12 centimetres) and thickness for plaiting. The finished mane should be an even length and thickness, and have a natural, rather than blunt, edge.

- **FAKE-PULLING:** While having a thin and tidy mane offers a professional look, regardless of your discipline, pulling the mane out from the roots can be uncomfortable for horses and is only necessary for those competing in disciplines requiring them to have flawless plaits, such as showing, dressage and Show Hunter (for sensitive horses, this should be done under sedation). For horses competing at lower levels or in disciplines that only require a tidy level of presentation, a fake-pull may be sufficient — it offers the appearance of a pulled mane but without any discomfort, and is still suitable for creating tidy plaits.

Top left: The difference between a fake-pulled mane (left half) and a cut mane (right half).

Top right and middle left: Backcomb the mane so only the longest strands remain within your grasp.

Middle right: Cut the longest strands as close to the roots as possible, to resemble a pulled mane.

Bottom: A well pulled, or fake-pulled, mane will result in perfect plaits for the show ring.

> **TO FAKE-PULL A MANE**
>
> Start at one end of the horse's neck and take a small section of mane in one hand, holding it near the ends. With the pulling comb in your other hand, tease the hair towards the roots. The longest hairs, which should have remained in your grip, can then be cut close to the roots. Work up the entire length of the horse's mane, then brush out the teased hair, before repeating the process until the mane is at the desired length. To finish, use a pair of scissors to tidy up uneven hairs while striving to maintain a natural look.

TIPS FOR TIDYING YOUR HORSE'S MANE

- If parts of your horse's mane is already thin, it may only need to be shortened rather than fake-pulled. To do this, use clipper blades or a razor. Taking a small section of the mane at a time, slowly and carefully trim the ends of the horse's mane until it is the desired length, then make small vertical cuts with scissors to soften the edge so that it doesn't appear cut.
- Many horses have their mane lying on both sides of their neck, or on the near (left) side, so before you pull your horse's mane it is beneficial to train it to lie on the offside, since horses are traditionally plaited on the right side of the neck. To train the mane, brush the mane so that it is knot-free and lying on the offside, then dampen it and divide it into 2- to 3-inch (5- to 7.5-centimetre) sections. Loosely braid each section and secure it with an elastic band. The weight of the plaits should encourage your horse's mane to change sides. Some manes can be retrained in a week while others may take several weeks; generally, the longer the mane, the easier it is to retrain, which is why it's best to do this before it is trimmed.
- *Top tip:* Make sure the plaits are loose, otherwise your horse may feel discomfort and rub them out. This is the only time when your horse should be left with plaits in; normally if your horse is plaited for a show, these should be taken out as soon as you have finished competing.

Clipping

Over winter, horses grow thicker coats, which can cause excessive sweating if your horse remains in work over the colder months. The decision to clip your horse, and what clip pattern to choose, will depend on the type and frequency of the work you are doing with it, the weights of rugs you have available, how often you can attend to it, and whether your horse will be stabled or has shelter in its paddock.

CONSIDER CLIPPING IF:

- Your horse is in medium to heavy work and works up a sweat during most rides. If this happens, the horse can become chilled after it is worked as the hair takes longer to dry; clipping will help it dry faster and prevent chilling.
- You are able to check your horse regularly and change rugs as needed.

DON'T CLIP IF:

- Your horse will only be in light work or is turned out.
- Your horse is outside in the elements with no access to sufficient shelter.
- You aren't able to check your horse regularly and change rugs as needed.

WHEN TO CLIP YOUR HORSE

Most horses are usually clipped in early winter (if they are ridden all year round), or when they return to work before the competition season (if they are spelled over winter). These horses should be clipped before they start to shed their winter coat to prevent clipping the emerging summer coat, which can give the horse a dull, unhealthy appearance.

CLIP PATTERNS

Choosing a suitable clip pattern will depend on your requirements — the more hair you clip off, the more care will be required. Regardless of the clip style you choose, however, you will have removed at least some of your horse's natural source of warmth, so your horse must have a rug and suitable access to shelter to counter the loss of hair.

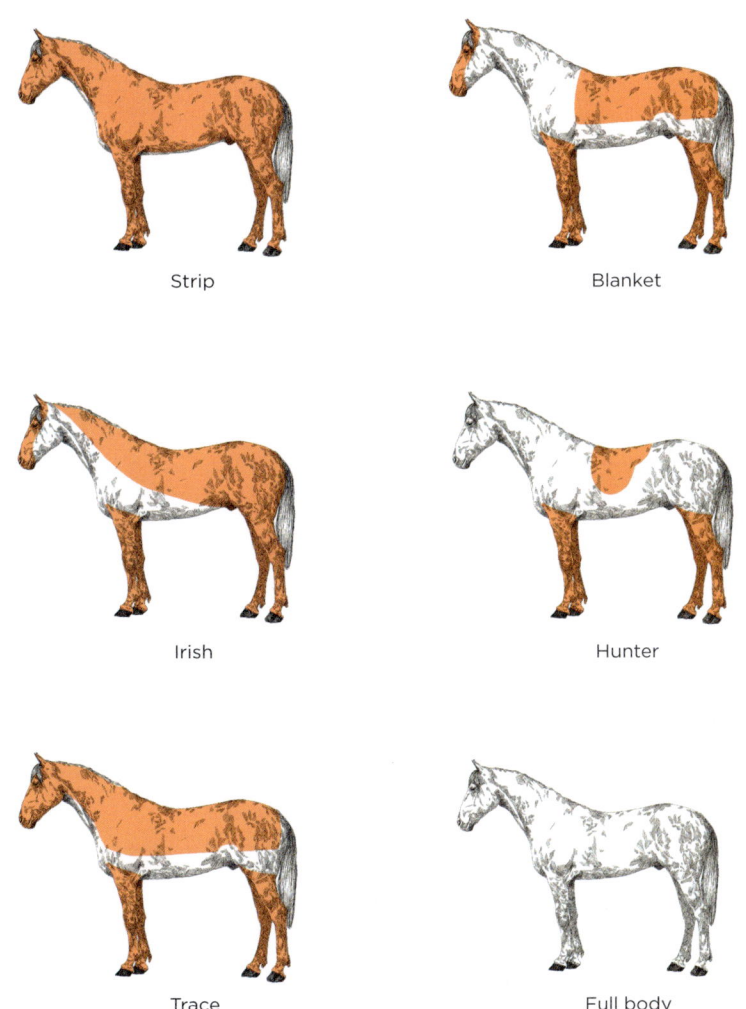

Common types of clip pattern.

A well-fitting synthetic rug.

RUGGING YOUR HORSE

Horses have evolved to regulate their own body temperature, with wild horses surviving in extreme conditions (hotter than 40°C in the Northern Territory of Australia, and colder than −40°C in the snow-covered Gobi Desert of Mongolia). They do this by growing a thicker coat in winter which stands on end when they feel cold, trapping a layer of warm air against their skin, then shedding it as temperatures increase. A horse in good condition (see page 101) will also store a layer of fat beneath the skin, which provides extra insulation over the colder months.

When driving rain, gusty winds or sleeting snow arrive, horses instinctively turn their hindquarters into the wind to minimise exposure to their extremities, and to keep the trapped layer of warm air against their skin. If cold weather is prolonged, their muscles shiver to generate additional heat, and blood is diverted away from the skin to the extremities, to give the horse the best chance of survival.

In the wild, horses also have the option of covering large distances to stay warm and find shelter, and can also huddle in their bands for extra warmth. For domestic horses, however, these options often aren't possible — horses may be paddocked or yarded in a small area, without shelter, or by themselves. A horse that has been rugged in the lead-up to winter may also struggle over the colder months if it is left without a cover, as its ability to grow a winter coat will have been compromised.

When deciding whether to leave your horse covered or uncovered, consider the following.

- **SHELTER:** Does your horse have sufficient shelter from both wind and rain (see page 67)?
- **COAT AND SKIN CONDITION:** If your horse grows a good winter coat it may be fine to leave without a cover. However, some horse breeds, like Thoroughbreds and Arabians, which often have finer coats and sensitive skin, may benefit from being rugged. If your horse is clipped during winter, a warm, waterproof cover is non-negotiable.
- **WEATHER:** Horses can struggle if they are exposed to long wet, windy or cold spells, with studies showing that they lose heat 20 times faster when they are wet through to the skin. Because of this, your horse will benefit from wearing a waterproof rug if your paddock has limited access to shelter. An unwaterproofed rug, or a rug that has insufficient fill, is worse than no cover at all — as your horse will still be wet or cold, but won't be able to have its hair stand on end to self-regulate its temperature.
- **WORKLOAD:** If your horse is in regular work over winter, it may be better off covered. Being turned out in a paddock on a cold and wet day after being ridden can cause your horse to chill — especially if it has worked up a sweat or has been hosed off.
- **AGE AND HEALTH:** Old, injured or sick horses can struggle to regulate their own temperatures and may benefit from being rugged in poor conditions. Covering foals and yearlings often isn't possible, so young horses should always have a paddock with sufficient shelter, plenty of grass to maintain good condition, and companions to share their body heat with.

Types of rug

TURNOUT RUGS: Turnout rugs are durable and waterproof to keep your horse dry, clean and warm while out in the paddock. They come in two main types of material:

- **CANVAS RUGS:** Made from natural fibres like cotton, linen, jute or wool, these covers are tightly woven to create a breathable but durable rug. The canvas is treated to make it water-resistant and UV-resistant, and comes in different weights for the different seasons: no fill (summer), jute (spring or autumn) or wool-lined (winter). Every few seasons your canvas rug may need to be treated with a product designed to restore its water- and UV-resistant properties.
- **SYNTHETIC RUGS:** These are made from synthetic materials and come in different grades measured in denier (usually ranging from 400 to 1200) — tougher fabric will have a higher denier. A synthetic rug's warmth comes from a layer of polyester fill, measured by the weight of fill in each square metre of material: no fill (summer), 100 to 200 grams (spring or autumn), 100 to 400 grams (winter, depending on the climate). Synthetic rugs, however, don't breathe as well as canvas ones and can leave horses slick with sweat on hot days. Because of this,

HOW TO MEASURE YOUR HORSE'S RUG SIZE

In New Zealand, horse rugs are measured in a straight line from the horse's wither to the base of the tail. In most other parts of the world, including the USA, UK and Australia, they are measured from the centre of the horse's chest, along the horse's side and to the point of the buttock where the rug ends.

CONVERSION CHART FOR RUG SIZES

The difference between a New Zealand-sized rug and a Australia/UK/USA rug is 1 foot, 3 inches (1'3") or 38 cm.

NZ	AUS/UK/USA
FEET + INCHES	FEET + INCHES
3'9"	5'0"
4'0"	5'3"
4'3"	5'6"
4'6"	5'9"
4'9"	6'0"
5'0"	6'3"
5'3"	6'6"
5'6"	6'9"

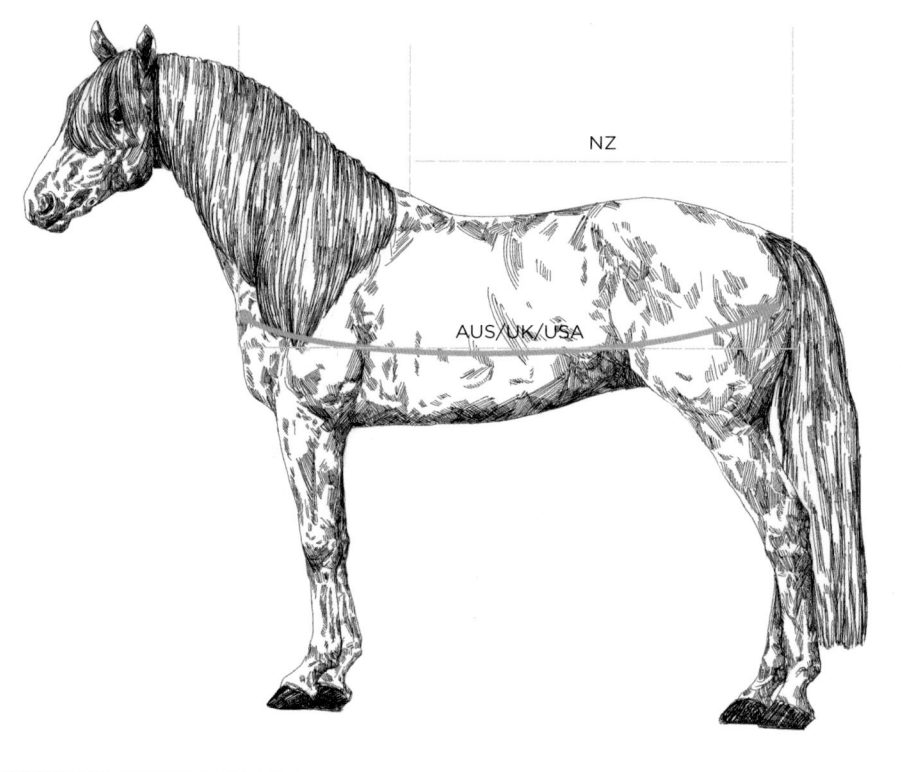

horses wearing synthetic rugs need to be carefully managed and should have the cover taken off, or changed to a lighter one, on warm days to prevent overheating or sweating.

> **WHAT WEIGHT TURNOUT RUG IS BEST IN WINTER?**
>
> The climate, available shelter, and the weather on any given day will all influence which weight of rug is best suited to your horse.
>
> A warm cover (i.e. a wool-lined canvas rug or a 200+ gram synthetic rug) might be needed to keep your horse warm on a chilly winter night, but that same cover is likely to be too warm in the midday sun and may cause your horse to sweat. When variations in weather occur, owners should be available to remove the rug or exchange it for one that is appropriate for the shift in temperature.
>
> If your schedule doesn't allow you to do this, however, be aware that over-rugging your horse can cause excessive discomfort (it's easier for a horse to warm itself up than cool itself down). In this situation it's best to leave your horse with no cover (provided that they have sufficient shelter, room to exercise and a good winter coat) or use a mid-weight canvas rug as these are more breathable, allowing the horse to regulate its own temperature.

SUMMER SHEETS: In summer, the need to keep your horse warm isn't a priority unless it is clipped. Instead, horses are usually left without rugs, or lightweight sheets are used to keep the horse clean and shiny or to offer protection from sun and insects. These covers usually aren't waterproof, so when it rains it's important to remove the lightweight sheet or switch your horse to a no-fill turnout rug; no cover is better for your horse than one that isn't waterproof.

- **COTTON SHEET**: Made from natural fibres, these lightweight rugs are ideal for keeping your horse clean while also offering protection from both sun and insects. It can be used by itself, weather permitting, or under a turnout rug.
- **FLY SHEET**: These lightweight and breathable mesh rugs offer protection from both sun and insects during the summer months.

STABLE RUGS: Stable rugs are designed to keep your horse warm while stabled, and are usually quilted or padded, in varying weights, to offer something for every season. Because they aren't waterproof, stable rugs aren't suitable for outdoor use, although can be used underneath a turnout rug to provide added warmth.

SHOW RUGS: Usually made from cotton or fleece, show rugs are extremely versatile and can be used as a light stable rug, a travel rug, or underneath a turnout rug after the horse has been washed. Show rugs often come with hood and tail bag attachments (or these can be added), making them ideal under a turnout rug on the evening before a horse show.

EXERCISE RUGS: Usually made from waterproof fabric and designed to fit under the saddle and over the loins, exercise rugs are ideal for keeping your horse warm and dry while being ridden in wet or cold conditions; especially if it has been clipped.

Cover accessories

To ensure your horse's comfort or cleanliness, additional cover accessories might be required.

ANTI-RUB VESTS: Usually made from nylon, satin, Lycra or quilted fabric, anti-rub vests are designed to prevent rugs from rubbing the coat across your horse's shoulders and wither. Anti-rub vests should be used only as a last resort — if your horse's coat is rubbing, it means that the cover is not fitting well and it should ideally be replaced with one that better suits your horse's size and shape to prevent further discomfort.

TAIL BAGS: Made from nylon, satin or canvas, tail bags are designed to keep your horse's tail clean and detangled. They attach to a summer sheet or show rug with Velcro fastening or ties. Alternatively, tail tubes can be used; these have self-ties which attach to the base of the dock when the tail is braided (offering protection to the lower half of the horse's tail).

HOODS: Made from Lycra, fleece or cotton canvas, hoods are ideal for keeping your horse's neck and head clean before a show, or to protect plaits. Because horses are unpredictable creatures that are easily distressed if their vision is obscured, it's important that the hood is securely and correctly fastened. A safe environment is also important, as a horse can panic and go through fences if a hood slips over its eyes.

Fitting a cover

Having a well-fitting cover is important for your horse's safety and comfort. A cover that is too big or small, or the wrong shape, can cause rubbing on the shoulders or chest or abscesses on the withers, or may slip and cause discomfort or come off your horse entirely. Your horse's shoulder angle, the width of its chest and its overall size will determine which style of cover will best fit it, so take care when selecting a cover — especially heavier covers, as they add more weight on to pressure points.

When fitting a cover, consider the following:

SIZE: The cover should sit nice and high from the base of the neck (about 5 to 10 centimetres up past the withers) and all the way back to the top of the tail. If the cover is too small, the horse will likely develop rub marks on the shoulders; if it is too big, the horse will likely develop rub marks on the front of the chest from the rug sliding back behind the withers. The cover should also come far enough down the horse's sides that its belly isn't visible or exposed to the elements.

SHAPE: A cover with a very deep-cut neckline is most suited for stocky horses with a broad chest, but will cause issues on a narrow horse that is more suited to a smaller neck opening. Gussets can also influence a cover's shape — a well-positioned gusset can offer a better fit and added comfort, especially if your cover has belly surcingle straps. An appropriate gusset allows the fabric to mould around the horse's shoulders,

Top: A cover rub, caused by an ill-fitting cover.

Bottom: A show pony dressed in a cotton show rug, hood and tail bag, to keep it clean the night before a competition.

relieving pressure on the chest, withers and shoulders.

CHEST STRAPS: The cover should be roomy enough to do up the chest straps without putting pressure on your horse's chest — once the straps are fastened, there should be space for you to slide your hand easily inside the rug, down the side of the shoulder and around the chest. The chest straps should ideally be done up on one of the tightest holes, so that there is plenty of overlap on the front of the cover; if your horse's chest is showing, you may need a cover with roomier shoulders or an adjustable neck opening.

SURCINGLE (BELLY) STRAPS: If your cover has surcingle straps, these need to be adjusted to custom-fit your horse. You should be able to fit the width of your hand between the straps and your horse's belly. Any looser than this and the horse can catch a hind leg in the straps when rolling or scratching, or snag the straps on something; any tighter will cause discomfort.

LEG STRAPS: If your cover has leg straps, these need to be adjusted so that the horse can move freely. Once fastened you should be able to fit the width of your hand between the straps and your horse's leg. If they are looser than this then the cover is likely to slip to the side, while tighter straps may cause discomfort or restrict the horse's movement. Note that not all rugs have leg straps; some just have a fillet strap that goes under the horse's tail.

NECK COVERS: Neck covers should be long enough to protect your horse's neck from the elements (but not touch the horse's ears when it's grazing), and loose enough that it doesn't rub out your horse's mane or restrict its ability to lower its head to eat.

COMMON CAUSES OF COVER RUBS

- **INCORRECT COVER SIZE OR SHAPE**: Covers that are the wrong size or shape are the most common cause of rub marks on the chest, shoulders or mane, as well as abscesses on the withers.
- **WEARING THE COVER FOR EXTENDED PERIODS**: Horses should never wear a cover for weeks or months on end. Leaving the cover on for long periods of time may cause rubs or abscesses to develop on pressure points and can also restrict the horse's ability to move correctly.
- **FINE COATS**: Some horses have finer coats that are more susceptible to rubbing; for these horses, an anti-rub vest is advised.
- **PRONOUNCED PRESSURE POINTS**: Horses with high withers, or with poor condition, may be more susceptible to rubbing. If so, an anti-rub vest may be needed to provide extra padding, and on sunny days the cover should be removed to relieve pressure.

A pony grazes in the field, wearing a synthetic turnout rug.

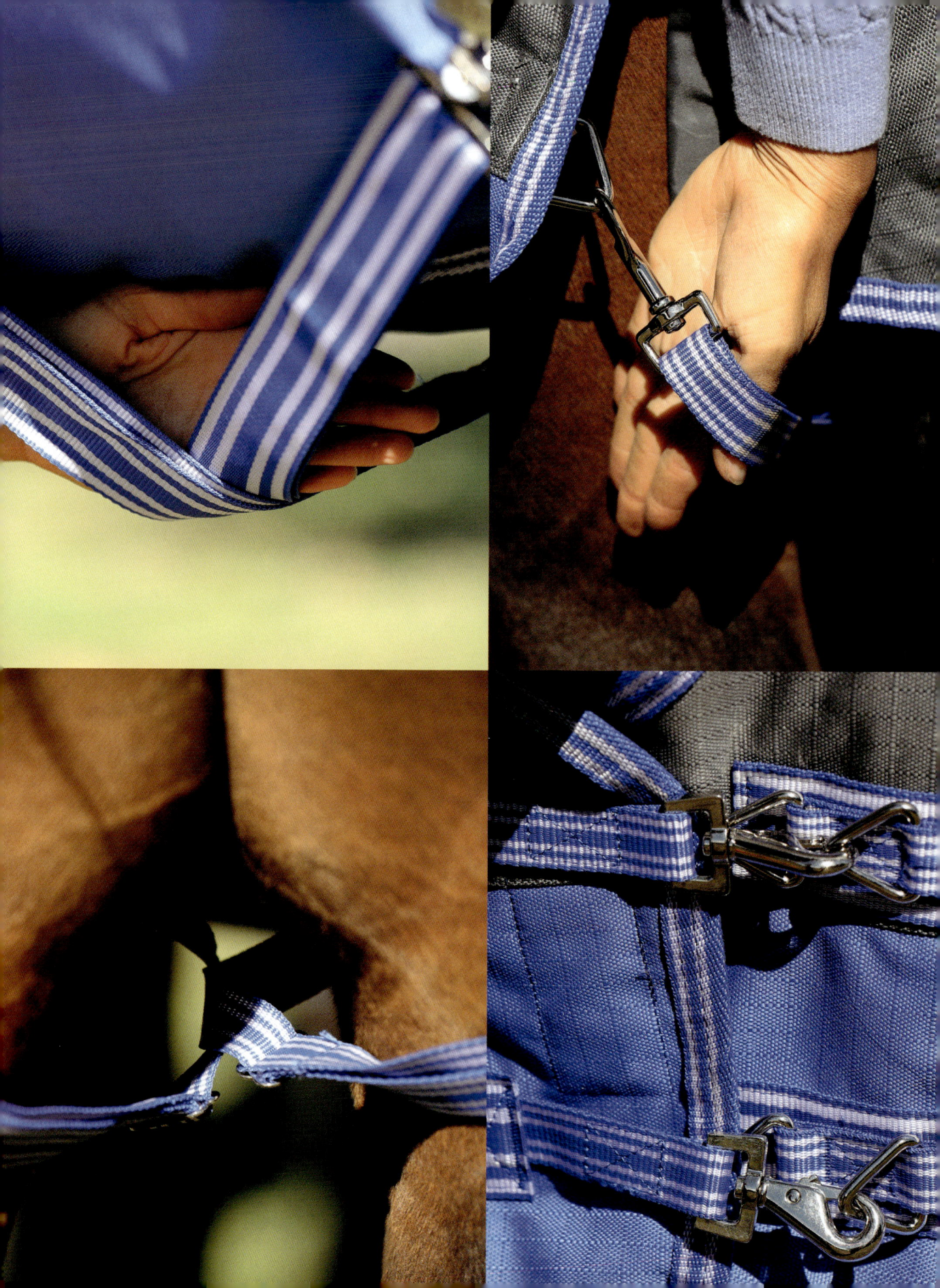

HOW TO FIT A RUG

Rugging a horse is easy once you've learned the correct order for doing up the straps. This order is important, as doing up the cover incorrectly can result in serious accidents if the horse takes off partway through being covered. If this happens, the cover may slip over the horse's neck and obscure its vision, or get dragged behind it, which can cause the horse to panic.

To keep both you and your horse safe, follow these tried and true steps to cover your horse.

STEP 1: Put a halter on your horse and tie it up, have someone hold it or hold the lead securely with your spare hand.

STEP 2: Check that the chest and surcingle straps are undone, and that the leg straps are fastened to their D-rings so they don't hit the horse as the cover is placed over its back.

STEP 3: Gently place the cover over the horse's withers, then smooth it into place. If the cover is heavy, or the horse is unsettled, you can fold the cover in half before gently placing it on the horse, then unfold it into position.

STEP 4: If your cover has leg straps, do these up first. Start with the right hind leg, looping the strap around the leg before fastening it back on to the D-ring on the right side. Ensure that the clips are done up facing inward so that they can't get caught on anything. Next, move around to the left side of the horse and loop the strap around the left hind leg, looping it through the other strap so that they are crossed before fastening it onto the D-ring on the left side — looping it through is critical to prevent the cover slipping when the horse rolls or lies down.

STEP 5: Next, fasten the chest straps.

STEP 6: Fasten the surcingle straps if your cover has them, making sure that you cross them to form an 'X' under the horse's belly.

STEP 7: If your cover has a neck cover, fasten these straps last.

TO REMOVE THE COVER: When removing the cover, undo the straps in the opposite order — start with the neck cover straps, then the surcingle straps, then the chest straps, and finally the leg straps, clipping them back onto the D-ring so that the buckle won't swing and hit your horse when the cover is taken off. Once all the straps are undone, stand at your horse's left shoulder and gently pull the cover off.

Correctly fitting straps, including the surcingle straps (top left), back cover straps (top right and bottom left) and chest straps (bottom right).

Loading a horse onto a float.

TRANSPORTING YOUR HORSE

The ability to transport your horse will open up a whole world of new opportunities, from riding at nearby forests, beaches and equestrian venues to attending Pony Club rallies or clinics, taking your horse to a vet, moving properties or competing at horse shows.

Choosing the right mode of transport, with a stall space that is sufficient for the size of your horse, will ensure that it has a comfortable ride. Cramming a large horse into a narrow or short space can cause it to rub its tail, chest and hips against the walls, dividers or benches, and can also cause unnecessary stress or muscle fatigue from bracing when the horse isn't able to stand balanced. The trailer or truck you use should also allow your horse enough room to load and travel without bumping its head on the roof, as well as room to spread its legs to find balance (without having to lean or scramble).

Vehicle safety

Whatever mode of transport you decide to buy (or hire), it will need to have regular safety inspections to keep it on the road and be safe for a horse to travel in. Here are some common issues and what to check for.

FLOOR: Accidents involving trailer floors are tragically common, with horses' legs going through floorboards and onto the road below, which can result in serious injury or death. At the start of each season, lift the rubber matting and inspect the wood and metal floors; do this more often if you travel a lot. Look for signs of wear or rust, especially on weld sites and underneath the trailer. It's also important to check the structure of the ramp, as this takes the full weight of the horse when it is loading and unloading, as well as hard impacts if the horse kicks the ramp while travelling.

NON-SLIP FLOORING: Trailer and truck floors should be covered with rubber mats, but even these can become slippery if they become wet from rain, urine or sweat. It's therefore important to have sawdust, shavings or straw on the ground for added grip. While some people like to put bedding on the entire floor, generally a 1-metre strip, under the hind legs, is sufficient.

TYRES: Check the tyres for signs of wear, that they are inflated properly and that they have been manufactured to carry heavy loads. If you have a blown or flat tyre, pull over to the side of the road, preferably into a rural driveway where you can unload the horses into a paddock or yards while the tyre is changed, as horses can become unsettled by the sound of a jack. If, however, you're in a busy urban area with lots of traffic, you may need to keep the horses loaded while the tyre is changed, to avoid the risk of a horse getting loose or injured.

TOWING GEAR: Ensure that the tow bar is the correct size, is correctly fitted and is greased every few months.

LIGHTS: Check that all the lights are working, especially if you are travelling at night.

WEIGHT: Check your vehicle's towing capacity and the trailer's (or truck's) tare weight — with a full load it may be overweight once you factor in the weight of your horses, hay, water and all your gear. If you're loaded incorrectly, you may be fined and your insurance will be void.

PARTITIONS: Make sure that the partitions are suited to the size and height of your horse. If they are not set correctly, the horse may be able to rush backwards (under the rump guards) when the ramp is lowered, or it may try to jump over the front partition if it is stressed or panicked.

CAMERA MONITOR: If you're concerned about how well your horse travels, a live camera feed — mounted to your dashboard — will allow you to keep an eye on it and provide ease of mind while driving.

> ### THINGS TO CARRY IN CASE OF AN EMERGENCY
> - A fire extinguisher — and knowledge of how to use it; fires are often caused by trailer brakes being left on and seizing, or from perished tyres
> - Tools to change a tyre (including a heavy-duty jack and tyre iron), and a spare tyre
> - Torch
> - Cell phone and charger, so that you can call a vet in an emergency
> - Knife or scissors to cut a rope or halter
> - First aid kits for both horses and humans
> - Spare halter and lead rope (in case your horse breaks one)

Preparing and loading your horse

BE PREPARED: Before you load, have your trailer ready to travel. It should be fully packed, have sawdust or a strip of carpet on the floor, windows open, and the partitions tied back (so they don't swing shut or clang if the horse bumps them).

SEPARATE HORSES: If you have horses that dislike each other or are poor travellers, avoid placing them beside each other to reduce the risk of injury. If they do have to travel side by side, have them separated by a head grille so that they can't bite, and rubber kick mats to prevent them kicking each other.

LEG AND TAIL PROTECTION: A well-fitting and correctly applied tail wrap or tail bandage will protect the tail from rubbing during travel. Travel boots and bandages (see page 200) are also available to protect the legs, although their use is controversial as they can cause the tendons to overheat if they are left on for too long. If used, a tail wrap and travel boots are more suited to inexperienced owners, as poorly applied bandages can loosen and fall off or cause pressure sores, irritation, swelling or permanent damage.

DON'T OVER-COVER YOUR HORSE: It can get very warm inside a truck or trailer, and because the horses are continually moving to maintain balance, they can overheat easily. No rug or a very light show rug or cotton sheet, is sufficient — you don't want your horse sweating in the trailer.

CLOSING THE RAMP: Stand to the side while you are raising the ramp (in case the horse rushes backwards and hits the ramp, causing it to flatten you). Banging the ramp can startle the horse and cause it to jump forward, or even go over the front partition, so close it gently before securing it into place. (*Note:* In a front-loading trailer, the horse should be tied up only once the ramp has been closed, and untied before the ramp is lowered for unloading.)

TYING YOUR HORSE: Once your horse is loaded, tie it to a piece of twine or breakaway ties; it's safer for a horse to be able to break free if it gets into a dangerous situation. The rope should be short enough that your horse can't get its head around the head divider, or turn its neck and get it trapped, or be able to bite another horse.

> ### TOP TIPS FOR LOADING YOUR HORSE
>
> Horses often have issues with loading and travelling — usually due to previous negative experiences — so it is worth investing the time and money to have a professional retrain them, to ensure they are able to travel with confidence in the future.
>
> - **PRACTICE MAKES PERFECT:** If you have a young horse, or one that's difficult to load, train (or retrain) it to load calmly well before you need to travel. Ideally give it several short trips, with a relaxed travel companion, to build up its confidence.
> - **ALLOW PLENTY OF TIME:** It's important to allow plenty of time to load; if you have an early start, it may be better to travel the night before, as your horse will be less likely to load if you have time restraints that cause you to rush or stress it.
> - **PARK DOWNHILL:** If your horse isn't good to load, park slightly downhill so that the ramp isn't as steep.
> - **MAKE SURE THE RAMP IS LEVEL:** If the ramp isn't level with the ground, or sits off the ground, it can feel unstable or cause it to make a clanging noise when the horse steps on it, which may cause the horse to lose its confidence.
> - **GAIN CONFIDENCE WITH OBSTACLES:** Before asking your horse to load onto a trailer or truck, increase its confidence by navigating a variety of obstacles on the ground (see pages 293–98). Getting your horse confidently approaching and stepping up onto bridges or boxes, or walking through narrow spaces, will be useful as these will mimic the actions required to step onto a ramp, then walk into your truck or trailer.

Drive slow and safe

A bumpy or rough drive, or going too fast around corners, will tire and stress your horse and increase the chances of injury; it can also have long-term consequences for your horse's confidence, or even make it difficult to load for future trips. The slower and more considerately you drive, the better your horse will be able to balance, as there will be less stress on its joints.

To ensure that your horse has a good experience, make sure that the driver:

- drives smoothly and at a reasonable speed, going about 10 kilometres below the recommended speed limit (and reducing speed by a greater margin on sharp corners or in bad conditions)
- doesn't brake suddenly, instead reducing speed gradually (especially on corners, or when braking for traffic lights)
- is in the appropriate gear to stop, go around corners or drive up and down steep hills.

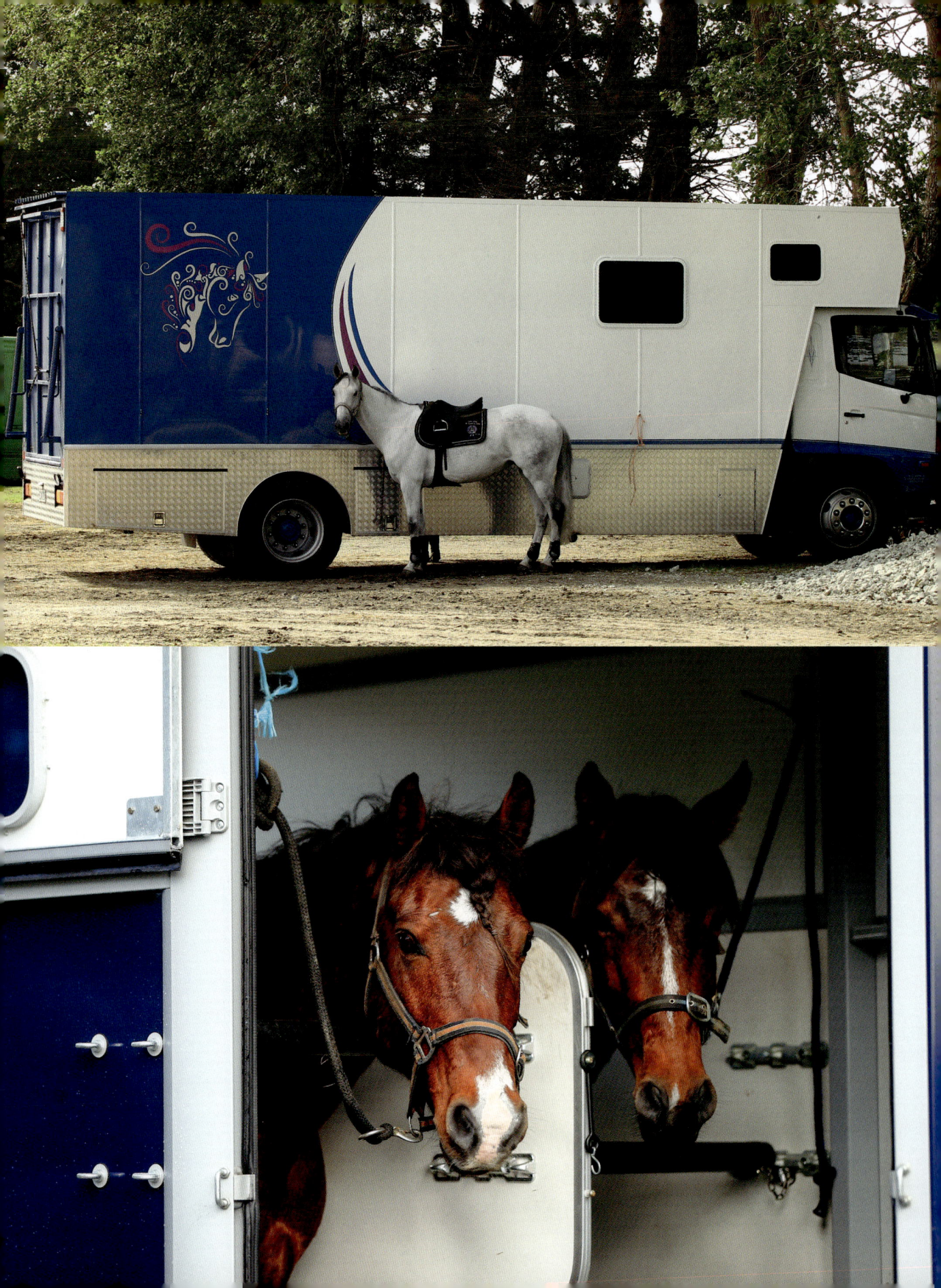

TOP TIPS FOR LONGER JOURNEYS

Here are some of our top tips for a stress-free trip.

- **REST STOPS:** Ideally stop every 2 to 3 hours for a rest break, allowing the truck or trailer to stand idle for 15 minutes (this can be while you refuel or stop to get food). During this time, your horse should be checked to make sure it is standing calmly.
- **LONGER BREAKS:** You should plan to have a suitable place to stop every 4 to 5 hours, where you can safely unload your horse, take it for a walk and allow it to graze for at least 30 minutes. This is vital so that your horse can lower its head and clear its nasal passages, loosen its muscles by walking and be offered food and water. It's also a good opportunity to muck out.
- **OVERNIGHT STOPS:** If your journey is longer than 5 hours, or the terrain is hilly or windy (meaning that the horse has to work extra hard to maintain balance), it's important to break the trip into multiple days. Have a suitable resting stop — with safe stables, yards or paddocks — organised well in advance. Plan to arrive before dark to get your horse settled into its new surroundings. If your horse is going into an unknown paddock, it's important to lead it around the fence line to reduce the risk of injury.
- **ARRIVE A NIGHT EARLY:** If you are driving a long distance to attend a clinic or show, arrive a night early to allow your horse to rest and recuperate before it is expected to perform.
- **AVOID ULCERS:** If you are travelling a long distance to a horse show or clinic, or buy or sell a horse that has to travel a long way (multiple trips longer than 5 hours, over several days), it is quite possible that it will develop ulcers during transit. To help minimise this, it's important to give your horse 2 kilograms of roughage immediately before each trip (if a hay net isn't available to it during the trip) and ensure it is fed and watered as soon as its unloaded. It can also be beneficial to put the horse on an ulcer-prevention product for a few days before, during and following travel, or to have it scoped for ulcers a few weeks after the trip if you notice a change in its behaviour or ulcer symptoms become present.

Top: A horse tied to a horse truck at a competition.

Bottom: Two ponies tied within a double straight-loading float.

HOW TO BANDAGE YOUR HORSE

Stable or travel bandages, which come in sets of four, are made from wool or polar fleece material and are designed to be used over Gamgee or leg wraps. Together, these work to protect your horse's legs while being stabled or yarded, during travel, or as support for horses recovering from injury.

In the wrong hands, however, bandages can cause serious damage if they are applied too tightly, unevenly or without Gamgee or leg wraps, or if the bandages are made from the wrong material (including elastic bandages).

Top tip: Before you begin bandaging your horse, make sure the bandages are rolled correctly, starting with the Velcro in the middle of the roll.

STEP 1: Wrap the Gamgee or leg wrap around the horse's leg, making sure that it lies smooth and flat, starting on the outside of the tendon and wrapping towards the back of the leg (resulting in the Gamgee or leg wrap being doubled over on the outside of the horse's legs and at the back of the tendon).

STEP 2: Start rolling the bandage midway down the horse's cannon bone, wrapping the leg counter-clockwise on left legs and clockwise on right legs (so you're working from the front to the back of the leg, and from the outside to the inside). Applying an even pressure, wrap down towards the fetlock, overlapping the previous layer by 50%.

STEP 3: At the horse's fetlock, wrap under the back of the fetlock, allowing the bandage to make a natural turn upwards. Continue wrapping up to the base of the knee, making sure you maintain an even gap between each layer, with no lumps or ridges forming.

STEP 4: Secure the Velcro.

STEP 5: Check to make sure that the bandage isn't too tight: you should be able to fit a finger between the horse's leg and the Gamgee or leg wrap at the base of the knee and also the fetlock.

Opposite page: How to bandage a horse's legs for stabling or yarding.

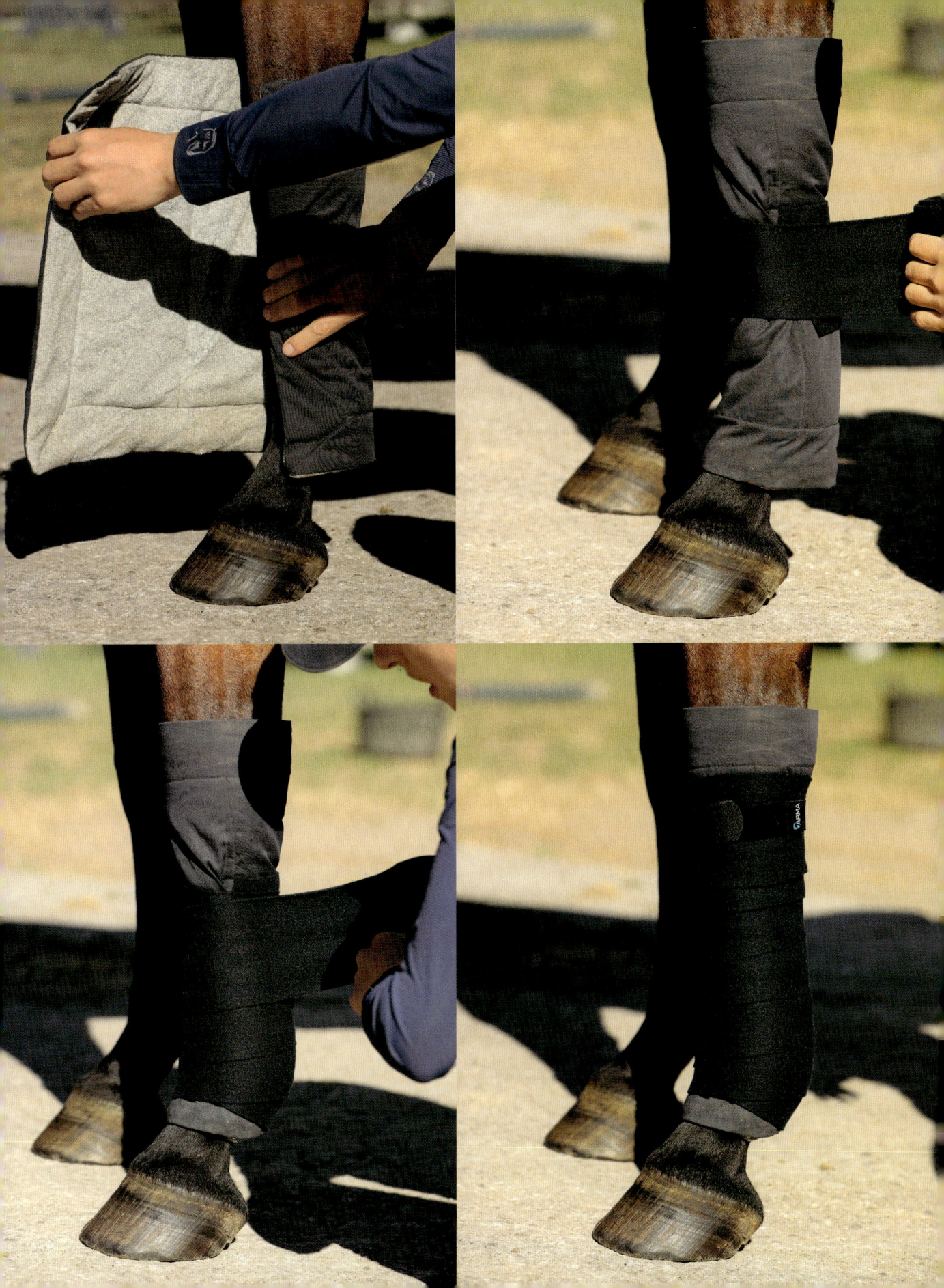

SECTION 4

Saddlery and Clothing

Before you start thinking about riding, it's important to make sure you have the right saddlery and clothing to ensure the comfort and safety of both horse and rider. In this section you'll learn the importance of saddle fit, which bit is best suited to your horse, why the safety of your gear is important, and what to wear while riding at home and in competitions.

SADDLES

A well-fitting saddle is one of the most crucial investments you will ever make. A saddle that doesn't fit properly will negatively affect your horse's performance, create behavioural and pain-related issues that will limit both you and your horse's enjoyment of riding, and also compromise your horse's mental, physical and emotional well-being.

An ill-fitting saddle can be compared to a person having to wear shoes that are the wrong size for their feet; the longer you wear them, the more likely the shoes will cause you pain or restrict your movement.

If a saddle doesn't fit — because it's too narrow or wide, crooked, rocks back and forwards, bridges or extends beyond the eighteenth rib — it will cause pain-related issues that negatively affect the way your horse moves and behaves.

While humans have the skills to identify what's causing them pain and do something about it, horses aren't able to make the same decisions for themselves. Instead, they will usually communicate their discomfort by misbehaving, which is often misinterpreted as the horse being naughty or bad tempered; these behavioural signs (see pages 54–59) can vary greatly depending on the horse's tolerance of pain, how much pain they are in, and their nature.

For the welfare of your horse, and its ability to perform the tasks you ask of it, it cannot be stressed enough how important a correctly fitting saddle is.

DOES THE SADDLE FIT YOUR HORSE? Every horse, no matter its value or purpose, should have a saddle that fits its unique shape, to prevent the development of behavioural and pain-related issues.

Signs of an ill-fitting saddle include the following.

PHYSICAL SIGNS
- White hairs under the saddle area, caused by intense pressure on the hair follicles which prevents pigment from being dispersed to the hair shaft
- Abnormal muscle definition or swelling under the saddle area
- Hard, sore muscle knots, especially on either side of the withers, or inflammation
- A hollow, tense or sore back, especially noticeable if the horse's back dips or flinches when you run your hands over the area where the saddle sits
- Rubs on the withers or spine, caused by the gullet not having enough clearance or a channel that is too narrow
- Gait abnormalities, including lameness, bridle lameness or a four-beat canter
- Head nodding
- Tail swishing
- Toe dragging

BEHAVIOURAL SIGNS
- Girth- or saddle-shy horse, including the horse laying its ears back, flinching, humping its back, biting or rearing while being saddled

Top: A well turned-out horse wearing a snaffle bridle, flat seat jumping saddle and breastplate.

Bottom: White hairs from a poorly fitting saddle.

- Poor work attitude
- Resistance to moving forward, or rushing
- Refusing or rushing into jumps
- Vices such as bucking, rearing, napping or head flicking
- Cold backed (the horse displays sensitivity or pain to being saddled, mounted or ridden, especially before it has been warmed up)
- A poor jump technique — a horse will often hang its front legs if the saddle restricts its ability to use its withers or shoulders correctly

Buying a saddle

When looking for a saddle, consider the following.

SADDLE TYPE: Your preferred equestrian discipline, whether it be jumping or dressage, will help determine the type of saddle you need, as will your future aspirations. There are three main types of English saddles:

- **GP (GENERAL PURPOSE) SADDLES**: General purpose saddles are designed for use in most equestrian disciplines, and are a good choice for young or inexperienced riders who want to do pleasure riding or low-level competition. They have a deep seat with slightly rounded knee flaps, with little to no knee pads, allowing the rider to change between a jumping and a dressage position by simply adjusting the length of their stirrups. A GP saddle will be sufficient for the needs of most low-level riders; however, it can make it hard to achieve the ideal position or balance for either dressage or jumping. Because of this, most competitive riders will use a saddle designed for their specific discipline.
- **DRESSAGE SADDLES**: Dressage saddles are designed for use in dressage, flatwork and showing. They have a deep seat to aid the rider in adopting an ideal position for flatwork, as well as longer and straighter saddle flaps to enable the horse's shoulder to move freely. If you enjoy competing in a range of disciplines, however, a dressage saddle is the least versatile, as it isn't designed for jumping.
- **JUMPING SADDLES (ALSO KNOWN AS FLAT SEAT SADDLES)**: Jumping saddles offer riders the ideal position for jumping and greater security in the saddle by placing the rider's weight over the horse's centre of balance, allowing the horse freedom of movement over jumps. To achieve this, jumping saddles have 'forward cut' flaps (which allow the rider to adopt a forward seat over the jumps), supportive knee rolls and a 'flat seat' (which helps prevent the cantle from flicking the rider out of the saddle on landing). Although designed for jumping, most riders use jumping saddles for general purpose use and simply adjust their stirrup length for hacking or flatwork.

MATERIAL: Saddles are traditionally made from leather, although synthetic saddles are also widely used for pleasure or low-level riding.

- **LEATHER SADDLES**: The quality of both leather and craftmanship varies greatly, which will be reflected in the price of the saddle and its expected lifespan.

Top: A brown dressage saddle with long billet points and a short girth (left). A black flat seat jumping saddle with short billet points and a long stud girth (right).

Bottom: A fleece saddle cover, with a slit for the stirrup leathers and irons, which is suitable to ride in (left). A fleece-lined canvas saddle cover, to protect the saddle between rides (right).

A good-quality leather saddle is always worth the investment, and if well looked after (see pages 236–38) should last a lifetime.

- **SYNTHETIC SADDLES:** There is a wide range of saddles made from synthetic materials, including artificial leather and suede. Synthetic options are much cheaper than leather, and are lightweight and easy to clean.

NEW OR USED? If you're buying a new saddle, expect to pay anywhere from $1000 for a low-budget saddle or up to $8500 for a good-quality saddle, with the final price often determined by the brand that best fits your horse. Be aware that some options lack the craftsmanship needed to ensure a good saddle fit, and by cutting costs you may end up with a horse that develops behavioural or pain-related issues.

For those unable to afford a new saddle, purchasing a used saddle can be an affordable way of getting the best saddle for your horse. Used premium-brand saddles generally cost between $500 and $4500, making them a similar price to brand-new saddles of lesser quality. Provided that a used saddle has been well maintained, it can still have a long lifespan. However, there is a risk that a used saddle might be worn or damaged, so it is important to carefully inspect it prior to purchasing.

Here are the things to look out for when buying a saddle.

- **EXAMINE THE SADDLE TREE:** Saddle trees can be twisted, broken or fractured, even when purchased brand new. Damage can occur during the process of constructing the saddle, widening the gullet size, from a horse rolling or flipping onto the saddle, or by using a narrow saddle on a horse that is too wide. There are several signs that a tree may be damaged — a crease in the leather on the seat or panels, a popping or clicking sound when you're riding, too much flexibility in the saddle, or the saddle sitting unevenly on the horse. If you suspect that the tree is damaged, it needs to be checked by a professional saddler; using a saddle with a damaged tree can cause your horse severe discomfort, which can result in dramatic behavioural issues.
- **ASSESS THE LEATHER CONDITION:** Check the quality and condition of the leather on both the saddle and the stirrup leathers to ensure that it is soft and supple. If there are cracks in the leather, it may have dry rot.
- **CHECK THE STITCHING:** The stitching holds the saddle together, so is very important to the overall strength of the saddle. Check to make sure that the stitching hasn't frayed or worn out, especially on the girth straps and stirrup leathers. If the stitching is compromised, you will need to have it restitched by a saddler.

ASK FOR ADVICE: Unless you are experienced and knowledgeable about saddle fitting, it is essential to seek the advice of a professional saddle fitter. Not all professionals are equally skilled, however, so it's important to gain an understanding of what a well-fitting saddle should look like. If you are unsure about the saddle fit, get a second or even a third opinion; a well-fitting saddle really is that important.

Top left: Checking the clearance over the horse's withers.

Top right: Checking the clearance at the horse's shoulders.

Middle left: The deepest part of the seat should be in the centre of the saddle.

Middle right: Checking to make sure the saddle doesn't rock on the horse's back.

Bottom: Checking for even panel pressure by running the back of a hand along the horse's back under the saddle.

HOW TO SADDLE FIT

Before you begin, check that the saddle is symmetrical and the tree isn't damaged. Once you are confident that the saddle is in good condition, make sure your horse is standing squarely on a level surface and place the saddle directly on the horse's back, without a saddle blanket.

SADDLE POSITION

- Place the saddle slightly forward on your horse's withers, then use the palm of your hand to gently bump it backwards until it comes to a natural resting place, behind the horse's shoulder blades.
- The exact saddle position will be dictated by your horse's conformation and the shape of the saddle.

WITHER CLEARANCE

- Ideally, you should be able to fit the width of 3 to 4 fingers between the top of your horse's wither and the pommel of the saddle. If there is too little space, the saddle can damage your horse's muscles and spinal processes.
- Horses with long withers can be deceptive — the saddle may clear the withers at the pommel but have contact in the channel, which will be equally painful for the horse.
- Always recheck there is still plenty of clearance once a saddle blanket is in place, the girth is done up and the rider is mounted.

SADDLE LENGTH

- The weight-bearing surface of a horse's back is the area that is supported by the ribs. The lumbar region, which begins after the eighteenth rib, has no support structure and should never bear the weight of a saddle or rider. Feel your horse's ribcage to locate the last rib, then follow it up to the spine; this is the location of the eighteenth vertebra and the end of the horse's weight-bearing area. The panels of your saddle should roll upwards and not extend past this point. If your horse has a short back, you will need to find a shorter saddle that rolls off the back before the eighteenth rib.
- *Top tip:* For heavier riders who may need a bigger saddle size, it's important to purchase a horse or pony with a large enough weight-bearing surface to accommodate the longer saddle length you'll need.

SEAT BALANCE

- The deepest part of the saddle seat should be in the centre of the saddle, and it should be level, allowing the rider's weight to be distributed evenly in a correct, balanced position (see page 256).

CHANNEL WIDTH

- When you turn over your saddle, you'll see a channel between the panels that runs the length of the saddle. This channel must be wide enough to allow the panels to sit on the horse's back muscles, so it can move freely, rather than on the spine and ligaments.
- A good rule of thumb is for the channel to be the width of at least 4 to 6 fingers, for the entire length of the saddle. Many old-fashioned or low-budget saddles are too narrow, especially at the back.

EVEN PANEL PRESSURE

- The panels of the saddle are designed to distribute your weight evenly along the horse's back. To achieve this, they should be wide and evenly packed, with no hard lumps or bumps caused by the packing balling up, and should be in full contact with your horse's back.
- You should be able to run the back of your hand along the horse's back, under the saddle, on both sides, and feel even pressure the whole way. Uneven pressure or areas with no pressure (known as bridging) will cause the rider's weight to be unevenly dispersed, creating painful pressure points for the horse.

SADDLE STABILITY

- The saddle should remain stable on the horse's back when you press down, in turn, on the pommel and then the cantle. There should be no rocking back and forth or shifting from side to side — if there is, the rider's weight on the saddle will create painful pressure points on the horse's back, as it will shift with every stride.

ONGOING FIT

- A horse's shape constantly changes through ageing, training, diet, injury or illness, so it's important to check the fit of the saddle at least twice a year.
- If your horse develops signs of tension when it's being saddled or ridden (see page 54), it's worth having its saddle checked before investigating other pain-related issues that may have developed.
- If you buy a new saddle with wool-flocked panels, the wool will compress and mould to your horse over time; this means you will need to continually monitor wither clearance and saddle fit.

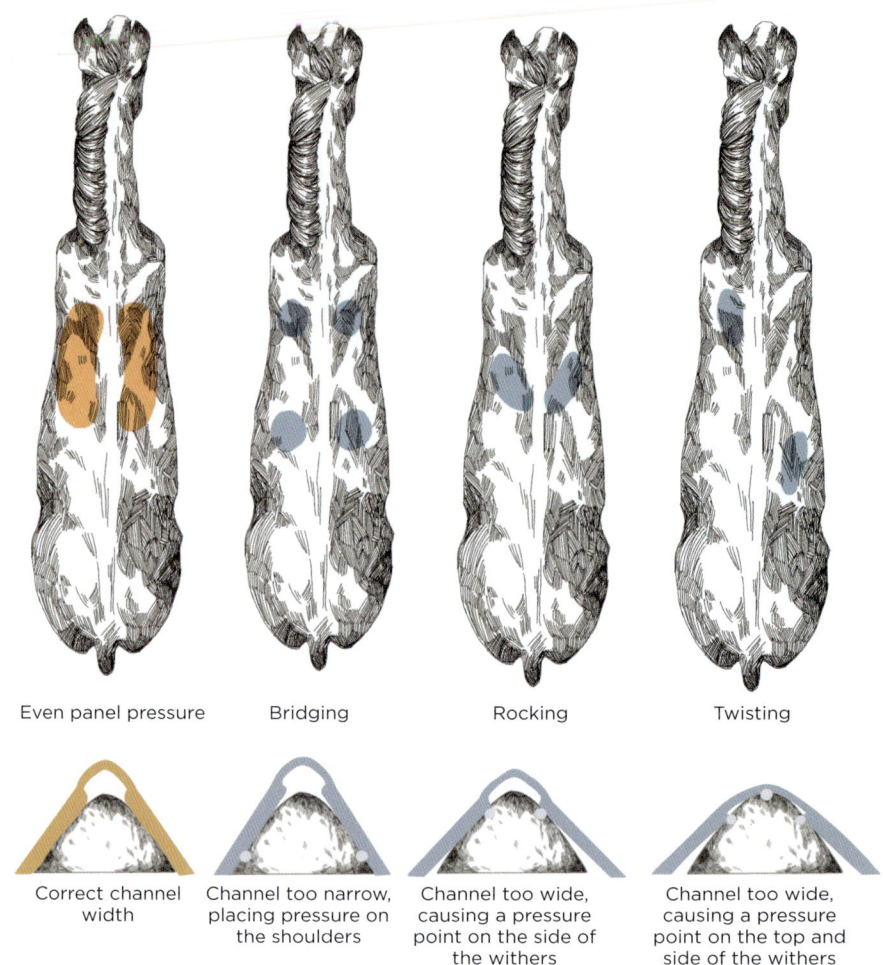

Top: Even and uneven panel pressures.

Bottom: Correct versus incorrect saddle channel widths.

Opposite page: Checking for even panel pressure; the light shining through indicates bridging (an area where the saddle isn't making contact with the horse's back).

DOES THE SADDLE FIT THE RIDER? As well as fitting your horse, it's also important that the saddle fits you. A saddle that suits your size and shape will allow you to sit in balance with the horse, ensuring that you can maintain an effective and balanced position, maximising the harmony between horse and rider.

Common signs that a saddle doesn't fit the rider are:
- a swinging or unstable lower leg, particularly at the trot and canter, or over jumps
- an unbalanced seat, causing the rider to either tip in front or behind the movement of the horse
- knee rolls that don't mirror the angle of the rider's leg
- the saddle flaps are too long, compromising the effectiveness of the rider's leg aids
- struggling to maintain the correct rider position (see page 256)
- feeling insecure in the saddle, or slipping backwards and forwards in the seat — the saddle is too big
- the rider's legs are pushed over the front of the knee flaps, or the cheeks of the rider's seat protrude over the cantle of the saddle — the saddle is too small.

Saddle accessories

GIRTHS: A properly fitting girth will keep the saddle securely in place and also ensure your horse's comfort when being ridden. Girths can be made out of a variety of materials, including leather (preferred for many disciplines such as showing, dressage and Show Hunter), neoprene, synthetic (popular for their easy care and affordability, but can crack and pinch the horse's skin if not well cared for) and fleece-lined (useful for horses with sensitive skin).

Common types of girth include:

- **TRADITIONAL GIRTHS:** Traditional-length girths are generally used on GP and jumping saddles and are designed to buckle up on short billet straps, underneath the saddle flap.
- **DRESSAGE GIRTHS:** Dressage girths are generally shorter, for use on dressage saddles, which have long billet straps. An ideal length would allow the width of at least 3 to 4 fingers between the top of the girth and the bottom of the saddle flap on both sides; any less and the horse's skin can become pinched.
- **STUD GUARDS OR JUMPING GIRTHS:** Stud guards have large oval panels in the middle of the girth to protect the horse from hitting its belly with its hooves, or studs, when jumping.

An anatomically shaped stud girth, designed to offer the horse freedom of movement while jumping.

HOW TO FIT A GIRTH

Before saddling your horse, make sure that it is well groomed so that there is no mud, dirt, dried sweat or wounds to aggravate it once the girth is done up. Poorly groomed horses can quickly develop girth galls (see below), which can lead to behavioural or pain-related issues, and also affect their performance.

Signs of a well-fitting girth:

- The girth should sit in the groove behind the horse's shoulder and when attached to the billet straps it should hang perpendicular to the ground. If the girth hangs on an angle, it's a red flag that the saddle doesn't fit and the seat balance is compromised.
- The girth should be done up on similar billet holes on each side of the horse.
- The girth should have at least two billet holes above and below the girth buckles so there is room to adjust it if your horse's weight changes.
- The girth should not cause open sores, chafing or rubbing (known as girth galls) — these will cause extreme discomfort to a saddled horse. If your horse gets a girth gall, you can use a fleece-lined girth or a sleeve over the girth to provide some protection and cushioning to relieve the pressure points; it is crucial that these are clean, as dirty fleece can rub the horse further.

Top tip: Girth galls are often caused by insufficient grooming, especially when the horse is ridden on sandy or abrasive surfaces or for long periods of time.

STIRRUP IRONS. There is a wide range of stirrup irons available, from the traditional irons to quick-release options (which are designed with the rider's safety in mind).

- **FILLIS IRONS:** The classic appearance of stainless-steel Fillis irons means they are an economical and common choice for casual riding and competition. During a fall, however, the rider's foot can become caught in them, increasing the risk of being dragged.
- **SAFETY STIRRUPS (ALSO KNOWN AS QUICK-RELEASE STIRRUPS):** Safety stirrups are designed to minimise the risk of a rider's foot getting caught in the stirrups in the event of a fall, and are a popular choice for both beginners and professionals.

> **HOW TO SELECT THE RIGHT SIZE STIRRUP IRONS AND LEATHERS**
>
> **STIRRUP IRONS:** When your foot is in the stirrups, you should have 1 to 1.5 centimetres clear on each side of your riding boots, at the ball of your foot. A too-snug fit can cause your boots to become stuck, while a too-loose fit can allow your boot to slide all the way through the iron; both can be very dangerous in the event of a fall. *Top tip:* Remember to check that your stirrup irons fit all the boots you ride in; yard and paddock boots are usually wider than the types of riding boots used in competition.
>
> **STIRRUP LEATHERS:** The correct length of leathers will allow you to comfortably ride with the buckle on a stirrup hole that has at least three holes above and below your comfortable length. This will allow you to lengthen your stirrups sufficiently for flatwork, or shorten them for jumping.

Top: Examples 1 and 5 are safety stirrups, which are designed to release the rider's foot in the event of a fall. Examples 2 and 4 are Fillis iron stirrups (example 2 also features a flexible joint to ease ankle discomfort). Example 3 is a plastic stirrup.

Bottom: Uneven stirrup length will cause the rider to sit unevenly in the saddle and can cause the horse pain.

SADDLE PADS: Saddle pads (also known as saddle cloths, saddle blankets or numnahs) are used to protect your saddle from sweat and grime, as well as enhancing your horse's comfort by providing cushioning underneath the saddle and absorbing shock from the rider's weight. For every discipline there are preferred styles and colours of saddle pads, which are important to adhere to for correct turnout at competitions.

Common types of English saddle pads include:

- **FULL PADS:** Full pads are the most common and are used when riding your horse during training sessions, out on trails and in most competitions. They are usually made of a quilted fabric, with rounded or 'swallow-tailed' corners, and have synthetic loops that you can put a girth through to stop the pad from slipping. White is always the correct colour for dressage, while white, grey, navy or black are generally preferred in showjumping. In the cross-country phase of eventing, riders often match their saddle pads to their riding shirt or body protector. In competitions, the space behind the rider's leg can be decorated with the rider or stud's logo, a sponsor's brand or the horse's name, although some national equestrian federations restrict the size and placement of these.

- **SHAPED PADS:** Shaped pads (also known as numnahs) mirror the shape of the saddle and can be made from a wide range of materials. For showing or Show Hunter competitions, a shaped pad made from either natural or synthetic fleece should be used, either in white, honey or the same colour as your saddle. Shaped pads often slip or bunch, so it's common for these to have loops that can be attached to the saddle flaps or billet straps.
- **HALF PADS:** Half pads are usually made from fleece, gel or foam and cover a small area of the horse's back, under the saddle tree. They are often used on top of a full or shaped pad to further absorb shock or to aid saddle fit, or under a dressage saddle in showing classes. They can change the fit of the saddle, however, so should be used only if necessary.
- **RAISER PADS:** Usually made from gel or foam, raiser pads are designed to improve the fit of a saddle, compensate for muscle wastage, and absorb shock. Front raisers lift the front of the saddle and back raisers lift the back of the saddle.

> **USING RAISER PADS TO COMPENSATE FOR MUSCLE WASTAGE**
>
> If a horse has muscle wastage from a previously ill-fitting saddle, having a saddle fitted to their current shape is counterproductive as they need the room to redevelop their natural topline (see pages 275–77). In these instances, we use a front raiser gel pad to create a 'fake muscle' for the saddle to rest on, allowing the saddle to be fitted to where the horse's topline *should* be; as the horse develops the correct muscle and topline, the front raiser should no longer be needed.

BRIDLES AND BITS

Bridles are used to control and direct the horse, acting as an important method of communication while riding. They come in different styles and sizes (including pony, cob, horse and warmblood) and need to be properly fitted to ensure your horse's comfort while allowing clear communication of your hand aids.

These are the main types of English bridle.

SNAFFLE BRIDLE: Snaffle bridles are almost always made from leather and are the preferred choice in most English disciplines, as well as for pleasure-riding, due to their versatility. Contrary to the name, snaffle bridles can be used with any bit. The functionality of the snaffle bridle can be further influenced by a variety of nosebands, including the standard cavesson noseband (a traditional look for showing or Show Hunter) or drop, flash and grackle nosebands (which have straps that sit below the horse's bit to prevent its mouth from opening).

DOUBLE OR WEYMOUTH BRIDLE: Double bridles use two bits at once — a bradoon (a small snaffle) and a Weymouth curb (a shanked bit, with a curb chain) — as well as two sets of reins. Double bridles are usually seen only in the highest levels of dressage

Top, from left: A sheepskin pad, for a jumping or general purpose saddle; two different types of front raiser gel pads; a full pad, for a jumping or general purpose saddle; a back raiser; and a sheepskin half pad.

Bottom: A jumping saddle, with a full pad and front raiser gel pad.

and showing competitions, and should only be used by experienced riders since the curb can be extremely harsh if used incorrectly.

BITLESS BRIDLE: Bitless bridles describe any headgear that allows the horse to be controlled without the use of a bit. They can include the more common hackamore or bosal, through to side-pull or cross-under designs, or a rope halter. Although considered kinder on the horse than a bit, in the wrong hands they can be harsh if the noseband is positioned too low on the nasal bones or the rider applies excessive pressure with their hands. *Note:* Some disciplines don't allow the use of bitless bridles in competitions.

THE USE OF NOSEBANDS

For us, a noseband is for looks more than anything else. It adds a level of professionalism to the horse's overall appearance at competitions, and for that reason our horses generally wear a cavesson noseband — although they are done up quite loosely. We have never found a horse that benefits from having its jaws cranked shut to keep its mouth from opening.

If a horse presents as 'gaggy' in the mouth, we see it as a symptom of an underlying issue. Rather than tying the horse's mouth shut to prevent this behaviour, we instead look at dental or skeletal issues that may be causing the horse to behave this way. These behaviours can also result from a lack of schooling, especially if the horse doesn't know how to balance properly, or wasn't trained how to correctly soften to the pressure of a bit when it was first mouthed. Using tight straps to mask these problems, rather than addressing them, will almost always lead to long-term behavioural issues.

HOW TO FIT A SNAFFLE BRIDLE

- **BIT:** The bit should fit on the bars of the horse's mouth, the gap between the incisors and the first molars; its position can be adjusted by tightening or loosening the cheekpieces. Traditionally, people look for two wrinkles at the corner of the horse's lips to determine a good bit fit, but since every horse's mouth is different, this should be used as a guideline only.

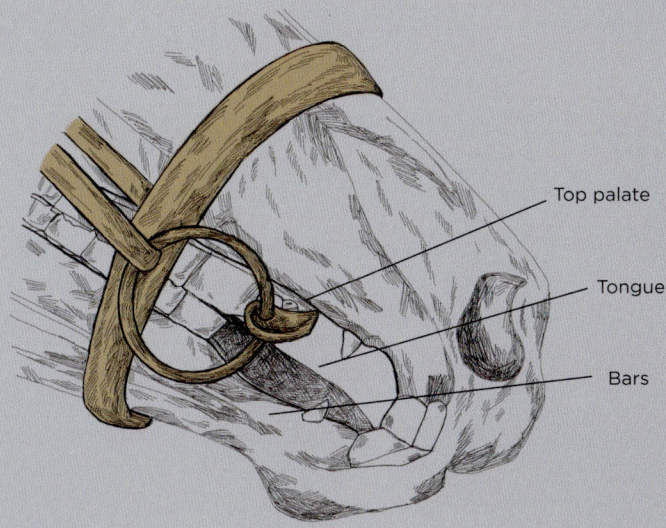

- **NOSEBAND:** The noseband should sit 1 or 2 fingers' width below the horse's cheekbones. It is important not to do it up too tightly: the general rule of thumb is that you should leave the width of at least 2 fingers under the noseband, and one finger under any flash, drop or grackle straps that circle the horse's mouth. If any of these straps are tighter than this, they can cause the teeth to press against the inside of the mouth, which can result in difficulty breathing, an elevated heart rate and long-term skeletal damage or affect the horse's ability to salivate; all of which can result in behavioural and pain-related issues developing.
- **THROATLATCH:** Once fastened, you should be able to fit 4 fingers between the throatlatch and the horse's jaw.
- **BROWBAND:** Allow the width of 1 to 2 fingers to fit beneath the browband; any tighter and it will place pressure on the ears and forehead, as well as sensitive nerves and blood vessels, while any looser can cause the bridle to slip off.

A snaffle bridle with a cavesson noseband and a double-jointed full cheek snaffle bit.

Bridle accessories

Bits

A bit is usually made from metal, rubber, plastic or leather and goes in the horse's mouth. Applying pressure to the bars and tongue (and sometimes poll or jaw) allows the rider to control the horse's speed and direction.

Things to consider when choosing a bit.

THICKNESS OF THE MOUTHPIECE: Every horse has different-sized gaps between their incisors and molars, so when choosing the thickness of a bit, the size of the horse's bars should always be considered. The thickness of the bit determines how well the horse will respond to the contact of the reins. Generally, the thinner the bit, the more sensitive the horse will be to the hand aids. Because of this, thicker bits were traditionally thought to be kinder, but if they are over 16 millimetres in diameter (measured at the thickest point, by the bit ring) they can cause their own issues — including limiting the horse's ability to breathe, swallow or close its mouth properly, and they can also cause damage to the tongue and upper palate.

TYPES OF MOUTHPIECE: The mouthpiece of a bit is generally made from a solid, smooth bar, often broken up by one or multiple links. Metal mouthpieces are the most common and are usually made from stainless steel, to prevent rusting, although copper or sweet iron are also used specifically to cause rusting (as this gives off a sweet taste and encourages horses to salivate). Plastic, rubber or leather bits are also popular for sensitive horses that don't like an inflexible mouthpiece or the cold sensation of metal in their mouth.

- **NO JOINT (ALSO KNOWN AS A MULLEN MOUTH)**: A snaffle bit featuring a straight or curved bar (to accommodate the horse's tongue). These are considered milder than a single-joint bit, since they have no nutcracker action, although not as kind as a double-jointed bit.
- **SINGLE JOINT**: These bits have only one joint in the mouthpiece, which can cause extreme discomfort to the horse due to its 'nutcracker' action, and should be avoided as much as possible. When pressure is applied to the reins, the bit creates a sharp 'V' shape which puts excessive pressure on the horse's bars, tongue and lips, and the joint can also dig into the roof of the horse's mouth.
- **DOUBLE-JOINTED**: These bits feature two joints, with a link, oval lozenge, level plate or a roller in the middle, which allows each side of the bit to work independently. They are designed with the horse's comfort in mind as the double joint reduces the 'nutcracker' effect; a tilted plate, like a Dr Bristol, has a more severe action.
- **MORE COMPLEX BITS**: Mouthpieces can have additional features which generally make them a more severe option. These bits include the Waterford (made up of multiple links), Cherry Roller (multiple links that roll), as well as mouthpieces made from twisted or corkscrewed metal. These bits should only be used by experienced riders, who have achieved an independent seat and steady hands (see pages 256–265).

TYPES OF BIT RING: Some of the most common types of bit rings, and their intended purposes, are covered below.

- **EGGBUTT**: Considered to be one of the gentlest types, the rings are fixed to the mouthpiece to offer the horse some consistency in rein contact and to prevent the horse's lips from being pinched.
- **LOOSE RING**: The rings are not fixed to the bit, instead rotating through a hole in the mouthpiece. This allows the mouthpiece to remain independent from the rein contact and follow the angle of the horse's tongue. It discourages the horse from leaning on the bit and promotes a relaxed jaw and mobile tongue. A correct fit is essential, however, to avoid the lips becoming pinched from the rings (rubber bit guards are recommended to avoid this issue).
- **FULL CHEEK**: Similar to an eggbutt, with the addition of long bars to reinforce the turning aids. The bars also prevent the bit from being pulled through the horse's mouth, which can be an issue with both eggbutt and loose ring bits.
- **D-RING**: Similar to an eggbutt, but as the name suggests, the rings are shaped like a 'D' to aid with turning and to prevent the bit sliding through the horse's mouth. When paired with a double-jointed mouthpiece, the D-ring can be ideal for children or novice riders.

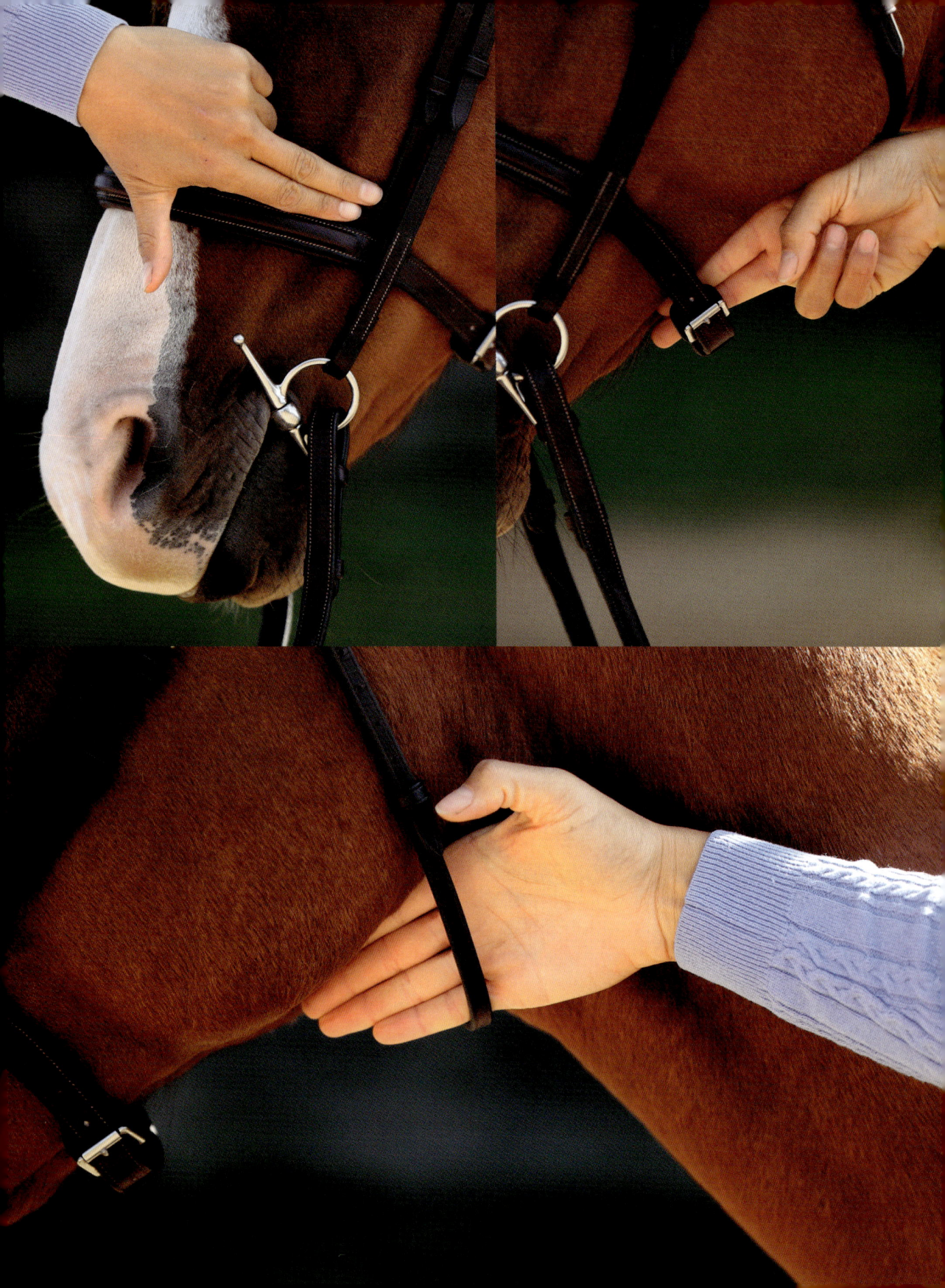

- **HANGING CHEEK (ALSO KNOWN AS TWO-RINGS OR BAUCHERS):** Similar to an eggbutt but with the cheek pieces attached to a second, smaller, fixed ring above the bit ring. When contact is applied to the reins, the mouthpiece tilts forward, which can increase pressure across the horse's tongue and bars and may make some horses overbend through their neck. Hanging cheek bits offer more braking control than an eggbutt.
- **BEVEL:** These are often used by riders who want a mild gag-like action while still enjoying some of the benefits of a snaffle bit ring. The subtle poll pressure provided by the bevel helps with strong horses and also encourages horses to soften onto a contact.
- **RUNNING GAG:** Gags are often used by experienced riders for horses that are strong, difficult to control or bear down on the reins, since it discourages them from leaning on the bit. They can be used with one or two reins (one rein works like a snaffle, while the second rein attaches to a cheek strap which runs through the bit rings and provides leverage on the poll). There are several types of running gags, named according to their snaffle bit ring; Cheltenham Gag (eggbutt), Balding Gag (loose ring) and Nelson Gag (full cheek).
- **FAUX GAGS:** There are many different styles of bits that provide a similar effect to a gag, but without being a true gag. They generally include a ring above the mouthpiece, which causes poll pressure, along with one or more rings below, which create leverage (encouraging the horse's head to lower). Some gags have two rings below the main bit ring, while others have three; the lower down the rings you attach the reins, the more severe the bit. Gags can be ridden with two reins (one rein on the snaffle bit ring, with the second rein attached to the lower rings to provide leverage on the poll), or with roundings (a small semi-circle of leather that joins two different rings together, but only needs one rein) for a softer effect.
- **CURB (ALSO KNOWN AS A WEYMOUTH):** A curb bit with a shank that creates leverage against the horse's poll; the longer the shank, the more severe the bit. As well as providing pressure on the horse's mouth and poll, a curb chain also applies pressure under the chin (using a curb guard, made from either rubber or leather, will reduce its severity). Because of its severity, a curb bit should only be used alongside a snaffle as part of a double bridle, and only by experienced riders with soft hands.
- **PELHAM:** Combining the action of the bradoon (eggbutt or loose ring snaffle) and Weymouth, this bit mimics the effects of a double bridle. Pelhams can be ridden with two reins, or with split reins or roundings for a simpler and softer effect. There are several types of mouthpiece for Pelhams, with the kindest being those with two joints, or a plastic (known as a Happy Mouth) or rubber mouthpiece with no joints. *Note:* The curb chain of the Pelham should always be encased in a curb guard, made from either rubber or leather, to reduce its severity.

Top: The correct fit for a cavesson noseband.

Bottom: The correct fit for a throatlatch.

Types of bits.
1. Neue Schule, double-jointed (with Turtle lozenge) loose ring snaffle.
2. Neue Schule, double-jointed, full cheek snaffle.
3. Neue Schule, double-jointed, loose ring snaffle (with extra small bit ring for ponies).
4. Stubben Full Cheek Snaffle, double-jointed snaffle (with sweet copper link to promote chewing and salivation).
5. Happy Mouth Full Cheek Snaffle.
6. Myler Comfort, double-jointed, D-ring snaffle.
7. Bomber Happy Tongue eggbutt snaffle.
8. Bomber Happy Tongue loose ring snaffle.
9. Loose ring flexi Happy Mouth, cheek ring guards.
10. Trust flexi-soft loose ring snaffle, with rubber bit guards.
11. Happy Mouth running gag, with rubber bit guards.
12. Stubben EZ Control Pelham, double-jointed, with chain and leather roundings.
13. Dutch Gag, 4-rings, double-jointed (with French link).
14. Neue Schule Waterford.
15. Running Lever Balding Gag Waterford full cheek.

ISSUES CAUSED BY INCORRECT BITS

Regardless of the mouthpiece, bit ring or material you choose for your horse's bit, it is always important to ensure that your horse is comfortable and the bit fits correctly.

The wrong type or size of bit can cause considerable damage to your horse's mouth, especially when ridden by a rider with harsh hands.

PHYSICAL ISSUES

- Damage to the upper palate
- Thickened or loose skin across the bars
- Bruising or lacerations in the soft tissue
- Bit-induced bone spurs
- Erosion of the first lower-cheek teeth
- Skeletal damage

If the bit is causing your horse discomfort or pain, it may show the following behavioural issues:

BEHAVIOURAL ISSUES

- Tension in the neck and jaw
- Tongue over the bit
- Fussing with the bit
- Struggling to take a contact
- Grinding or chewing the bit
- Opening the mouth
- Difficulty breathing or swallowing
- Head tossing
- Running through the bridle
- Ridden vices like rearing, bucking, napping or bolting

Top tip: If you suspect that behavioural issues in your horse are caused by bit damage, ride the horse in a bitless bridle and see whether the behaviour improves; if it does, continue to use a bitless bridle or change to a different bit (preferably non-metal). It is also important to have your horse seen by an equine dentist or veterinarian to see if dental issues are a contributing factor (see page 111).

> ## HOW TO FIT A BIT
>
> Your horse's bit should fit across the bars of its jaw and rest comfortably at the corners of its mouth. A bit that is too narrow can pinch and rub the skin on the horse's lips, while a bit that is too long can slide from side to side, damaging the sensitive bars in the horse's mouth.
>
> When shopping for a new bit it's important to purchase the correct size. If your horse's current bit fits, simply measure the mouthpiece of the bit from just inside the bit rings. If it's a new horse and you are unsure of the bit size, use a piece of thin rope and mark where it meets the outside corners of the horse's lips, then hold the string against a ruler to determine the length.
>
> Sizes go up in increments of a quarter of an inch or 1 centimetre at a time, with ponies generally being ridden in 3½-inch to 5-inch bits and horses being ridden in 5-inch to 6-inch bits.
>
> *Top tip:* For loose ring snaffles, you will need to go up a bit size to ensure that your horse's lips are not pinched when the ring rotates. This will also allow enough room for bit guards to sit comfortably on each side of the bit, if required.

> If you feel the need to 'bit your horse up' and select a stronger bit so that you have more control, it's important to consider why your horse is being unresponsive to subtle hand aids. It may be that the horse hasn't been mouthed correctly and doesn't understand how to respond to pressure from the bit, or that's rushing from other pain-related issues. Often, fixing the underlying cause will mean that your horse will become more comfortable and responsive to the contact.

Reins

Reins attach to the bit and allow the rider to control the horse's direction and speed. What type of reins to ride in will be determined by both your discipline and personal comfort.

Common types of reins available are:

- **PLAIN REINS**: Made from plain, smooth leather, they offer a traditional look and are most often used in showing or dressage competitions. They can, however, become slippery in wet conditions.
- **LACED REINS**: Made from plain leather plaited together, laced reins provide good grip and are most often used in Show Hunter and Saddle Hunter competitions.
- **WEB REINS**: Made from cotton webbing, these reins feature leather stops at regular intervals for added grip, and a leather end that attaches to the bit. They are a popular choice for riding at home and for competing in most disciplines.
- **RUBBER REINS**: These reins offer a firm grip in all weather conditions.

From left: Laced reins for showing; rubber grip reins; clip-on leather reins; leather reins; clip-on rubber grip reins; web reins.

- **RUBBER-LINED REINS:** Made with leather to look like traditional reins, these have a thin rubber lining on the inside of the leather for added grip. They are most often seen in dressage competitions.

Other accessories

BREASTPLATE/BREAST COLLAR: A breastplate (with a girth attachment) or breast collar (with no girth attachment) attaches to the D-rings of the saddle and is used to keep the saddle from slipping back while riding. Often horses will need a breastplate or breast collar due to their conformation (particularly horses with large shoulders or a narrow ribcage) or when jumping large fences, to keep the saddle in place.

MARTINGALES: A martingale attaches from the horse's breastplate to the reins, and is used to control the horse if it has a high or erratic head carriage. These behaviours, however, are usually caused by underlying issues like teeth problems, pain, a poorly fitting saddle or a lack of schooling; in these instances, it's much more ethical to correct the issue than to use a martingale to mask the problem. If a martingale is used, it must be fitted correctly: too loose, and the horse risks getting a leg entangled in it; too tight, and the horse will have its neck and head overly restricted, affecting its ability to balance or correctly bascule (form the correct shape with its body as it jumps) over a jump.

Common types of martingale are:

- **RUNNING MARTINGALE:** Two forked straps attach to the horse's breastplate and up to the reins through metal rings. It works in conjunction with the bit to encourage the horse to lower its head by applying pressure to the mouth if the horse raises its head too high. When using a running martingale it is important to use reins with rein stoppers, to prevent the rings from sliding forward and getting caught on the bit. It is not legal to use in dressage and it should never be used in showing.
- **STANDING MARTINGALE:** This is a strap that attaches to a cavesson noseband and puts pressure on the horse's nose if it raises its head. Due to their severity on the horse's nasal bones, some national equestrian federations restrict their use.
- **BIB MARTINGALE:** Similar to the running martingale, but featuring a solid leather 'V' between the forked straps.

JUMPING BOOTS: Designed to protect the horse's legs, primarily while jumping or doing strenuous workouts. These come in a variety of styles for both the front and hind legs. There are, however, strict welfare regulations for jumping boots, so check the latest guidelines from your national equestrian federation.

Common types of jumping boot are:

- **OPEN-FRONT BOOTS (ALSO KNOWN AS TENDON BOOTS):** Usually made from hard-wearing plastic, neoprene or leather, with Velcro or stud fastenings, and shaped to wrap around the side and back of the cannon bone, while being open at the front. They protect the tendons, ligaments and fetlocks, as well as absorb impact; some also come with gel capsules or sheepskin lining for added comfort. They are primarily

Top: A horse wearing a hackamore bridle and running martingale.

Bottom left: Open-front jumping boots, classically used for showjumping.

Bottom right: Hind jumping boots.

used for jumping, although are also a popular choice for general riding.
- **BRUSHING BOOTS:** A popular choice for schooling and some competitions, these are primarily used on the hind legs and offer protection to the cannon bone, tendons, ligaments and fetlocks. They also protect a horse with poor conformation from rubbing if its legs brush together.
- **OVER-REACH BOOTS (ALSO KNOWN AS BELL BOOTS):** Made from rubber or neoprene, these encircle the horse's hooves, protecting the lower pastern and coronet band from the hind hooves forging or striking the horse's front heels. They are also commonly used in the paddock, or when ridden, for horses that over-reach and are prone to pulling shoes off.
- **SPORT BOOTS:** Usually made from neoprene, these are used on both the front and the hind legs, encircling the entire cannon bone and fetlock and reaching to just below the knee or hock. Often used in Cross Country, when galloping, for dressage training, in Western disciplines or for trail riding.
- **HIND FETLOCK BOOTS:** Usually made from hard-wearing plastic, neoprene or leather, with Velcro or stud fastenings, and designed to protect the hind fetlocks from brushing or damage from studs. Most often paired with open-front boots and used in showjumping competitions.
- **EVENTING BOOTS:** Usually made from advanced fabrics or leather to keep the legs cool, and designed to protect the tendons, ligaments, cannon bone and fetlock. They are generally used during the strenuous Cross Country phase, or by racehorses, to give the horse high impact protection and maximum freedom of movement.

TACKING UP YOUR HORSE

Before tacking up, ensure that your horse is tied safely (see page 148). Next, thoroughly groom your horse, taking special care of the saddle and bridle areas to ensure that dirt won't rub or cause sores, then pick out and oil your horse's hooves.

Saddling your horse

1. **PUT ON THE SADDLE PAD:** Place the saddle pad on to your horse's back, slightly further forward on the withers than needed.
2. **PUT ON THE SADDLE:** Check that the stirrups have been run up the leathers, to avoid them hitting your horse's side, then place the saddle gently over the saddle pad. Next, gently bump the pommel of the saddle back until it naturally comes to a stop. This will make sure that the horse's coat hairs are lying in the right direction and the saddle is in its natural resting place. Lastly, lift the front of the saddle pad well up into the gullet to relieve pressure on the horse's withers, and check that the back of the panels aren't sitting on the seam of the saddle pad (as this will create painful pressure points).
3. **BUCKLE THE GIRTH:** Buckle the girth onto the billet straps of the saddle, on the

The correct way to carry a saddle and bridle.

right side of the horse first, before moving around to the left side. Carefully reach under the horse's stomach and bring the girth towards you. Slowly tighten the girth — once it is tight, you should only just be able to slide your fingers between the girth and the horse's side. *Top tip:* The buckles on both sides should be on similar holes, to ensure that the pressure from the girth and saddle is evenly spread.

4. **RECHECK THE GIRTH:** Some horses will hold their breath while the girth is being done up, so double-check that the girth is still firm before you mount, then again once mounted, and tighten it if necessary. Be sure not to over-tighten the girth, however, as this can restrict your horse's movement and cause discomfort.

Bridling your horse

1. **UNDO THE HALTER:** Untie your horse, then undo the nose strap of its halter, leaving the halter still secured around the horse's neck.
2. **HOLD THE BRIDLE IN PLACE:** There are two main ways to hold the bridle when you are ready to place the bit in your horse's mouth. One option is to hold the headpiece of the bridle in your right hand and place your arm gently between the horse's ears. If your horse is too tall for you to do this, or is head-shy, you can instead hold the cheekpieces in your right hand, just below the horse's eyes.
3. **PUT THE BIT IN:** Place the bit in your left palm and guide it between your horse's lips, inserting your thumb into the corner of the lips to encourage it to open its mouth, before gently lifting the bit into place. *Never* force the bit into your horse's mouth, or bang its teeth with the bit, while bridling or unbridling your horse. Once the bit is in place, lift the bridle over the furthest ear, then the one closest to you. *Note:* When removing the bridle, don't let the bit fall from the horse's mouth — instead, gently lower the bridle in your right hand and wait for your horse to open its mouth.
4. **BUCKLE UP THE BRIDLE:** Do up the straps on the noseband and throatlatch, and adjust the cheek pieces if needed, ensuring a correct fit (see How to fit a snaffle bridle, page 221).
5. **PULL THE FORELOCK OUT:** Ensure that the horse's mane is sitting smoothly in place under the headpiece, then lift the forelock so that the hairs are hanging over the browband.
6. **PUT THE REINS OVER THE NECK:** Once you are ready to mount, place the reins quietly over your horse's neck.

The correct order for saddling and bridling. First put the saddle blanket in place, then the saddle, and then the bridle.

SADDLE AND BRIDLE MAINTENANCE

Proper care and maintenance of your leather saddlery will greatly enhance its appearance, suppleness and lifespan. It is important to keep your saddle and bridle free of excess grime and sweat, and conditioned regularly, to ensure that the leather remains healthy.

Protecting your saddlery

STORE ON RACKS: In between rides it is important to store your saddlery correctly to preserve its shape and prevent damage. Saddles need to be supported from pommel to cantle (on racks that are neither too narrow nor too wide), while bridles should be hung up on a rounded hanger (rather than a nail or a hook).

KEEP YOUR SADDLE COVERED: To minimise wear and damage, and keep out excess dust and dirt, it is important to keep your saddle covered. A padded saddle cover is ideal to use between rides and can be left on any time your saddle is stored. However, if you ride a lot of miles in the saddle you can buy specially-designed saddle covers, usually made from fleece or waterproof material, to ride in at home (these have a slit for the stirrups to fit through). They need to be removed to clean your saddle, or when you're riding in lessons or at competitions.

KEEP YOUR SADDLERY CLEAN AND DRY: To maintain healthy leather it is important to store your saddlery in a clean, dry place and at a comfortable temperature. Too much heat can dry out leather and cause it to crack, while too much moisture can cause mould and mildew. If you aren't planning to use your saddlery for an extended period, store it in a cloth bag at room temperature (preferably in your house, rather than in a shed or garage), along with some silica gel sachets to absorb moisture.

DRY AND CONDITION WET GEAR: If your saddle gets wet, don't stress. Straight after your ride, remove your stirrups and any accessories, towel-dry the leather, then condition your saddlery (the oil will prevent the water bonding to the protein of the leather and cause cracking), before allowing it to air-dry. It is important to do this immediately after the saddle gets wet, as leaving it wet for days can cause long-term damage. If you know in advance that you're going to be riding in the rain, it is recommended that you condition your saddle beforehand.

INSPECT YOUR GEAR: Every time you tack up your horse, look over your saddlery and take note of any frayed stitching or elastic, worn leather or enlarged holes. Damaged or cracked saddlery not only risks injury or discomfort to your horse, but can also be dangerous for the rider if something were to break. Points of wear to watch out for on a saddle are the tree, billet points, D-rings, stirrup leathers and girth; on the bridle check the stitching, studs and buckles (especially in the areas where the leather is folded or the buckles rub), as well as the joints of the bit.

REPAIR YOUR GEAR: If your saddlery shows signs of wear, have it repaired or replaced before it breaks. Most saddleries offer repair services at very affordable rates, which is usually much cheaper than buying new gear.

A well-organised tack room, with suitable racks for the saddles.

Cleaning your saddlery

Saddlery has to withstand some very challenging conditions. Dust, mud and sand can build up and become abrasive, causing stitching and leather to wear, while the acidity of sweat can leave marks on leather or even corrode it. To ensure the longevity of your saddlery it's important to give it a quick wipe over after every ride (removing any dust, mud, sand or sweat) and regularly clean and condition it.

HOW TO CLEAN LEATHER SADDLERY

1. **DISMANTLE YOUR SADDLE AND BRIDLE:** Begin by removing the stirrups and any other accessories attached to your saddle, and undo all the straps on your bridle.
2. **CLEAN WITH SADDLE SOAP:** Dampen a small sponge or cloth with warm water (wringing out any excess water) and rub into the saddle soap until you've formed a lather. Using this damp cloth, wipe it in small circular motions over every piece of leather to remove any sweat, dust or grime. Once you're done, use a clean damp cloth to rinse off the soap (like you would rinse soap from your own hands, or shampoo from your hair), since it causes leather to become brittle if left on.
3. **MOISTURISE WITH A LEATHER CONDITIONER:** After rinsing off the saddle soap, allow the leather to air-dry (or use a towel to dry it). Next use a leather conditioner to replenish the moisture that has been stripped out of your saddlery from sweat and soap. A beeswax product or speciality leather cream is ideal for this — oil should only be used sparingly, as it will darken the leather, can stain clothing, and if overused can cause leather to soften and change shape. Use a dry cloth or sponge to apply the conditioner in light layers, on both sides of the leather, until the leather stops absorbing the conditioner. Take care not to over-condition your saddlery, as excess product will leave the leather greasy and can lead to a build-up of dirt and grime.
4. **REMOVE JOCKEYS:** If you find lumps forming on your leather saddlery or riding boots, you likely have a build-up of dirt and grime, known as jockeys. These should be removed regularly to prevent damage to the leather. They can, however, be difficult to remove with a cloth or sponge during the cleaning process, so special attention needs to be given to them. A soft toothbrush, or a few strands of your horse's mane or tail hair rolled into a compact ball and dampened with water, will be coarse enough to exfoliate the jockeys but gentle enough to avoid scratching the leather.
5. **CLEAN METAL AND RUBBER:** Bits, stirrup irons (including the rubber stirrup insets) and spurs (with the leather straps removed) can be soaked in warm water, then scrubbed clean. Once clean, you can use baking soda or a speciality product to polish metal or remove stains from rubber.

Reassemble your saddlery and store it as recommended (see page 236).

To correctly clean your leather saddlery, dismantle your saddle and bridle in a clean place; a towel or newspaper on the ground is sufficient.

HOW TO ASSEMBLE A BRIDLE

1. **START WITH THE HEADPIECE:** Hold the headpiece so that the side with the throatlatch is furthest away from you.
2. **ATTACH THE BROWBAND:** Thread the browband on upside down, placing the upper throatlatch and cheek straps on the right side of the crownpiece through the loop on one side of the browband. Next, slide the browband over the crown (the browband will now be the correct way up), then thread the upper throatlatch and check straps through the second loop on the browband.
3. **ATTACH THE CHEEKPIECES:** Attach the cheekpieces so that the buckles face outwards, away from the horse. If you've used the bridle before, there will be wear marks to show you which hole to buckle it onto to ensure the correct fit for your horse.
4. **ATTACH THE NOSEBAND:** If the noseband is separate from the headpiece, attach it by threading the strap through the loops of the browband so that it lies flat underneath the headpiece, then buckle it in place.
5. **ATTACH THE BIT:** Before attaching the bit, make sure it is facing the right direction and is the right way up — most bits are contoured to the horse's mouth and if attached the wrong way can cause the horse severe discomfort. Ensuring that the curve of the bit faces forward and up (to allow it to sit comfortably on the horse's tongue), place the ends of the cheekpieces through the bit rings and buckle them in place. If your cheekpieces are secured with studs they should be done up to face inwards, and those with buckles should face outwards.
6. **ATTACH THE REINS:** Finish by attaching the reins to the bit rings, underneath the cheekpieces. Like the cheekpieces, reins that are secured with studs should have the buckles facing inwards, while reins secured by buckles should face outwards.

RIDER CLOTHING

Helmets

Helmets are one of the most essential pieces of riding equipment. They are designed to reduce the impact to the rider's head in the event of a fall or if they are knocked by a horse, and must, by law, meet specific and stringent safety standards.

When shopping for a helmet, keep the following in mind.

SAFETY STANDARDS: Legally, all helmets must be certified. Check the box, or inside the helmet, for a label to ensure that it is not only safe to ride in but also legal for competition.

DON'T BUY SECOND-HAND: The effectiveness of a helmet is compromised once it has sustained a hard impact, so only buy helmets brand-new — there is no way of knowing how often the previous owner may have fallen off. Likewise, if you have a fall in a helmet and knock your head, it's essential to check or replace your helmet to ensure that the internal structure hasn't been dented or cracked. If it has been compromised, you will need to replace it so your head is protected the next time you fall.

GET THE FIT CHECKED: Always have someone knowledgeable help you check that a helmet fits you correctly. Start by having your hair in the same style you would when you ride (normally a low ponytail or bun if you have long hair, or tucked up under your helmet). Place the helmet on the front of your forehead before sliding it down and back over the crown of your head. The helmet should sit level on your head, and about the width of 1 finger above your eyebrows. It should also be snug but not tight, so that when you shake your head back and forward (without the straps being done up), the helmet remains in place. The longer you wear a helmet, the more comfortable and less noticeable it should get; if it starts to give you a headache, it is too small. *Top tip:* A loose helmet is a safety risk, as it can fall over your eyes and obscure your view, increase the risk of concussion, and compromise the protection provided. Never buy a larger size in the hope that you'll grow into it.

CHECK THE SHAPE: Not every head is the same shape, with some being slightly rounder or more oval. Fortunately, different brands of helmets also vary in shape, so finding a comfortable fit is usually possible. If the helmet presses uncomfortably against your forehead, the helmet is likely too round for you, and if it presses against your temples it is likely too oval for you.

ADJUST THE CHIN STRAP: Lastly, adjust the chin strap to provide a custom fit, allowing 2 fingers to fit between your chin and the strap.

HELMETS ARE NON-NEGOTIABLE

When we were younger we didn't give much thought to the importance of wearing helmets, but after seeing family and friends suffer the long-term effects of bad concussions, we are careful to wear a helmet at all times when riding. It doesn't take much to have an accident — we've seen or experienced head injuries from horses slipping over on slick grass surfaces, being banged into the stable wall, having the horse trip while walking on a loose rein, the horse flipping over a jump, and so much more. Fortunately, in all of these instances a helmet was worn, but several of these accidents still cause ongoing side effects from concussions; for some, a month off from riding was sufficient, but other people we know are still suffering from health issues years later. Had they not been wearing a helmet the damage could have been much worse, or perhaps even fatal.

Just because your horse is quiet, it doesn't mean that an accident can't happen. By wearing a helmet you are protecting the most important asset you have — your brain.

Boots and safe footwear

Second only to a helmet, one of the most important safety aspects when riding is your footwear. A closed riding boot, with a smooth heel (between 1.5 and 2.5 centimetres high), will protect your toes if a horse stands on you, while also reducing the chance of your foot sliding through the stirrups and you being dragged in the event of a fall. Good riding boots will also support your legs and ankles, helping you maintain a correct leg position when you ride.

The types of riding boots are:

LONG OR TALL RIDING BOOTS: This traditional style of boots come to just below the rider's knee and are used for competition in most equestrian disciplines. They are usually made from leather; cheaper materials can include plastic, neoprene or rubber, but these aren't recommended as they can be bulky and stiff and don't promote a good lower leg position. Of all the styles of equestrian footwear, long riding boots offer the most ankle and leg support, encouraging a better leg position while also preventing the rider's calf from chafing and pinching on the stirrup leathers.

SHORT RIDING BOOTS (OR JODHPUR BOOTS): Favoured for children, or for use at home by riders of all ages, these shorter boots are usually made from leather and stop at the ankle. To offer more grip, and prevent the rider's calf from chafing and pinching on the stirrup leathers, this style of boot is usually paired with half-chaps (made from leather, suede or neoprene, with a zip on the side — suitable for use at home) or gaiters (made from smooth leather, with a zip at the back, to give the polished look of a long riding boot — acceptable in the competition arena). In the competition ring, short riding boots are only acceptable for younger riders (on ponies) and should always be used with jodhpur clips.

YARD OR PADDOCK BOOTS: These come in both long and short styles, and are designed for everyday wear around the stable or paddocks. Usually waterproof (or water-resistant) and made from durable material, they are more sturdy and comfortable for walking than traditional riding boots but can offer a compromised lower leg position when in the saddle. Some come with steel-capped toes, which offers greater protection when handling horses. Although designed for riding, they are not encouraged for competition use or in lessons.

Clothing at home

In addition to a helmet and boots, it's important to wear suitable clothing when riding your horse at home, or in lessons, to ensure your comfort and safety.

TOPS: Any comfortable, well-fitted shirt is suitable for riding at home, although materials made from a breathable fabric are ideal. A polo or long-sleeved riding shirt (which offers sun protection) is most suited for riding lessons.

BOTTOMS: Any comfortable pants are suitable for riding at home, although you should avoid a thick inner seam which may rub your saddle. Leggings or jeans can be a good option for a casual and cheap look, but riding tights or jodhpurs (normally navy, grey or black) are best and should always be used for riding lessons.

Top left: A correctly fitting helmet should sit level and about 1 centimetre above your eyebrows.

Top right and bottom left: A helmet that is too big will tilt forwards or backwards and won't provide adequate protection in the event of a fall.

Bottom right: A well-fitting velvet helmet, suitable for the show ring.

SAFETY VEST: An approved safety vest is compulsory for riding over cross-country jumps, but is also recommended for most beginners while they are learning to ride or jump. It can also be a good idea for professional riders when they are starting or training a young horse under saddle.

GLOVES: Riding gloves offer a professional look and can be useful for providing extra grip on the reins and warmth, and also to prevent your fingers rubbing together.

Clothing at competitions

The clothing you wear at equestrian events will be determined by the official rules of your chosen discipline, your age and the level at which you're competing. Presentation is very important, and what you wear makes a vital first impression on your fellow competitors, judges and show officials. Long before you compete, therefore, it's important to familiarise yourself with the specific dress codes for each discipline.

General dress code

Regardless of the type of competition, the following items are considered essential.

RIDING BOOTS: Long riding boots, usually black or brown and made from leather, are the most traditional choice for adults (or for children riding horses), regardless of the discipline. Short riding boots, either black or brown and made from leather, are acceptable for children on ponies; if leather gaiters aren't used, they should be paired with jodhpur clips so that your jodhpurs don't ride up your leg and show your socks. On show day, your boots should always be clean and polished.

BELT: A belt in brown or black (to match the colour of your saddle and bridle) is a classic choice for most disciplines; in showjumping, belts with bold colours and patterns are often worn.

JODHPURS OR BREECHES: For competitions you should always wear jodhpurs, breeches or competition tights. The colour and style will be dependent on your discipline.

RIDING JACKET: For most competitions, a short riding jacket should be worn. Navy or black are the most traditional and versatile option for adults, and navy for children. Depending on the discipline, however, specific colours and styles of jacket may be acceptable.

RIDING SHIRT: Underneath your jacket, a long- or short-sleeved riding shirt should be worn. The colour and style will depend on your discipline.

GLOVES: In most disciplines, black, brown or navy gloves (to match your riding boots or jacket) offer the most traditional look; in dressage it is also acceptable to wear white or ivory, and in showing tan or canary may also be worn.

HELMET: A black or navy helmet (to match your riding jacket) is the most traditional and versatile look for most disciplines. To be legal for competition it must meet the approved safety standards.

HAIR NETS AND BOWS: If you have long hair it should be in a tidy bun and contained within a hair net for a polished look, or tucked up under your helmet. For girls, a plait is also acceptable.

TIE, STOCKS AND STOCK PINS: If a tie or stock is used with your riding shirt it should complement your riding jacket. When using a stock, a stock pin should always be used; either silver or gold to match the buckles on your saddlery.

SAFETY VEST: An approved safety vest is compulsory for the Cross Country phase of eventing, and optional for most other disciplines.

Discipline-specific dress codes

In addition to the clothing and accessories mentioned in the previous section, the following recommendations are specific to each of the various disciplines.

SHOW PONIES OR HORSES OR RIDING HORSES
- **JODHPURS OR BREECHES:** cream, canary or beige
- **RIDING JACKET:** navy or black for adults, and navy for children.
- **HELMET:** navy or black velvet (to match the jacket) with fawn leather straps.
- **RIDING SHIRT:** a long-sleeved riding shirt is acceptable, in any pale colour; usually paired with a tie (no tie is required if the shirt is ruffled, and instead a stock pin should be used); a waistcoat is optional.
- **SADDLERY:** snaffle or double bridle with a decorative 'show' browband (with a matching lapel on the jacket); a shaped pad or half pad made from either natural or synthetic fleece (in white, honey or the same colour as your saddle); as well as a number holder and leather cane (both in the same colour as your saddle).
- **GROOMING:** quarter marks on the horse's hindquarters, stitched plaits, false tail (optional), make-up on the horse's points and white markings.

SADDLE HUNTER
- **JODHPURS OR BREECHES:** cream, canary, white or beige.
- **RIDING JACKET:** tweed (with a brown, hunter green or navy pinstripe and collar) are most common.
- **HELMET:** navy, brown or hunter green velvet (to match the jacket), with fawn leather straps.
- **RIDING SHIRT:** a long-sleeved riding shirt, with ruffles or a stock, is acceptable, in white, beige, cream or canary; paired with a stock or tie; a waistcoat is optional.
- **SADDLERY:** snaffle or double bridle with a plain leather or plaited browband; dressage saddle; shaped pad made from either natural or synthetic fleece (in honey or the same colour as your saddle); as well as a number holder and leather cane (both in the same colour as your saddle).
- **GROOMING:** quarter marks on the horse's hindquarters, stitched plaits, false tail (optional), make-up on the horse's points and white markings.

SHOWJUMPING
- **JODHPURS OR BREECHES:** white and beige are most often seen in showjumping (although any light colour is acceptable).

- **RIDING JACKET:** navy or black are most common for both adults or children, although other colours are allowed (including grey, forest green, brown or royal blue); red is traditionally only worn by people who have won a prestigious national title (such as the Olympic Cup) or represented their country in a Nations Cup or at international level.
- **RIDING SHIRT:** any colour of riding shirt, usually with a choker collar.
- **SADDLERY:** full-pad saddle blanket in white, grey, navy or black (although any colour is allowed); flat-seat saddle; stud guard (recommended regardless of whether your horse is wearing studs); breastplate; open-front jumping boots, fetlock boots (optional).
- **GROOMING:** for higher-level classes plaiting is optional.

SHOW HUNTER
- **JODHPURS OR BREECHES:** tan, fawn or beige.
- **RIDING JACKET:** tweed (with a brown, hunter green or navy pinstripe and collar) is most common.
- **HELMET:** navy, brown or hunter green velvet (to match the jacket) with fawn leather straps.
- **RIDING SHIRT:** a beige or cream stock is usually worn, paired with a stock pin.
- **SADDLERY:** snaffle bridle with a plain leather or plaited browband; flat-seat saddle; shaped pad made from either natural or synthetic fleece (in white, honey or the same colour as your saddle); stud guard (optional, but recommended if your horse is wearing studs); breastplate (optional); open-front jumping boots (optional).
- **GROOMING:** stitched plaits, quarter marks on the horse's hindquarters (optional), make-up on the horse's eyes and muzzle (optional).

DRESSAGE
- **JODHPURS OR BREECHES:** white, although any light colour is acceptable.
- **RIDING JACKET:** navy or black, in the standard short style, although for adults it is also acceptable to wear tailcoat jackets (in black or navy) at the highest levels of competition — these are not allowed on ponies.
- **RIDING SHIRT:** white button-down riding shirt with a collar is preferred, paired with a stock or tie.
- **SADDLERY:** plain leather snaffle or double bridle; dressage saddle; white full pad
- **GROOMING:** stitched plaits, quarter marks on the horse's hindquarters (optional), make-up on the horse's eyes and muzzle (optional).

Top: Suitable attire for the dressage phase of Eventing.

Bottom: Suitable attire for showjumping.
NED DAWSON

Top left: Suitable attire for a child competing in Show Hunter classes. For Saddle Hunter classes, you would change the jumping saddle to a dressage saddle.

Top right: Suitable attire for a child competing in show pony classes (minus the garland, of course).

Bottom left: Suitable attire for a child competing in dressage.

Bottom right: Suitable attire for a child competing in Pony Club competitions.

PONY CLUB

- **JODHPURS OR BREECHES:** white, beige or fawn (although any light colour is acceptable).
- **RIDING JACKET:** not required for some Pony Club competitions; if they are allowed, follow the same clothing recommendation for either Showing or Saddle Hunter, depending on your pony or horse's type.
- **RIDING SHIRT:** long-sleeved Pony Club uniform for rallies and some competitions; in the Cross Country phase of eventing a long-sleeved Pony Club uniform, riding shirt or polo shirt should be worn underneath a safety vest. (At Pony Club level, the riding shirt or safety vest is traditionally coloured to match your saddle blanket).
- **SADDLERY:** generally a GP or flat-seat saddle is used at Pony Club rallies, with a Pony Club saddle pad; snaffle bridle; open-front jumping boots (optional)
- **GROOMING:** tidy fake-pulled or pulled mane, or plaits (allowed at only some Pony Club competitions).

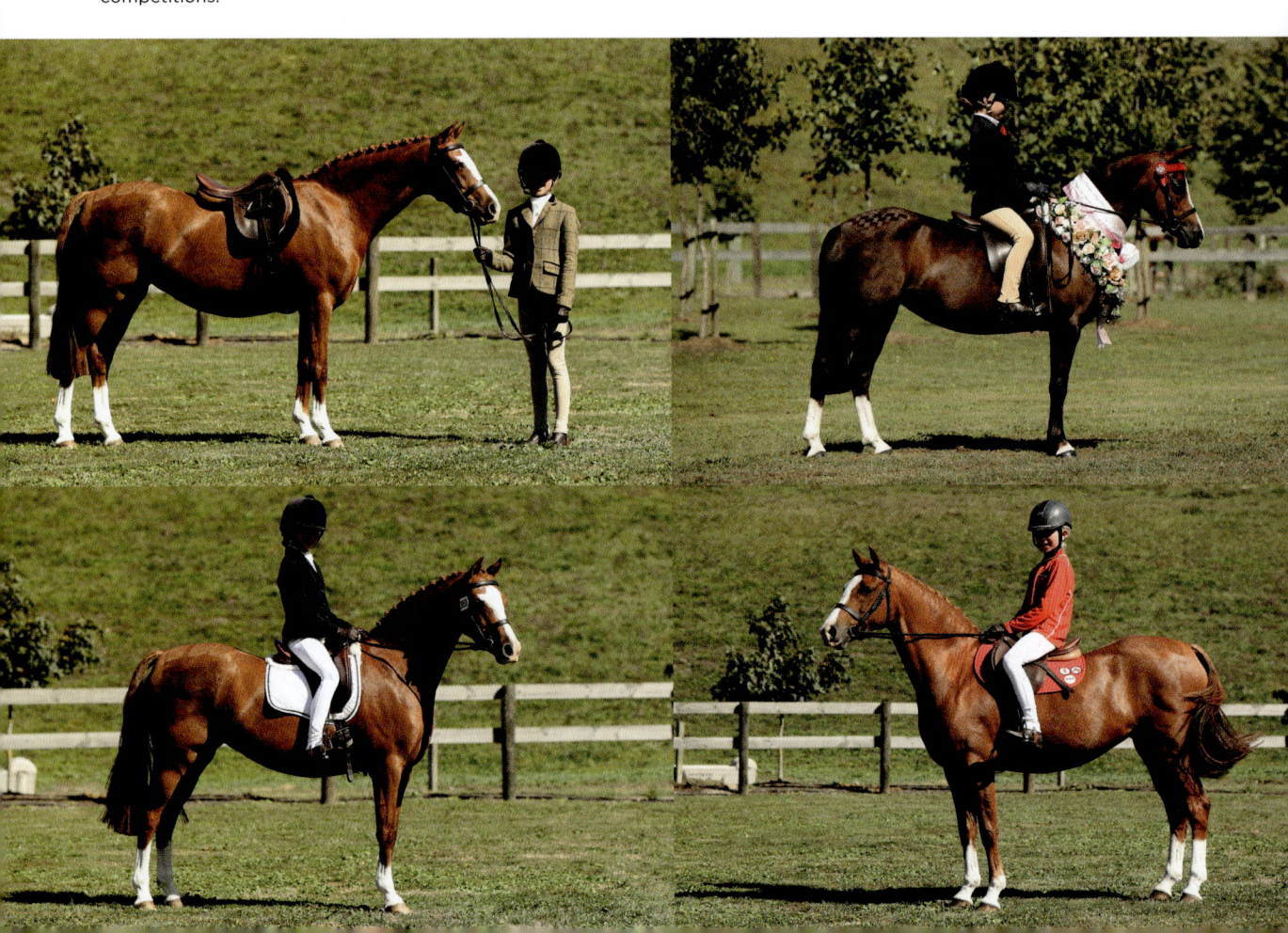

TIPS AND TRICKS TO TURN OUT YOUR HORSE FOR THE SHOW RING

Preparing your horse for showing, dressage or Show Hunter classes requires a high level of presentation and attention to detail — far beyond what is needed for any other discipline. From applying make-up to using false tails or quarter marks, these tips and tricks will help you stand out in the show ring.

- **QUARTER MARKS:** Quarter marks are patterns that are stencilled, combed or brushed into the horse's hindquarters to offer a polished level of presentation and flatter the horse's conformation. They are mostly used in showing and can range from simple to very detailed designs.
- **MAKE-UP:** Make-up is used to enhance your horse's natural features or adjust or whiten markings, and is usually used for showing classes. Different make-up colours are available to suit your horse's colour. Make-up is usually applied to the horse's eyes, ears and muzzle, and may even be used on the legs or body to darken or define points.
- **FALSE TAIL:** If your horse's tail is thin, short or rubbed out this can affect your horse's overall appearance. A false tail, which is made from real horse hair and plaited into the dock, can be used to increase volume or disguise damage.
- **FALSE MANE:** If your horse's mane is thinner at one end, or rubbed out, this will affect your ability to create perfect plaits for showing classes (or a perfect mane, for breeds presented unplaited with a long mane). A false mane, made from real horse hair and plaited into the crest of your horse's neck, can increase volume or disguise damage. To save money and get a perfect colour match at the same time, make your own false mane by keeping your horse's excess mane hairs when you trim it.

SECTION 5

Riding your Horse

Becoming a good rider takes both practice and a willingness to continually learn and improve. In this section you'll gain an understanding of the correct riding position and how to establish an independent seat at walk, trot, canter and over jumps, as well as gain insight into the different disciplines you may wish to compete in. Most importantly, you'll learn key skills to keep yourself safe while riding.

MOUNTING AND DISMOUNTING

Horses are traditionally mounted from the near (their left) side, although at times it can be useful to be able to mount from both sides. While mounting from the ground is an important skill to master, you should use a mounting block or get a leg-up as much as possible to protect your horse's back from unnecessary strain. The ease of mounting will depend on your height and weight, strength, flexibility, stirrup length and the height of your horse.

Top four: How to mount your horse from a mounting block: run down your stirrups (top left); put your horse's reins over its head (top right and middle left); put your left foot into the stirrup and swing into the saddle (middle right).

Bottom: Always check your stirrup length before you mount. Here, the stirrups are too short, which has compromised the rider's hip-heel-shoulder alignment.

HOW TO MOUNT

1. Before you mount, make sure that your girth is tight and your stirrups have been run down the leathers (and are the correct length).
2. If you're using a mounting block, your horse should be positioned parallel to it, with its shoulder and wither in line with where you are standing. Your horse should be close enough that you don't have to reach for the saddle.
3. Stand on the left side of your horse (either on the ground or on the mounting block), with your body adjacent to its wither.
4. Hold the reins with your left hand and place your hand on your horse's neck for balance, grabbing a handful of mane if needed. Hold the stirrup in place with your other hand, then lift your left foot into it.
5. Once your left foot is in the stirrup, move your right hand to the pommel or seat of the saddle. Don't hold the cantle, as this can twist the saddle, placing unnecessary strain on your horse's back.
6. Hop on your right foot, to help build up the momentum needed for you to spring into the saddle. Don't pull yourself into the saddle; instead, push off the sole of your right foot, using your leg muscles to propel your body up and over the saddle until you're positioned over your horse's centre of gravity.
7. Next, swing your right leg over your horse's rump (making sure not to kick it with your foot), then gently lower yourself into the saddle. Settling yourself into the saddle in a controlled and smooth manner is important, as thudding your weight down can damage your horse's back, especially if you are a heavier rider. 'Up fast and down slow' is a useful concept to remember when mounting.
8. Once you're in position, use your right toe to search for the stirrup iron, then put your foot into position. If you need to, you can reach down and use your right hand to hold the stirrup in place. The ball of your foot should sit evenly across the bar (bottom) of the stirrup iron; any more than this will increase the risk of your foot getting trapped in the stirrup if you fall off.
9. To finish, check your girth is tight then sit up tall, with a correct ear-shoulder-hip-heel alignment (see page 256 and pages 260-61), then organise your reins so that you're ready to ride.

With practice, these steps will be able to be done in one fluid motion and will become second nature to you.

> **HOW TO DISMOUNT**
>
> Dismounting is similar to mounting, except done in reverse.
> 1. To begin, take both feet out of your stirrup irons so that you don't get your foot caught if your horse moves away.
> 2. Hold the reins with your left hand and place your hand on your horse's neck for balance, grabbing a handful of mane if needed.
> 3. Swing your right leg over your horse's rump (making sure not to kick it with your foot), then slowly slide down the saddle and onto the ground on the near (left) side, bending your knees on landing to help absorb the shock. Don't unmount onto a mounting block, as it's easy to miss your mark and fall, or lose your balance.
> 4. Take the reins over your horse's neck, then give your horse a rub on the neck to thank it for the ride!

RIDING POSITION

If you want to achieve a good connection with your horse under saddle, a correct riding position is the most important foundation you can strive for, no matter what your preferred discipline, or level of ambition.

Your body position can influence how your horse stands and moves, in both positive and negative ways. A crooked or unbalanced position will cause the horse to adjust its way of working to compensate, resulting in it becoming unbalanced, uneven or sore, which can cause ridden issues to develop. It is therefore important to take the time to establish a balanced and independent seat, so that you aren't unbalancing your horse while riding.

EAR, SHOULDER, HIP, HEEL: From the side, your body should form a straight line from your ear, dropping straight down through your shoulder, to your hip and heel. This ear–shoulder–hip–heel alignment, which ensures that your upper body is perpendicular to the ground, is critical because it allows you to remain in your horse's centre of gravity and move in harmony with its movement. *Note:* If you are struggling to achieve the correct alignment, your saddle may be putting you in the wrong position.

ELBOW, HAND, REIN, BIT: From the side, your elbow and hands should form a straight line along the reins to the bit, to ensure a clear line of communication to your horse's mouth. Your hands should be positioned at the width of the horse's shoulders, about 5 to 7½ centimetres (2 to 3 inches) above its neck, and they should be stretched forward, towards the horse's mouth, to allow the horse to work freely.

SPINE: Your spine should be straight, but relaxed, with a slight hollow in your lower back. While you should sit tall, it is important not to become stiff, as this will negatively affect how your horse moves.

SHOULDERS: Your shoulders should be relaxed, back and down. Riders can be prone to slumping their shoulders forward, or lifting them up towards their ears if they become tense; both of these compromise the correct riding position. To get a feel for where

Top: An incorrect elbow–hand–rein–bit alignment, caused by the rider's leg being too far forward.

Bottom: A better elbow–hand–rein–bit alignment although the rider's hands could be marginally higher.

your shoulders should sit, lift them towards your ears, then push them back and down as if you're trying to push them down into your heels.

ELBOWS: Your upper arms should be relaxed, with a soft bend in the elbows so that they can flex with the horse's movement, which will allow you to establish steady hands. Tensing your elbows will make your hands bounce up and down, placing inconsistent and painful pressure on your horse's mouth. If you are struggling to get a correct bend in your elbows, usually you just need to lift your hands a little higher or move them forward to re-establish a correct elbow–hand–rein–bit alignment.

HANDS, WRISTS: Your hands and wrists should be relaxed, holding the reins with a soft grip, with your thumbs 'on top' as the highest point.

CHECK YOUR POSITION

As a general rule, if you glance down (without leaning forward) and can see the toes of your boots, then your legs are positioned too far forward. This will put you behind the motion of the horse — if you were plucked from your horse in this position and placed on the ground, your centre of gravity would be compromised and you would fall backwards. Riders in this position put unnecessary strain on their horse's back and are often left behind the horse's movement when jumping, which can cause their horse to either rush (if they are sensitive) or become unresponsive to the hand and leg aids (if they are more laidback in nature).

At the other extreme, if your leg is positioned too far back, you will be in front of the motion of the horse. This can make it difficult for your horse to maintain its balance (as extra weight will be loaded on its forehand), can cause your horse to rush or become anxious, and will also increase your chance of falling off. *Note:* An incorrect saddle fit can be a contributing factor to an incorrect rider position, especially if the deepest part of the seat isn't in the centre of the saddle (see page 210).

REINS = BABY BIRDS

When we were younger we were taught to hold the reins as if they were baby birds — tight enough so we didn't drop them on the ground, but not so tight that they got squashed. Ideally you should apply pressure to your horse's mouth only if you need it to slow down or stop, turn or work on a contact, relaxing the pressure as soon as your horse has given you the correct answer. The rest of the time your hands should maintain a soft neutral contact on the reins, or no contact at all if you are riding on a loose rein.

SEAT BONES, PELVIS: Bearing your weight evenly on your seat bones and pelvis will allow your horse to use its body correctly. This can be challenging for many riders, as often they think they are sitting balanced when in fact they are crooked. Often a dressage instructor, who focuses on the biomechanics of the rider, will be useful to help determine where you may be unbalanced and be able to offer advice on how to improve your posture.

You should also sit deeply into your horse's back, while having a light seat. When sitting in the saddle, it can be helpful to imagine your pelvis is the heaviest part of your body (it should feel like your pelvis is sinking towards the ground), while your spine is the lightest part of your body (it should feel like your head, neck and spine are being lifted up into the air). This will help you create a deep but light position on your horse's back. Some people ride with both a heavy pelvis and a heavy spine, giving them a heavy position on the horse's back. Others have a light spine and a light pelvis, making the rider appear as if they are sitting 'on the top' of the horse, which produces a weak and unstable position.

> To check whether the angle of your seat bones is correct, imagine that your pelvis is a bowl of water. When the horse is both standing and in motion, the rim of the bowl should remain level, not allowing any water to spill out.

KNEES, TOES: From the front, your thighs should be flat against the saddle with your knees and toes pointing forwards. When your horse is both standing and in motion, your lower calves should have a neutral contact against the horse — just enough pressure that you feel the horse's sides, but not squeezing unless you require more speed or collection (see page 293) from your horse. If you grip with your knees, or your toes turn in, you'll likely have an inactive or swinging lower leg which can make you tip forward in front of your horse's movement, negatively affect your balance or make your horse overly sensitive and reactive to leg aids if they are sensitive, or desensitised and heavy if they are more laidback in nature.

A correct position is important and something that you should be constantly assessing and improving. If your riding position is out of balance, your horse will likely be unbalanced beneath you; this can result in numerous riding and behavioural issues developing, including rushing, bucking, drifting and napping, as well as causing the horse to become heavy in the mouth (unresponsive to the hand aids).

Stirrup length

Having stirrups at the correct length is important to help you maintain the ideal riding position.

If your stirrups are too long it will make it difficult to keep your heels down, which will cause an unstable lower leg, as well as making it difficult to maintain an independent seat or effectively communicate with your leg aids. It can also cause you to fall back in the saddle, which will compromise your ear–shoulder–hip–heel alignment and can result in you falling behind or in front of the movement of the horse — especially when cantering or jumping.

Stirrups that are too short should also be avoided, as they can cause you to be perched precariously in the saddle, above the horse's movement, or at the back of the saddle in a 'driving' position. This not only makes it difficult for you to maintain an ideal position, but will also affect the balance of your horse and may even cause it to develop a sore back.

To find your ideal stirrup length, sit in the saddle with both feet out of the irons. As a general rule, the bar of each iron should be in line with your ankle, with the length then varying a hole or two depending on the width of your horse (on a narrower horse your legs will hang longer, while on a wider horse your legs will hang shorter) and your chosen discipline (for jumping, riders generally ride with their stirrups two to three holes shorter than for dressage). The correct length is one that allows you to maintain the correct riding position, have a secure seat to keep yourself safe, effectively use your leg aids and maintain the balance of both horse and rider.

TOP TIPS FOR STIRRUP LENGTH

ARMPIT TEST: Before you mount it's best to have your stirrups at approximately the right length. A good way to determine this is to stand next to your horse and place your fingertips on the stirrup bar of your saddle. Using your other hand, pull the stirrup leather taut along your outstretched arm. Adjust the length so that the stirrup iron fits comfortably in your armpit. This will provide you with more or less the right length, which you can further adjust once you are mounted, if needed.

VISUAL TEST: Once your stirrups are the correct length, have someone do a visual check from the ground to ensure the length allows you to maintain the ideal ear-shoulder-hip-heel position. It's also important to check your stirrups from the front to ensure they are level; even if they are on the same hole, the stirrup leather on one side may have stretched from excessive mounting or general wear and tear. If they are uneven, adjust as needed to ensure they are an equal length on both sides.

Left: The correct stirrup length will help you maintain an ideal ear–shoulder–hip–heel alignment.

Right: An incorrect ear-shoulder-hip-heel alignment, caused by the rider's leg being too far forward (short stirrups can also be a contributing factor).

ADJUSTING YOUR STIRRUPS AND GIRTH WHILE MOUNTED

ADJUSTING THE STIRRUPS

1. Hold the reins with one hand, resting them on your horse's neck if needed for balance.
2. Hang your foot out of the stirrup you are wanting to adjust, then use your spare hand to lever the stirrup leather away from the stirrup bar, until there is enough room to adjust the length.
3. Adjust the stirrup to the correct length and re-buckle it.
4. Grasp the stirrup leather and pull down until the buckle sits firmly against the stirrup bar, then put your foot back in the stirrup.
5. Once your stirrup is the correct length, adjust the other side, remembering to switch your reins to your opposite hand.

ADJUSTING THE GIRTH

1. Hold the reins with one hand, resting them on your horse's neck if needed for balance.
2. Keeping your foot in the stirrup, lift your leg over the front of the saddle flap. This will allow you to quickly return to a normal riding position if your horse were to spook or shoot forward suddenly, ensuring that you have the best chance of remaining balanced.
3. With your free hand, lift the saddle flap and tuck it under your thigh.
4. Grasp a billet strap, with your fingers pointing towards the ground, then pull it up until the buckle undoes.
5. Once the buckle is in line with another hole, use your index finger to settle the girth buckle into the hole. Repeat on the second billet strap, so that both of the girth buckles are done up on the same holes.
6. Lower the saddle flap and return your leg to its normal position.

Opposite page: The correct way to adjust your girth while mounted.

Achieving steady hands

The first step towards achieving steady hands is to develop an independent and balanced seat; something that can only be achieved by establishing a correct position (see pages 256–59).

Steady hands are not rigid. Instead, they should consistently follow the horse's motion, with the elbows opening and closing at the walk and the canter, as the horse's head and neck move back and forth with every stride. At the trot, however, the horse's head and neck remain fairly still — so the rider's hands should mirror this.

If your hands are inconsistent or hard, the horse can develop behavioural issues, including yanking at the reins, gaping its mouth open, head-tossing, leaning on the bit, tilting its head, hollowing the neck, tensing through the jaw and neck, or even bucking, rushing, napping or rearing.

While these issues can also be caused by dental or body issues, a poorly fitting saddle, mineral imbalances and a lack of schooling, it's important to understand that a rider with inconsistent or hard hands can be one of the biggest causes of pain to the horse. For this reason, it is important that beginner riders use forgiving bits (or a halter or bitless bridle) and have a slight loop in their reins when they are learning to ride — especially when learning how to rise to the trot or jump.

HOW TO HOLD THE REINS

When holding a single set of reins, on a snaffle bridle, your hands should stay level, with one rein held in each hand. The reins should be positioned between your ring finger and your little finger, passing inside a gently closed fist (with your fingers loose, not gripped tight) and with the reins coming out above your index finger. Hold the reins in place with your 'thumbs on top' (similar to how you would hold an ice-cream cone). It's also important the reins aren't twisted, to ensure there is a clear line of communication to your horse's mouth.

The excess loop of the rein should lie underneath the right rein, resting against your horse's offside (right) shoulder.

USE A WALL TO STEADY YOUR HANDS

If you find that you move your hands up and down while trotting, try this exercise.

Dismount and take up your riding position on the ground in front of a wall. Press your hands against the wall, holding them as if you were holding the reins (with thumbs on top, at the height where your hands would naturally sit while riding). Then practise rising up and down without moving the height of your hands. Next, strive to keep your hands steady without having them touching the wall. Ultimately, you should be able to rise up and down around your hands, rather than have them rise with you.

Top: How to hold the reins, with thumbs on top and the reins sitting above your index finger.

Bottom: How to hold the reins when carrying a cane or whip.

Following hips

When the horse is in motion, your hips should be gently moving backwards and forwards to follow the swinging motion of the horse at the walk and canter, and rise up and down in the tempo of the trot. To do this, you must be completely relaxed through every muscle and joint in your body.

To establish following hips, try our top tips below.

- Sink your weight deep into the saddle (or into the horse's back, if you are bareback) — the more relaxed you are, the smoother your position will become.
- Straighten your spine, put your shoulders back and check your ear–shoulder–hip–heel alignment is correct (see page 256 and pages 260–61).
- Relax and loosen your joints and muscles — especially your knees, so they are not gripping onto the horse. Any tension in your body will 'lock' your knees and hips, causing you to bounce or go against the horse's movement, which will result in your hands becoming unsteady.
- Establish your hips following the movement of the horse at the walk before progressing to a faster pace.
- At the trot, your hips don't need to follow the horse's movement, and instead should rise up and down in time with the horse's beat and on the correct diagonal (see pages 283–85). While rising, it is important to open up your core and keep your shoulders back, allowing your hips to rise up and slightly forwards towards the pommel of the saddle (rather than directly up and down).
- At the canter, imagine that you are sweeping the saddle with your seat, moving in a rhythmical backwards-and-forwards motion in time with the horse's beat, while keeping a slight hollow in your back.
- To truly feel the swing of the horse's movement, it can be beneficial to ride bareback. If you haven't ridden bareback before, try it while you are being led or lunged and ensure your horse is safe to ride bareback; if a horse is not used to being ridden without a saddle it may pick up speed if you accidentally lose your balance or grip tightly with your legs.
- To get a feel for your horse's rhythm, it can be helpful to close your eyes and focus on the movement of the horse beneath you. This is also easier to do while being led or lunged, so that you're able to keep your eyes closed without having to worry about controlling your horse.

Riding bareback is a great way to improve your riding position.

RIDING BAREBACK TO IMPROVE YOUR POSITION

Riding bareback improves your skills as a rider, fine-tunes your balance, improves your stickability and enhances your communication with your horse, so it's a valuable skill to gain if you want to improve your riding position.

BENEFITS OF RIDING BAREBACK

- Bareback riding is a great way to develop your position and core strength. Without a saddle to give you support, you must rely on an independent seat to keep yourself balanced and on the horse.
- Riding bareback will allow you to feel your horse's muscles shifting, making it easier to anticipate when something is about to go wrong. In these instances, you can often avoid a potential accident by correcting the horse or quickly dismounting.
- Bareback riding is a lot of fun — and can save lots of time saddling up.

TOP TIPS FOR RIDING BAREBACK

- Mounting your horse bareback, without the aid of stirrups, can be difficult. The best way is to get a leg-up or use a mounting block, or learn how to vault onto your horse's back from the ground.
- When trotting bareback, keep your muscles and joints relaxed, and let your weight sink down through your seat and heels.
- If you start to lose your balance, don't suddenly clench the horse with your legs — your horse may think you're asking it to go faster.
- Don't use the reins for balance; instead hold onto your horse's mane if needed.
- When riding uphill, lean forward and grab a handful of mane to stop yourself sliding backwards; when riding downhill, lean backward and push your legs further forward to prevent you from sliding onto the horse's neck.
- When you first start trotting and cantering bareback, it can be helpful to have someone lunge your horse; that way you can concentrate on maintaining your seat without having to worry about controlling your horse. Before you begin, however, make sure that your horse knows how to lunge, and is confident being ridden bareback at a faster pace (some horses can become unsettled if an unbalanced rider is bouncing on their back).

Top: Vicki and Showtym Spotlight competing bareback and bridleless at the New Zealand Horse of the Year Show in 2011. NED DAWSON

Bottom: Amanda and Showtym Viking competing bareback and bridleless at Equifest in 2022.

Riding out over farmland is a fun change from arena work, for both the horse and the rider.

WHERE TO RIDE

When it comes to ridden work, variety is key to ensure your horse doesn't become sour or bored; ideally your training sessions should be a mix of flatwork, polework and jump schooling, as well as ridden adventures and obstacle training.

- **SCHOOLING:** When schooling your horse, whether it be groundwork (including lunging), flatwork or over poles, obstacles or jumps, an arena or flat paddock is ideal. The schooling surface needs to be firm, but soft enough to provide cushioning for your horse's joints, and it should be even, with no sudden dips or hollows. In the summer months you will know that the ground is too hard to ride on if you can hear it echoing beneath your horse's hooves. Riding on hard ground can cause your horse to 'jar up' and become sore from excessive concussion on an unforgiving surface.
- **RIDDEN ADVENTURES:** While you are learning to ride it is sensible to remain in an enclosed arena or paddock, but once your basic riding position is established and you are safely able to control your horse, it's very beneficial to get out on ridden adventures. Not only will this allow your horse a change in scenery, but these adventures will also increase your horse's fitness and give you the opportunity

to become a versatile rider. Ideally ride your horse out over farmland, through forestry or along the beach regularly; these rides should be anywhere from 20 minutes to an hour in length. Longer, sporadic rides are fine, as long as your horse has sufficient fitness.

Key things to consider when you're out on the trails:

RIDING UP AND DOWN HILLS: Your body position is very important when riding up and down hills, as it affects your horse's ability to remain balanced. A good position will allow the horse to compensate for the rider's weight on uneven terrain, making it less likely to stumble or slip. As you ride uphill you should lean slightly forward to stay in front of the horse's movement; when you ride downhill you should lean slightly back to stay behind the horse's movement. *Note:* When riding up particularly steep hills it's important to stand in the stirrups, in your half-seat jumping position (see page 300), with your hands holding the mane; this will reduce the chance of you slipping back and affecting your horse's centre of balance, or pulling on its mouth. When riding down particularly steep hills, your horse should walk in a slow and controlled manner, so it's best to keep your reins short. Riding in a zigzag pattern can be useful if the horse is unbalanced, the hill is very steep or the rider is nervous.

RIDING ALONE: Riding by yourself is necessary at times and can be a lot of fun if your horse is confident and independent out on the trails by itself, but it does have increased risks if there is an injury to yourself or your horse (since there will be no one to ride for help), or you get lost. If you're planning to ride alone, here are some safety rules to heed:

- Always tell someone where you are going and when you'll be back.
- Take your phone with you (and make sure it's charged). Keep it on your body (not in a saddle blanket pocket) in case the horse bolts when you fall off.
- Ride a dependable horse, which is confident and relaxed being ridden alone.
- Always wear a helmet.

RIDING IN COMPANY: Riding your horse out in a group can be a fun and social experience for both horse and rider. If you don't have anyone to ride with, it is worth seeking out local riding groups to join so you have like-minded people to ride with.

RIDING ON ROADS: Riding on roads can be highly dangerous, especially if the horse or rider is inexperienced, and should be avoided at all costs. If you must ride on the road take into consideration the road rules:

- Stay on the opposite side of the road to the oncoming traffic (in New Zealand you need to ride on the left side of the road).
- If you are leading another horse, lead it on the side furthest away from the road, to keep it away from the traffic.
- Always ride in single file, keeping your horse as far off the road as possible.
- If you are riding on the road in low-light conditions, make sure both you and your horse are kitted out with reflective gear.
- Keep off footpaths, lawns and gardens.

RIDING AT BEACHES OR PARKS: Horse riders are welcome in many regional parks and beaches, but careful consideration must be given to the following.
- Make sure you adhere to the local council, Department of Conservation (DOC) or iwi regulations, which will include when and where you can ride.
- Make sure you remove all manure and hay from the parking area.
- When riding on a beach, keep below the high-tide mark and never ride in sand dunes; this will keep you away from fragile areas and nesting sites, as well as ensure any manure is washed away. This is also crucial for the well-being of your horse as riding in deep sand, especially at a trot or canter, can risk injury to its tendons, ligaments and bones.
- Make sure to show consideration for other beach or park users, including pedestrians, cyclists and fellow horse riders.

BRINGING A HORSE INTO WORK

When your horse is coming back into work after a break, or is being started under saddle, it's important to get it physically and mentally fit so it's able to complete the tasks asked of it. Overworking an unfit or poorly conditioned horse to the point where it's laboured or sweating will affect its ability to build muscle, put excessive strain on its body and increase the risk of potential injury. Doing too much, too fast, before the horse is sufficiently muscled and conditioned, will not only cause damage to the horse's body, but also its mental well-being.

When bringing your horse into work, it's important to increase its fitness gradually over a period of 6 to 8 weeks, or longer if it's been out of work for an extended period of time (especially if it's been confined in a yard, stable or small paddock), has a weak topline (see page 275), is under- or overweight, or is being rehabilitated after an injury.

LOW LEVEL OF FITNESS: Young horses that are being backed, and lead-rein ponies, won't need a high level of fitness as only light work is expected of them. Older, semi-retired horses that are ridden only sporadically may also require a low level of fitness.

MODERATE LEVEL OF FITNESS: Horses that require a moderate level of fitness, for low-level competition or pleasure riding, should be ridden no less than three to five times a week. *Note:* It's important not to over-jump your horse; make sure your ridden work includes a balance of flat and jump schooling sessions, as well as ridden adventures. When you're jumping in group lessons, you'll often ride for an hour or more, but there is usually down time in between intensive periods for your horse to physically and mentally rest, while the instructor focuses on another rider.

HIGH LEVEL OF FITNESS: For higher levels of competition, your horse will require five to six rides per week; half of these should be schooling sessions (15 to 45 minutes of work), and the other half should be ridden adventures, ranging anywhere from 20 minutes to a couple of hours, to provide your horse with variety, while maintaining its fitness.

Trekking horses over farmland, through forestry or at the beach — or swimming in rivers or the ocean — is beneficial to their mental and physical well-being.

Topline

Whether your horse is returning to ridden work after time out in the paddock, or needing to be rehabilitated after an injury, establishing a strong topline (the muscles that support the horse's withers, back, neck and hindquarters) is crucial to your horse's long-term soundness and well-being. A good topline is developed from good nutrition and the right type of work, and is essential to support the weight of the rider, as well as give the horse the strength needed to perform the tasks being asked of it.

In order to assess your horse's topline, evaluate its body condition score (BCS; see pages 104–05); if it has a low BCS or any muscle atrophy (wasting away of muscle) along its spine, it has a poor topline. This will limit your horse's ability to use its body correctly or bear the weight of a rider, as well as making it difficult to saddle-fit and more prone to injury.

How to improve topline

A horse with a poor topline needs time to slowly strengthen and build muscle, so it's important to plan its training programme with that in mind. If the horse is asked to do too much, too soon, it can become weak and sore, which will lead to pain-related and behavioural issues developing.

To improve your horse's topline, first ensure it has an ideal BCS; if it is underweight, increase its feed as needed to ensure it has enough energy to build muscle (see pages 104–05). If your horse has a good BCS, however, muscle atrophy may be occurring because of specific pain-related issues, including skeletal damage or an ill-fitting saddle, or from the wrong kind of exercise. A sore horse, or one that is schooled incorrectly, will not build correct muscle. In order for these horses to improve their topline, they firstly need to be pain free, then begin training exercises that encourage muscle to build over the top of the neck, withers, back and rump.

Good exercises to improve topline include the following.

- **LUNGING:** Usually it takes 8 to 10 weeks for a horse to get to competition fitness, and 12 to 14 weeks for a weak horse. If your horse has a poor topline, spend the first 4 to 6 weeks lunging your horse to build fitness and strength, without the added weight of a rider on top. This is very important, as riding a weak horse can cause it to hollow its back, exacerbating any muscle atrophy and pain-related issues. Start with 3 to 5 minutes of trot on each rein, then gradually build up to 5 to 8 minutes of trot and 2 to 3 minutes of canter on each rein as the horse's fitness increases. When lunging to improve topline, it's important to use a lunging system (like the Soft Lunge Training Aid, Equisystem Bandage, Kinkade, Pessoa or Chambon) to encourage your horse to drop its head, engage its core, push from its hindquarters and lift the muscles over its back. *Note:* If you have a weak horse with a poor topline, avoid cantering it on the lunge initially, as it will lack the muscle needed to use its body correctly on such a small circle.
- **WORKING ON A LONG AND LOW CONTACT:** Once your horse has developed sufficient topline to hold the weight of a rider, gradually add in short schooling

Top: A horse with a well-conditioned topline.

Bottom: A young horse with a weak topline.

sessions (between 10 and 25 minutes). During these rides the horse should not be asked to work on a contact (see page 291), as it will lack the physical requirements to support itself, placing massive stress on its skeletal system; this can result in pain-related and behavioural issues developing, which can further compromise your horse's topline and strength. Instead, work your horse on a long and low contact (where its head is stretched out and down towards the ground), to encourage it to lift its back muscles and engage its core. These sessions should be short, never going beyond the point where the horse is sweating or labouring for breath — these signs indicate that the horse has been pushed past its level of fitness and strength. *Note:* If you are not skilled in rehabilitating sore horses or schooling on the flat, you may need to send your horse to a professional rider so it can be trained to use its body correctly, then have adequate lessons so you're able to maintain your horse's new way of going.

- **GYMNASTIC EXERCISES OVER POLES**: Polework is beneficial to increase your horse's strength and flexibility, as well as to encourage it to engage the muscles in its core, back and hindquarters. Start out with short sessions, as polework can be strenuous for a weak horse. As your horse increases in fitness and strength, you can progress to raised poles, which are even more beneficial to developing a good topline.
- **HILL WORK**: Riding your horse up and down hills is a good way to build your horse's topline as it requires the horse to engage the muscles in its core, back and hindquarters. Initially only walk and trot, progressing to the canter only once your horse has increased in strength and fitness.
- **SWIMMING OR WATER WALKING**: Swimming and walking in deep water will encourage your horse to engage its core, back and hindquarter muscles, without having to cope with the added weight of a rider. It can be particularly beneficial for a horse recovering from injury, as it will allow it to build muscle and fitness without requiring any of the limbs to bear weight.

FLATWORK

Flatwork refers to any schooling session that doesn't involve jumps or obstacles. It is an essential part of every horse's training and is not only important for riders wanting to compete in dressage and showing, but is the foundation for every discipline. When done well, flatwork improves your horse's relaxation, rhythm, suppleness, strength and obedience, as well as enhancing the connection between horse and rider.

Flatwork can provide many benefits, regardless of your ambitions or chosen discipline, including the following.

- **CORRECT BEHAVIOURAL ISSUES**: Many behavioural issues are a result of insufficient or incorrect flatwork training. If your horse hasn't been trained to respond to subtle rider aids or use its body correctly, its behaviour and performance (including over jumps and out on ridden adventures) will be greatly

Hill work is important for strengthening a horse's topline, especially for the cross-country phase of eventing.

improved by focusing on flatwork. If you don't have the skills needed to retrain your horse on the flat, it may be beneficial to send it to a professional rider for schooling.

- **INCREASE STRENGTH AND FITNESS:** Schooling your horse on the flat will improve its suppleness, strength and topline (see page 275), and also allow you to work on any physical weaknesses it may have.
- **ESTABLISH GOOD HABITS:** The greatest kindness you can offer any horse is to train it well; a horse with good manners under saddle will not only be a pleasure to ride, but will have the foundations needed to give it a good ridden life no matter who owns it. If your horse lacks the basic foundations, use your flatwork sessions to retrain it so that riding becomes a more enjoyable experience for both you and your horse, or send it away to be schooled by a professional.
- **FOSTER RELAXATION:** Good flatwork training is about keeping your horse relaxed and engaged so it's able to learn efficiently and retain information. In order to foster relaxation during your training sessions, it's important to develop good feel and timing (see page 168) and clearly communicate with your aids.

AIDS

Aids are used to communicate with your horse, to help you influence its speed and direction. The most common are natural aids, which come from your body; these include your hands, seat, legs and voice. Artificial aids, like whips and spurs, should only be used sparingly to reinforce natural aids if your horse isn't listening, and should never be used to punish the horse.

Most aids require the use of physcal pressure to communicate with your horse. For aids to be truly effective, it's important to know when to apply pressure (to ask it a question) and when to release it (to let it know it answered the question correctly). If the pressure is maintained or inconsistently applied (because the rider lacks an independent seat or has unsteady hands), the horse may learn to ignore the aids. This can cause a quiet horse to become dull to the aids, while a sensitive horse may become anxious or worried.

To know how much pressure to apply, use the 1–10 Pressure System (see pages 160–62). Ideally, you want your horse to respond off the lightest aid possible, increasing the pressure only if smaller forms of communication are ignored. If your horse continues to ignore you when the pressure is increased, or does the wrong thing, it might be because it doesn't understand what you are asking — perhaps because you asked the question in a confusing way, or because you asked your horse to do something it didn't know the answer to.

Leg aids

Leg aids are applied by squeezing the horse's sides with your inside lower legs and heels, and are primarily used to encourage the horse to move.

Regardless of your preferred discipline, good flatwork is important for developing a supple and well-balanced horse.

Leg aids can be used on different parts of the horse's sides, to ask for different movements. Depending on where your leg is positioned, you can ask your horse to move forwards or backwards, to yield its hindquarter or shoulder, or do more advanced lateral movements like side-passing.

Different pressures can also be used to mean different things. A 'driving' leg aid (in which pressure is applied from one or both legs) asks the horse for movement or to increase in energy, while a 'keeping' leg aid (where the rider maintains a light, neutral, contact on the horse's sides) asks it to maintain its current pace and collection.

DON'T CUT CORNERS

When it comes to flatwork, and horse riding in general, many riders try to learn skills beyond their capabilities; it is only when they reach the higher levels that they pause and realise they need to return to the basics and master the foundations, in order to have success at the highest levels.

Beginner riders try to master *intermediate* movements.
Intermediate riders try to master *advanced* movements.
Advanced riders try to master *beginner* movements.

THE GUITAR METAPHOR

When it comes to moving the horse laterally, think of the horse's ribcage as being like a guitar: pressure applied to different areas on the horse's side should mean different things, just as different chords on a musical instrument make different sounds. With correct training, a horse can be taught to move forwards, backwards or sideways in response to pressure applied to specific points on the horse's body.

The ridden cues for basic lateral movements are shown here.

Right circle — Position 1.

Middle circle — Position 2.

Left circle — Position 3.

REIN-BACK

Apply a gentle rein aid with both hands to ask your horse to soften to the contact, while applying both legs at Position 1 to ask your horse to step backwards. Gently bump your legs against your horse's sides with each step backwards.

HINDQUARTER YIELD

Apply a gentle pressure to the inside rein to ask your horse to flex its head to the inside, then apply your *inside* leg aid at Position 3 (right leg on means yield the hindquarters to the left; left leg on means yield the hindquarters to the right). The outside leg has a supporting role and should remain in Position 2, with only a light contact on the horse's side.

> **SHOULDER YIELD**
> Open your outside rein so your horse has an open space to step into, then apply your *inside* leg aid at Position 1 (right leg on means yield the shoulders to the left; left leg on means to yield the shoulders to the right). The outside leg has a supporting role and should remain in Position 2, with only a light contact on the horse's side.
>
> **SIDE-PASS**
> Open your outside rein so your horse has an open space to step into, then apply your *inside* leg aid at Position 2 (right leg on means side-pass to the left; left leg on means to side-pass to the right). The outside leg has a supporting role and should remain in Position 2, with no contact on the horse's side.

Hand aids (also known as rein aids)

Hand aids are applied to the horse's mouth, through the reins (or to their nose if they are being ridden in a halter or bitless bridle). Depending on whether the pressure is applied to one or both reins, and how much pressure is used, rein aids can tell the horse which direction to go, what gait to travel at (see pages 283–87), the rhythm and impulsion you want, to collect onto a contact (see page 291), or to move laterally.

A 'taking' hand aid interrupts what the horse is doing and requires it to decrease in energy, drop down to a lower gait, turn, work on a contact or rein back. It is usually applied by the rider moving one or both of their little fingers fractionally closer to their body. If the horse ignores this, then the pressure can be increased by moving the elbows closer to the body. When the horse responds correctly, the rider should immediately remove the pressure, using a 'giving' hand aid (in which the pressure is softened by returning the fingers or elbows back to their normal position). The amount you 'give', to reward your horse for doing the right thing, should be directly equal to how much rein you 'took'. At all other times a 'keeping' hand aid should be used; this can be either a loose rein, with no pressure on the horse's mouth, or a soft, consistent contact.

Seat aids (also known as weight aids)

Seat aids are used to ask your horse to increase or decrease its gait, back up, move sideways, change direction or adjust its length of stride within a pace just through a change of your body position. Your seat aids are also crucial for turning. Looking where you're going and guiding the horse with your reins may get it to turn or bend its neck, but if your hips are straight, your horse will interpret that it should continue tracking on a straight line. Instead, turn your entire upper body and pelvis before using your rein aids to let your horse know that you want it to turn. This will allow your horse to complete a smoother turn, without you needing to 'pull' on its mouth.

When you are learning to ride, your seat will likely be communicating a lot of confusing things to your horse if your position is unsteady or you're slipping around in the saddle. Because of this, the horse may become over-sensitised or desensitised to your seat aids, depending on its nature.

Once you have developed an independent and balanced seat, however, and are able to follow the horse's movement at each gait (see pages 283–87), your seat position should become neutral to your horse. Once you get to this point, you can intentionally and clearly communicate through your seat aids. If your hips are following the motion of your horse, you can slow the movement of your hips to encourage the horse to slow or stop. Alternatively, you can increase the tempo of your horse's movement and ask it to lengthen or shorten its stride by increasing or decreasing the amount that your hips swing at the walk and canter, or the speed at which you rise to the trot.

Artificial aids

Artificial aids, which include whips and spurs, are tools that can be used as an extension of the hand or heels to clearly communicate something to the horse.

Because some artificial aids can inflict harm on horses if used incorrectly, they should never be used in times of anger or frustration, and *never* as a form of punishment. In the wrong hands, and with the wrong timing, they can be unfair and painful to the horse, so should only be used by experienced riders or under supervision. While whips can be used with discretion by riders of all levels, spurs should only be used by experienced riders who have established an independent seat and a stable lower leg position.

As a general rule, artificial aids should only be used on horses that already know the answer to the question you're asking, and not when teaching the horse something new. Only if it ignores the escalation of pressure from your natural aids, should an artificial aid be used.

Often artificial aids are only needed if a horse has been desensitised to the rider's natural aids, usually through incorrect timing when applying or releasing pressure. If this has happened, the horse will have 'stitched off' to normal levels of pressure as a means of survival, and the need to use artificial aids has only come about because the horse lacks a good education. This is why it's important that horses are trained to be light and responsive from the very beginning. If your horse hasn't been trained to respond to subtle natural aids, it is worth sending your horse away to be retrained by a professional so it doesn't have to be continuously nagged with whips and spurs, and is able to have a better quality of life going forward.

Voice aids

Your voice can be used to reinforce your hand and leg aids, as well as to offer praise and reprimands as needed. With consistent training, horses can also learn to work off voice cues. This can be taught by combining a word with a natural or artificial aid. For example, every time you flick the lunging whip to ask your horse to trot while lunging, you could say the word 'trot' as it changes pace into a trot. With repetition the physical aid will be able to be faded out, so that your horse understands to change pace from the word alone.

GAITS

The four basic gaits of the horse are the walk, trot, canter and gallop (less common gaits include the tolt, pace and rack). They are distinguishable not only by their speed, but also by the pattern the horse's legs follow within each pace, known as beats or footfalls. Each time the horse completes a pattern of footfalls, it is known as a stride.

Walk

The walk is the slowest gait of the horse, averaging about 6 kilometres per hour. It has four beats, with no moment of suspension (when all four hooves are briefly off the ground at once), making it very comfortable to sit to.

 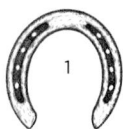

Trot

The horse trots at an average speed of 14 to 20 kilometres per hour. It has two beats, with the horse's legs moving in diagonal pairs, and also has a moment of suspension. To smooth out the bounciness of this gait, riders need to master both the rising and sitting trot.

During the rising trot, riders rise and fall in a *one, two, one, two* rhythm. The timing of when to rise and fall is important and is known as being on the correct diagonal. When the rider is riding on a circle, they should be sitting in the saddle as the horse's outside front leg swings back and hits the ground. When a rider changes direction, they need to change their diagonal by sitting to the trot for two steps (or two bounces). Riding on the correct diagonal is important, as it allows the horse to bend correctly and remain balanced going through a turn or around a circle, and also allows the horse to develop a good topline.

To check whether you are on the right diagonal, glance down at your horse's outside

The footfall pattern of the walk is outside hind leg (1), outside foreleg (2), inside hind leg (3), inside foreleg (4).

shoulder while you are trotting. As the outside leg swings backwards you should be sitting in the saddle, and as it swings forward you should be rising. With practice this should become instinctive, and you will no longer need to look down to see what diagonal you are on.

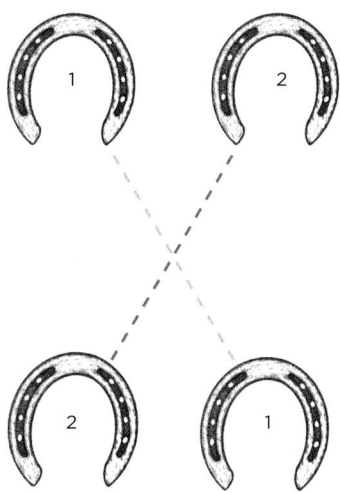

Canter

Horses canter at an average speed of 16 to 27 kilometres per hour. It has three beats, with a moment of suspension, and is usually quite a smooth pace to sit to if the horse is balanced and able to maintain its own rhythm.

When a horse canters, one front leg always strikes out further than the other, determining which lead the horse is on. Cantering on the correct lead is important, as it allows the horse to use its body correctly and stay balanced when going through a turn or around a circle, while also making it more comfortable to ride.

To check whether you are on the correct lead, look down at your horse's shoulders while cantering, taking the time to check each shoulder to determine which leg is striking the furthest forward. When riding on a circle, the inside leg should be leading. If your horse is on the wrong lead, ask it to trot for a few strides, before asking for the canter again, checking to see if it is on the correct lead. With practice, you'll be able to instinctively feel if your horse is on the correct lead, without the need to look down.

FLYING CHANGES: Flying changes are a more technical skill in which the horse changes its canter lead in mid-air as the rider changes the rein (i.e. from a left circle to a right circle). It is usually taught once a horse has established lateral movements at the canter and can effortlessly do walk-to-canter and canter-to-walk transitions.

COUNTER CANTER: A counter canter is an advanced dressage move in which horses are required to canter on the outside lead, with their heads bent to the outside of the circle or turn. A correct counter canter helps the horse develop rhythm, strength, balance and engagement of the hindquarters, and is very different from being on the wrong lead.

The footfall pattern of the trot consists of the horse's legs moving as two diagonal pairs — outside hind leg and inside foreleg (1), followed by a moment of suspension, then inside hind leg and outside foreleg (2).

Opposite top: The correct diagonal; the rider is sitting as the horse's outside leg swings backwards.

Opposite bottom: The incorrect diagonal; the rider is sitting as the horse's inside leg moves forwards.

DISUNITED CANTER: In a disunited canter, the horse is cantering with the incorrect pattern of footfalls (with both the right and left legs together, rather than as a diagonal pair), which can be very uncomfortable to sit to and affects the horse's balance. If your horse disunites, bring it back to a trot and then ask for the canter transition again. Horses that are prone to disuniting may be too weak to use their bodies correctly or have pain-related issues.

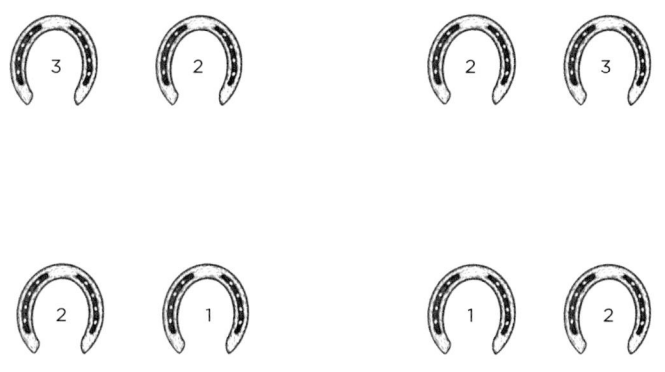

The correct footfall pattern of the canter on the left lead is right hind leg (1), then left hind leg and right foreleg moving together (2), left foreleg (3). The correct footfall pattern of the canter on the right lead is left hind leg (1), then right hind leg and left foreleg moving together (2), right foreleg (3).

Gallop

The gallop is the fastest pace and can reach speeds of up to 64 kilometres per hour. It has four beats, with a moment of suspension. *Note:* An in-hand gallop (commonly asked for in Saddle Hunter or Working Hunter competitions) is often a lengthened canter (three-beat gait), rather than a true gallop.

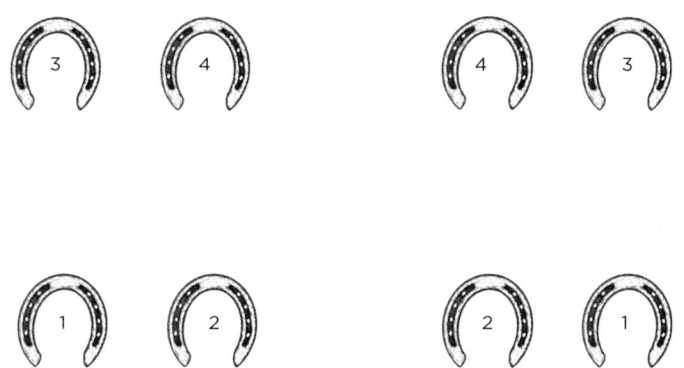

The footfall pattern of the gallop on the right lead is left hind leg (1), right hind leg (2), left foreleg (3), right foreleg (4), followed by a moment of suspension. The footfall pattern of the gallop on the left lead is the right hind leg (1), left hind leg (2), right foreleg (3), left foreleg (4), followed by a moment of suspension.

Opposite top: A horse cantering on the correct lead.

Opposite bottom: The moment of suspension in the gallop.

TRANSITIONS

A transition refers to any change between gaits (such as from walk to trot), or a change of speed or length of stride within a pace (such as from collected trot to extended trot). Riding correct transitions is important to help your horse remain balanced, supple and obedient, and to build up the muscles in its hindquarters.

Only ask for a transition when your horse is balanced at its current pace and is attentive to the rider's aids (asking your horse to canter from an balanced trot will likely result in a rough transition, or even the incorrect lead). It is also important to maintain a balanced position, as tipping forward will cause your horse to fall onto the forehand and become unbalanced as the majority of its weight will be carried by its shoulder and forelimbs.

With inexperienced riders and horses, transitions should be kept simple — only moving up or down one gait at a time (halt to walk, walk to trot, trot to canter, canter to trot, trot to walk, and walk to halt). As your skill level increases, you can skip a gait and progress to doing a halt-to-trot or trot-to-halt transition (with no walk steps in between) or a walk-to-canter or canter-to-walk transition (with no trot steps in between).

UPWARD TRANSITIONS: When used correctly, your aids for upwards transitions should encourage your horse to move forward with its hindquarters engaged.

- **HALT TO WALK**: Squeeze with both legs on the girth to encourage your horse to increase its gait, while softening your hands to give the horse space to move into.
- **WALK TO TROT**: This is ridden the same as the halt-to-walk transition, but when the horse picks up the trot, sit for four strides before rising to the trot on the correct diagonal.
- **TROT TO CANTER**: Sit to the trot for four strides, then squeeze with your inside leg on the girth and have your outside leg sitting just behind the girth. At the same time, open the inside rein slightly, while half-halting (see below) with the outside hand, to encourage the horse to engage its hindquarters and pick up the correct canter lead. *Note:* Some horses are trained to canter by squeezing with the outside leg, rather than the inside leg.

HALF-HALT

The half-halt is a combination of the hand, seat and leg aids, and is used to rebalance or collect the horse by transferring weight from its front end back onto its hindquarters.

DOWNWARD TRANSITIONS: When used correctly, your aids for downward transitions should encourage your horse to slow down, while remaining engaged through its hindquarters. To achieve this, use your leg, seat and hand aids in turn; never ask your horse to drop down in pace from a hand aid alone.

- **WALK TO HALT**: To prepare your horse for this transition, stop following your horse's movement with your hips 4 seconds before you want to drop down in pace. Next, drop your weight into your seat bones and close your legs to engage the horse's hindquarters. Lastly, use a 'taking' hand aid to ask your horse to stop; when it halts, 'give' with your hands to reward your horse.
- **TROT TO WALK**: Sit to the trot for four strides before using the same aids as the

walk-to-halt transition. When the horse walks, immediately allow your hips and hands to follow your horse's movement as it walks forward.
- **CANTER TO TROT**: Drop your weight into your seat bones and close your legs to engage the horse's hindquarters, while using a 'taking' hand aid to ask your horse to slow. When the horse trots, sit for four strides before rising on the correct diagonal.

BASIC EXERCISES ON THE FLAT

Adding variety into your flatwork sessions is important not only to keep your horse's mind stimulated, but also to improve its fitness, strength and rideability. Below are some basic exercises that can be included in your training sessions.

CIRCLES: Working your horse on circles is beneficial to improve balance and establish a correct bend (see page 292). Although an easy exercise, they are a difficult shape to ride correctly; the circle should be perfectly round, not oval. To accomplish a perfect circle your horse must not drift to the outside (making parts of the circle too wide) or to the inside (making parts of the circle too small), something that many inexperienced horses are prone to do when they are ridden past a gate or another horse. *Note:* As a general guideline, the minimum circle diameter for each gait are as follows.
- Walk: 5 metres
- Trot: 10 metres
- Canter: 20 metres

CHANGE OF REIN: A change of rein refers to changing the direction that you are riding. When a change of rein is done at a trot, the rider must change their diagonal (see page 283), and at the canter the horse will need to change leads; this is normally achieved through a simple-lead change (trot for three strides, before picking up the new canter lead) or a flying-lead change.

SERPENTINE: A serpentine is a series of half circles, changing from one direction to another. Each half circle should be the same size to create an 'S' shape.

FIGURE EIGHT: Figure eights combine two perfect circles, with a change of rein in the middle, to create an '8' shape.

ADVANCED FLATWORK

To have your horse work in perfect balance and perform to the best of its abilities, it needs to systematically learn rhythm, suppleness, contact, impulsion, straightness and collection. These six components are known as the German Scales of Training and while they are designed for dressage horses, they are beneficial to horses competing in any discipline if you are wanting them to develop a correct topline and reach their maximum potential.

The scales of training link together, and should be taught in a specific order:
1. Until your horse can maintain a *rhythm*, it is unlikely to be *supple*.
2. Until it is *supple*, it will be inconsistent in the *contact*.

3. Until it is consistent in the *contact*, it will not have true *impulsion*.
4. Until it has true *impulsion*, it cannot be *straight*.
5. Until it is *straight*, it will struggle to achieve *collection*.

Rhythm

Rhythm refers to the regularity and cadence of the horse's footfalls at each gait, and the speed of the footfalls (known as the tempo). In every pace, the tempo of your horse's strides should be purposeful but unhurried, and it should maintain an even speed without having to be constantly corrected by the rider.

Suppleness

Your horse should be both physically and mentally supple, something that can only be achieved when your horse is free from tension or constraint. You'll know if your horse is supple if it has a happy and relaxed expression, elasticity in its movement, a swinging tail, and it stretches forward and down when the reins are softened. In comparison, a horse that lacks suppleness will be tight through the back, have a clamped or swishing tail, an inconsistent rhythm, tense body language or lack correct bend on a circle.

Contact

Contact refers to the connection between the horse's mouth and the rider's hand, leg and seat. When a horse is working correctly on the contact (also known as working on the bit, or in a frame) its poll should be the highest point of its neck, with the jugular (throat) forming the shape of an upside-down 'U'. In order to create this, it's important the horse isn't forced onto the bit by excessive pressure on the reins, but rather ridden forward with the seat and leg aids, to create impulsion and therefore suppleness of the horse's head and neck. This allows the horse's energy to come from the hindquarters and over its back, so the head and neck can reach down and forward into the contact to seek the rider's hands.

A horse can only do this, however, if the contact on the reins is soft and consistent (often referred to as being elastic); if your hands are rigid or tense the horse is likely to evade the bit by breaking at the neck (resulting in the third or fourth vertebra being the highest point and the jugular forming a sharper, upside-down 'V' shape) or dropping behind the vertical (an overbent horse, with its nose too close to its chest, will have excessive strain placed on its poll — in extreme cases this is known as Rollkur or hyperflexion, which is an illegal practice in all equestrian sports). Riding with an incorrect contact will not only cause the horse's back to hollow, the hindquarters to disengage and the horse to become heavy in the hand, but it can cause long-term skeletal damage which can result in pain-related and behavioural issues developing.

Impulsion

Impulsion refers to controlled, forward energy. True impulsion is not only determined by the engagement of the hindquarters (which creates power to propel the horse

Top: A horse working correctly on the contact will have their forehead perpendicular to the ground, with a soft 'U' shape under its jugular.

Bottom: An overbent horse, with a sharper 'V' shape under the jugular.

forward), but also the horse's willingness to move forward and respond to the rider's aids, the elasticity of its paces and the suppleness of its topline. The aim of impulsion is to create expressive movement that is both forward (energy, not speed) and upward (the hind legs should step under the horse's centre of gravity, so its movement becomes 'uphill').

Straightness

Your horse should be even on both sides of its body; not only when it is working on straight lines, but also when working laterally (see pages 280–81). Young and inexperienced horses are wiggly when they are started under saddle and many are naturally one-sided, so straightness is something that needs to be fostered. *Note:* Your horse can't be straight if you're not *even* in your own riding position. A good rider should sit straight and balanced on the horse; if your posture is crooked, it's worth visiting a professional to try to realign your skeletal structure, or consider starting a fitness plan to improve the alignment of your own body.

A: Correct bend.

B: Incorrect bend, head and shoulders to the outside.

C: No bend.

D: Incorrect bend, hindquarters swinging to the outside.

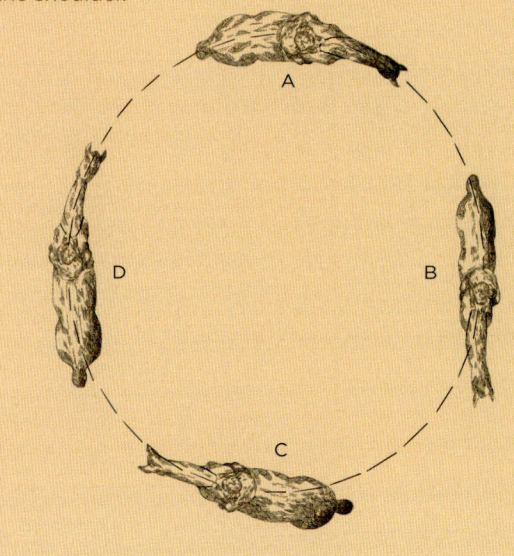

BEND = BALANCE

A correct bend is important to enable your horse to stay balanced when it is travelling on a curved line. When working your horse on a circle or going around a corner, it should bend its entire body (from poll to tail) into the arc of the line you are riding (example A below); you'll know if your horse is bent correctly if its ribcage is swinging and its jaw is flexed to the inside. To establish a correct bend use your inside leg aid combined with an open inside rein to flex the horse in the direction it is moving. At the same time use your outside leg to support the horse and prevent its hindquarters from swinging out on the circle (example D below), and place your outside rein against the horse's neck to prevent it falling out through the shoulder.

Collection

In the basic stages of training, collection can be referred to as balance. Your horse will be balanced when it has the majority of its weight on its hindquarters; if a horse isn't naturally this way inclined, its balance can be improved using the half-halt (see page 288) to increase engagement of the hind end and create lightness in the forehand. This shift in weight — from the front end to the back end — allows the horse's centre of gravity to be perfectly balanced, resulting in it being able to maintain a steady rhythm and self-carriage (where it can maintain working on a contact, without constant support from the rider). In comparison, an unbalanced horse will tend to have more weight on its forehand (known as being on the forehand), lean on the bit, may have contact issues or an inconsistent rhythm, and is more likely to develop behavioural issues.

OBSTACLE TRAINING

In between schooling sessions and ridden adventures it can be beneficial to ride your horse over, under, through and between obstacles — either man-made or natural — to increase its confidence in a variety of situations. Training with obstacles is a great way to teach your horse how to respond to pressure and learn how to positively work through anything it may be scared of or confused by. Each type of obstacle works as a metaphor for real-life situations that your horse may experience: including but not limited to loading on a truck or trailer, coping with banners and signage at shows, jumping (especially fillers, see page 305), opening gates, riding past spooky things (including letterboxes, tarpaulins or vehicles) or entering narrow spaces.

How to train your horse over obstacles

When training with obstacles it is important to foster relaxation and straightness on the approach to the obstacle and also while engaging with it. A horse that learns in a relaxed state will be more likely to retain information and be more confident on future attempts, while a tense horse will be reacting from their survival brain (see page 60) and will not only take longer to learn the same lesson, but may lose confidence and trust in its rider when asked to perform similar tasks in the future.

To counteract your horse's flight, fight, freeze and fawn response, follow these steps.

READ YOUR HORSE'S BODY LANGUAGE: On the approach to an obstacle, a relaxed horse should be able to maintain its rhythm and straightness, confidently navigating the obstacle with ease. In comparison, a tense horse will likely do one of two things: either stop or rush backwards (which would be considered a refusal, if it was a jump), or sidestep to avoid the obstacle (which would become a run out, if it was a jump).

In the moment you feel your horse tense on the approach to an obstacle (including hesitating or stepping sideways), halt your horse and wait for the tension to leave its body. Once your horse returns to a relaxed state, ask it for one step forward in a straight line; any attempt to move closer to the obstacle should be rewarded (see page 164). If

your horse maintains relaxation allow it to take another step, but if tension returns then make gradual progress through a series of isolated steps, allowing time for relaxation between every step. This slow but considerate approach allows the rider to slowly earn the horse's trust, while teaching it to stay straight and relaxed.

FOSTER A HORSE THAT TRIES, RATHER THAN QUITS: It's important that each attempt shows some improvement. As your horse learns to understands each micro-question and progresses, you can gradually expand your expectations, until it's able to navigate the entire obstacle in a relaxed manner. If, instead, you allow your horse to spook or avoid the obstacle, or become stubborn and switch off without working through it, your horse may learn that it can misbehave to avoid anything it perceives as scary or difficult in the future.

BREAK IT DOWN INTO SMALLER QUESTIONS: If your horse is struggling, break down the question into simpler steps; your expectations should be determined by your horse's body language (see page 54) — the more your horse is struggling, the smaller the questions you will need to ask of it. For example, rather than expecting a nervous horse to walk over a bridge on its first attempt, it might need this broken into several lessons, over several days; day one could be getting your horse to approach the bridge and stand in front of it in a relaxed manner; day two could be to step its front hooves up onto the bridge; and day three could be walking across the bridge.

HOPE FOR THE BEST, BUT PREPARE FOR THE WORST: While it's important not to micro-manage your horse, it's equally important to be ready to correct your horse's speed or direction at a moment's notice. Approach a new obstacle with short reins, but with soft hands, positioned slightly further forward than normal — this will ensure you're able to provide a correction the moment your horse starts to deviate from a straight approach. The longer your reins, and the faster you go, the less control you'll have over your horse.

KEEP IT SIMPLE: Set your horse up for success by working over simple obstacles first, then gradually build the degree of difficulty as your horse's confidence grows.

KEEP IT SAFE: It's also crucial to ensure you ask your horse to navigate only sturdy obstacles with a non-slip surface; if your horse is scared of an obstacle and the experience goes well, it will be more likely to trust you in the future, but if it goes wrong it will be less likely to trust you.

A variety of obstacles that you might find at Working Equitation or Cowboy Challenge events.

Types of obstacles

Basic obstacles that are beneficial to build at home, or that you may encounter in Cowboy Challenge, Working Equitation or Wild Horse competitions, include the following.

- **BRIDGE:** These can vary in length, width and height, and need to be solid to withstand the full weight of a horse, with a non-slip surface. They should be long enough for the horse to stand on with all four hooves, and can either be fixed or a teeter-totter style (tilting as the horse and rider cross it). A flat piece of plywood or carpet can be a good introductory obstacle to prepare your horse for a bridge.
- **HORSE BALL:** These balls are large and sturdy enough to withstand a horse hitting them. Usually the aim is to get the horse to move into the ball, pushing it with its chest or foreleg.
- **CAR WASH:** The horse must pass through foam noodles attached to two stands with the noodles creating a vertical wall, or with the noodles on a horizontal plane, at about the horse's chest height. It mimics the horse pushing through scrub.
- **BOX OR PEDESTAL:** A round or square platform, between 10 to 40 centimetres high, that the horse stands on with its front hooves (or with all four hooves for a more advanced option).
- **PIANO KEYS (ALSO KNOWN AS DOWNFALL):** A collection of logs or poles, fixed at irregular distances, for the horse to walk through. It mimics the horse needing to be surefooted when crossing rough terrain.
- **DRAGGING ITEMS:** A rope (long enough to keep the object away from the horse's hind hooves) is tied to an object, which can then be dragged behind the horse (or towards the horse, with the horse reining back away from the dragging object, for a more advanced option). It can be beneficial to try this while leading your horse on the ground first.
- **FLAG:** A flag on a flagpole positioned in a cone or stand, for the rider to pick up and carry to a set point, then place back into another cone or stand.
- **GATE:** Either a rope slung between two poles or a metal or wooden hinged gate, which is used to teach a horse how to open gates. Once the rider's hand comes into contact with the gate, they should open it, ride through it, and then shut it again (manoeuvring the horse with lateral movements, see pages 280–81). It mimics opening gates without having to dismount.
- **JUMPS:** These are usually lower than the horse's knee height and able to be jumped over from any pace. They may be solid (like a log, wall or barrel) or able to be knocked down (like poles set on jump stands). Ditches, banks or water jumps, which are typically seen in Cross Country (see Eventing, page 325), may also be used in an obstacle course.
- **CURTAIN:** An archway the horse passes under, with strips of fabric, ribbons, foam noodles or plastic hanging from it.
- **TARP:** A tarpaulin of any colour or size spread flat on the ground (and usually

Kelly working over obstacles at liberty with Conquistador, a wild Kaimanawa stallion she tamed in 2021.

pegged down) for the horse to be ridden over. Always be careful when riding a horse over a tarpaulin for the first time, especially if they aren't confident or of a spooky nature, as some horses can get a fright from the rustling noise and can leap suddenly (especially in windy conditions). If in doubt, teach them to lunge over a tarpaulin on the ground first.

Obstacle courses also use poles or markers placed at specific points to showcase your horse's body control (see page 156). These can include the following.

- **SIDE-PASS:** The horse straddles a single pole, while side-passing across it (or an 'L', 'V' or 'W' formation for more advanced options).
- **REIN-BACK:** The horse walks forward into a set of parallel poles, placed about 1 metre apart, and then rein-backs out of the poles (or through an 'L' formation for a more advanced option).
- **ROLL BACK:** The horse 'rolls' back along a fence line, at specific markers, by doing a 180-degree turn on the hindquarters or forehand to change direction.
- **360-DEGREE TURN:** The horse is asked to do a 360-degree turn on the hindquarters or forehand, within a confined area (often four poles positioned in a square).

JUMPING

Jumping position

Developing a correct jumping position will not only allow the horse to jump unhindered by the rider, but also enable it to use its body correctly. To jump effortlessly, the horse needs to be balanced on its hindquarters so it can lift its front hooves on take-off. While horses can naturally find this balance when free-jumping, an unbalanced rider, with a poor jumping position, can make it difficult for the horse to stay balanced and increase the chance of it refusing or running out, knocking rails, rushing into the fences, stalling or hesitating on take-off, drifting on the approach, twisting in mid-air or jumping with a poor technique.

This page: The four jumping positions: full seat, light seat, half seat and driving seat.

Opposite top: Amanda and Showtym Cassanova winning the New Zealand Speed Horse of the Year. KAMPIC

Opposite bottom: Vicki and Ngahiwi Showtym Premier competing at the New Zealand World Cup Finals. NED DAWSON

Therefore, it's your job to establish a secure position that allows your horse to find its natural balance over jumps. Once you have developed an independent seat, steady hands and a stable lower leg on the flat, you will need to master the four positions needed for jumping — full seat, light seat, half seat and driving seat.

THE FOUR POSITIONS

Riders use four positions at different stages of a jumping course, to adjust the quality of their horse's canter stride, to rebalance it as it approaches the jump, and then to allow the horse to use its body correctly in mid-air.

FULL SEAT: The full seat is the same as the position used in flatwork, with three points of contact with your horse — your seat, upper thighs and calves. Your upper body will be straight, with a correct ear-shoulder-hip-heel alignment. This position is usually used when going around corners, between the jumps and to rebalance the horse's canter.

LIGHT SEAT: In the light seat, your seat comes slightly out of the saddle and your upper body folds marginally forward, while keeping your shoulders tall and back. You will have only two points of contact with your horse — your upper thighs and your calves (which should maintain a hip-heel alignment). This position is usually used on the approach to the jump and on landing after the jump. *Top tip:* If you lean too far forward on the approach to the jumps, it will load your weight over your horse's shoulders and put it on the forehand. This will make it very difficult for the horse to jump well, as its front legs are the first things that need to come off the ground when jumping.

HALF SEAT (ALSO KNOWN AS TWO-POINT): Similar to the light seat, but with your body folding slightly further forward so that your hands can slide about halfway up your horse's neck to crest release (see page 301). This position is used as the horse takes off from the ground, and should be maintained as the horse soars through the air, with you returning to a light seat only after your horse's hind legs have landed. It is also used when galloping or riding up hills.

DRIVING SEAT: Similar to the full seat, but leaning slightly back (your spine may make a 'C' shape), with your seat and hips moving forwards in the saddle as if they are pushing a swing. The driving seat is seldom used, but is a good defensive position if your horse spooks, loses momentum into a jump, trips in front of a fence, or you desperately need extra speed or power to make it over the jump safely. Because this position places the rider at the back of the saddle, it should only be used when necessary; adopting a driving position too often can result in your horse rushing into the jumps or becoming sore (as your position is heavy on the horse's back).

Crest releasing allows the horse to use its body correctly while jumping.

Crest release

When you're jumping, it's important to soften the reins forwards to allow your horse to stretch its head and neck as it bascules over the fence. To do this, you need to slide your hands about halfway up the horse's neck, to lightly nestle on the crest (the upper ridge of the neck, where the mane grows). As you crest release, make sure you push your weight into your heels and have them lightly pressed against your horse's sides so your lower leg doesn't swing back as you jump.

Tips for improving your crest release

- When learning to jump it can be beneficial to tie a ribbon or hair tie halfway up your horse's mane, so that you know how far to slide your hands up the horse's crest as you jump. Initially, grab a handful of mane so that you're not relying on the reins for balance or yanking the horse in the mouth over the jump. Eventually you should be able to maintain a correct jumping position through core strength and a stable lower leg, without relying on your hands for balance.
- Once you have an established position, when and how much to crest release will depend on each individual horse and how expressive they are over a jump. If you're jumping a horse that you don't know, or a young horse that is learning to jump, hold the mane until you become accustomed to its unique jumping style.

HOW TO IMPROVE YOUR POSITION ON THE FLAT OR OVER JUMPS

ANOTHER PAIR OF EYES: The quickest way to improve your riding position is to have regular lessons so your instructor can advise you as needed. When you're just starting out, these corrections will need to be constant to prevent you developing bad habits which can take a lot of unlearning to fix. By learning correctly from the start, your body will become familiar with the feel of the right riding position and it will become second nature.

SELF-CRITIQUE: If you don't have a good instructor or can't afford regular lessons, it can be beneficial to have someone video you, so that you can self-critique your position. While reviewing footage, pause the video at each gait to check whether your ear–shoulder–hip–heel and elbow–hand–rein–bit alignment are correct on the flat. Over jumps, check you're using the correct jumping positions throughout the different parts of the course, and that you're crest releasing enough to ensure you are never pulling on the horse's mouth during take-off, in mid-air or on landing.

REPETITION: Over time, and with continual and correct practice, your riding position will become much more automatic and should be able to be done without thought, through muscle memory alone.

While muscle memory is beneficial, there is a downside to it. If you repeatedly do something *incorrectly*, then this will become your body's automatic response in similar situations and you will have developed a bad habit which can take a lot of effort and time to undo. That is why it is well worth getting the right training from the beginning, enlisting the best coaches you can afford.

PRACTISE OFF YOUR HORSE FIRST: Before you start to jump, it can be beneficial to practise changing between the four positions while you're standing on the ground. Once you have a grasp of them, mount your horse and practise them at the halt, then at the walk, trot and canter. When you are able to maintain these positions on the flat, without losing your balance or relying on the reins, practise them over a pole on the ground, then progress to a full course of poles. Once they become second nature, jumping will be a far more positive experience for both you and your horse, and you can progress to a small crossbar, then eventually a full course. If you still find you are getting ahead or behind your horse's movement over jumps, or are pulling on its mouth at any point on approach, take-off, in mid-air or on landing, you are not quite ready to jump, and should instead go back to improving your position on the flat or over poles.

WATCH TOP RIDERS ONLINE: By watching top-level jumping competitions online, such as the Olympics, Global Champions Tour or Nations Cup, you'll start to see where and when the world's top riders use the four different positions. Once you can see the pattern of when to change between the full seat, light seat, half seat and driving seat, you'll have a greater understanding of when to use each position and be able to replicate it more easily in your own riding.

Horse jumps

Whether you're wanting to attend a Pony Club rally, or compete in a showjumping, Show Hunter or eventing competition, a set of jumps will be necessary to train your horse. A basic horse jump is usually made from rails, jump cups and stands, which can be adjusted to vary the height, width and style of the obstacle. Multiple jumps can be used to create combinations, grids, related lines or entire courses (see pages 306–08).

Parts of a basic horse jump

POLES (ALSO KNOWN AS RAILS): These are posts, usually 10 centimetres in diameter and between 3 to 4.2 metres in length, used for horses to jump over. They are usually made from wood or UV-resistant polypropylene plastic.

STANDS AND JUMP CUPS: The sides of horse jumps, used to hold up the poles, are known as stands. They have holes — usually spaced about 5 centimetres apart — which jump cups slot into, to allow the height of the jump to be adjusted. While most cups have a dip for the pole to sit in, planks, walls and gates should be placed on flat cups.

Types of jumps (also known as fences)

The most commonly used jumps for training and competitions are as follows.

CAVALETTI: A traditional jump used for training that has a straight pole supported by an 'X' at either end. Unlike most jumps, cavalettis don't require stands or jump cups and can be set at only three heights (about 15, 30 and 45 centimetres) by turning the 'X'.

CROSSBAR (ALSO KNOWN AS A CROSS RAIL): An X-shaped fence formed by two poles that cross in a diagonal to form a low point in the middle. These are one of the first jumps that an inexperienced horse or rider will learn to navigate. At jumping competitions, a crossbar is usually used in the warm-up arena, even at the highest levels.

VERTICAL (ALSO KNOWN AS AN UPRIGHT): A straight fence formed by horizontal poles. It can have one or multiple poles in jump cups, a drop bar (a pole that rests in a cup on one side and on the ground on the other side), and/or a ground line (a pole placed on the ground, about 15 to 30 centimetres in front of the fence on the side you are approaching from, used to help the horse judge its take-off distance).

OXER: A wide jump, formed by having a vertical or crossbar in front, with a second set of stands and a single pole behind. As a general rule the back rail should be placed no wider than the height of the jump and 5 to 10 centimetres higher than the front rail (if it is placed at the same height, it is known as a square oxer).

TRIPLE BAR: An ascending spread, formed by having a smaller vertical or crossbar in front, with two additional sets of stands and poles behind, staggered in height. As a general rule these gradually ascend, with the back rail placed no wider from the front rail than the height of the jump.

PLANKS: Planks of wood can be used instead of rails and positioned on flat-jump cups (so they are easier to knock off). A plank jump usually consists of three or four planks and is built as a vertical; if used in an oxer or triple bar, the top rail/s should always be a pole, never a plank.

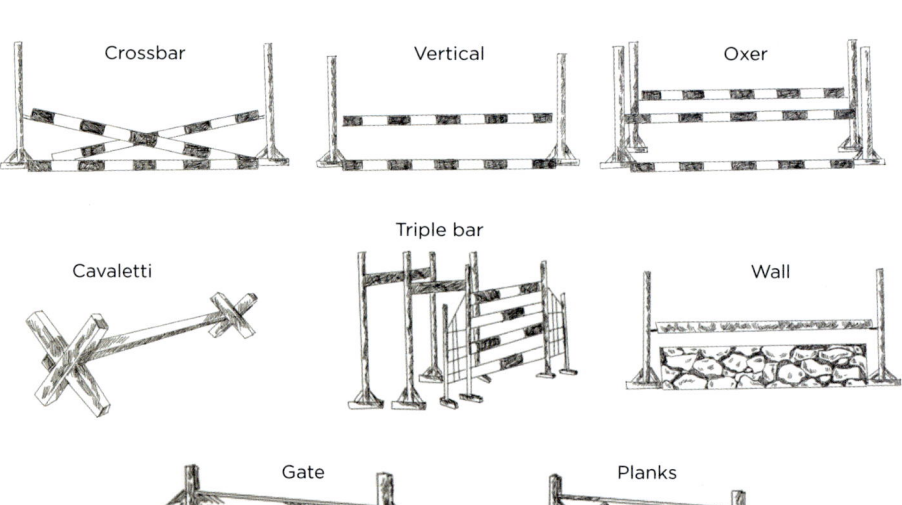

Types of horse jumps.

WALL: Traditionally made from lightweight wood and painted to resemble a brick or stone wall. They are constructed from blocks that can be layered to adjust the height.

FILLERS: Fillers are used to make a jump more attractive and challenging for your horse and are usually placed under a vertical or oxer.

- **WALL:** Smaller, lighter walls that hang on flat-jump cups.
- **GATES:** A filler constructed out of lightweight wood to resemble a gate, usually left rustic or painted white.
- **LIVERPOOL:** A small pool of water that sits underneath a jump. Liverpools are generally blue and made from vinyl, making them both portable and flexible if a horse stands on them.

Types of cross-country jumps

The most commonly used jumps for the Cross Country phase of eventing are listed below. Regardless of whether you event or not, cross-country jumps are fun to train over and can increase your horse's jumping confidence for any discipline.

LOG: One of the simplest jumps on a cross-country course, made from the trunk of a felled tree. They are usually placed on the ground or on stumps, or two logs may be used to form an oxer or combination.

BANKS: Banks or steps that require the horse to jump up or down to higher or lower ground. A bank may be presented as a single bank or as a combination (two or more in a row).

BRUSH: A solid box-style jump with brush (usually tea tree, spruce or cedar) on top, which makes the jump appear higher than it is; the brush, however, will give as the horse 'brushes' its legs through it.

DITCH: A shallow, rectangular hole in the ground, with poles on either side, designed for the horse to jump over. If a pole is placed *over* the ditch it is known as a trakahner, while a wall or brush *behind* the ditch is known as a palisade.

CORNER (ALSO KNOWN AS AN APEX): These jumps are in the shape of a triangle, from a bird's-eye view. It is a technical jump as the horse needs to jump as close to the point/apex of the corner as possible.

HOGSBACK: Three poles or logs, built with the middle pole being the highest and the outer poles being equally lower.

DROP DOWNS: This jump combines a log and bank, in which the horse jumps over a log that rests on the top of a bank so it lands on lower ground.

ROLL TOP: A relatively simple cross-country fence designed in the shape of a half-barrel.

SKINNY: A very narrow jump that requires accuracy from the rider.

RAMP: Similar to a wall, but with an ascending surface which looks like a right-angle triangle from the side, and can only be jumped from one direction.

STONE WALL: A wall built from stones or bricks.

WATER JUMP: An expanse of water, no more than 35 centimetres deep and surrounded by elements (including banks and drop downs) that the horse has to jump into and out of.

Setting up jumps

Polework

Working your horse over poles is beneficial for establishing balance, rhythm and stride length, as well as improving your horse's strength and fitness. The placement of the poles should match your horse's natural stride, although experienced riders will intentionally adjust the distance between the poles once their horse is confident, to encourage it to lengthen and shorten its stride.

WALKING POLES: At least three poles, set 0.8 to 0.9 metres apart for ponies, or 0.9 to 1 metre apart for horses.

TROTTING POLES: At least three poles, set 0.9 to 1.4 metres apart for ponies, or 1.2 to 1.5 metres apart for horses.

CANTER POLES: At least three poles, set 2.4 to 2.8 metres apart for ponies, or 3 to 3.3 metres apart for horses.

Jumping

Jumping can improve your horse's suppleness and strength, as well as provide variety to its weekly routine, no matter your chosen discipline.

DOES YOUR HORSE ENJOY JUMPING?

Most horses have the ability to jump, although not every horse enjoys it. If your horse becomes highly anxious, tense or stubborn while jumping, there is likely an underlying reason it struggles with the concept of jumping, which can include an undetected injury or illness, poor saddle fit, dental issues or even an incorrect rider position. These horses may need diagnostic work to help determine the cause. If nothing is obvious, a second opinion may need to be sought, or the horse may benefit from being schooled by a professional. *Note:* Although experienced riders may be able to get good results with a sore horse, it will likely regress again if underlying issues are present.

Top: Correctly placed trotting poles will allow your horse's hooves to land in the middle between each pole.

Bottom: Correctly placed canter poles will allow your horse to maintain its natural canter rhythm.

COMBINATIONS: A set of jumps set up on a straight line, allowing for a specific number of strides between each jump, plus room for take-off and landing. The standard stride length that is used in jumping competitions is 12 feet or 3.66 metres for horses, and 11 feet or 3.35 metres for ponies. Generally half a stride (6 feet or 1.83 metres for horses, or 5 feet 6 inches or 1.68 metres for ponies) is then added for both take-off and landing.

LINES	PONY FEET	PONY METRES	HORSE FEET	HORSE METRES
1 stride	22 feet	6.70 metres	24 feet	7.30 metres
2 strides	33 feet	10.05 metres	36 feet	10.95 metres
3 strides	44 feet	13.40 metres	48 feet	14.65 metres
4 strides	55 feet	16.75 metres	60 feet	18.30 metres
5 strides	66 feet	20.10 metres	72 feet	21.95 metres
6 strides	77 feet	23.50 metres	84 feet	25.60 metres
7 strides	88 feet	26.80 metres	96 feet	29.25 metres

There are many variations of a combination.
- **BOUNCE:** At least two small jumps, usually crossbars or uprights, with enough room for take-off and landing only (with no strides between). They should be set 2.9 to 3.3 metres apart for ponies or up to 3.3 to 3.6 metres apart for horses, depending on the natural length of its canter stride.
- **ONE-STRIDE DOUBLE:** Two jumps with enough room for the horse to take a single stride between them.
- **TWO-STRIDE DOUBLE:** Two jumps with enough room for the horse to take two strides between them.
- **TRIPLE:** Three jumps in a row, with enough room for the horse to take one or two strides between each jump.
- **GRID:** A combination of polework and jumps, with four or more jumps set up on a straight line, with varying strides between. Grids are used to practise your position and balance, improve your horse's strength and fitness, or to slow down or balance a horse that rushes over jumps or uses its body incorrectly. A simple grid uses basic jumps (with no fillers) and may include three trot poles, followed by two crossbars set as a bounce, followed by a vertical set one stride apart, and then onto an oxer set two strides apart. When training a horse through a grid, introduce each jump gradually; start with the entire grid as poles on the ground to check that the stride length suits your horse and to allow it to gain confidence, then raise the first fence into a crossbar, gradually adding in more elements.

RELATED LINES (ALSO KNOWN AS RELATED DISTANCES): A related line is formed by placing two jumps on a straight line, usually between 3 to 8 strides apart.

BROKEN LINES: A broken line is formed by placing two jumps on an offset or curved line, usually between 3 to 8 strides apart.

HOW TO MEASURE STRIDES

Course designers follow basic rules when measuring strides, to allow horses to get a set number of strides between combinations and related lines. The striding is important since the jumps are set so close together; how you jump the first fence will influence your take-off distance (see pages 310–11) to the second. Because of this, it's important to walk the course to measure the strides between jumps to help you determine how many strides your horse will naturally fit between the two elements. If the distance doesn't suit your horse's canter stride (enabling it to take a smooth number of strides to reach an ideal take-off spot), you will need to adjust your horse's canter. For example, if you walked a related line at 4.5 strides, you will either need to lengthen your horse's canter stride to fit in a smooth 4 strides, or shorten it to fit in a smooth 5 strides. For a broken line you could instead change the line you ride, by taking a shallower or deeper turn.

To measure the distances between the jumps, calibrate your walking steps so four human strides matches the length of one horse stride: make your step 3 feet or 91 centimetres for horses, or take a slightly shorter stride of 84 centimetres for ponies. To measure one horse stride you need to pace out four steps, then add two steps for both take-off and landing. For example, you would take eight human steps for a one-stride double: 2 steps (take-off) + 4 steps (1 stride [1 x 4] = 4 steps) + 2 steps (landing), or 32 steps for a 7-stride related line: 2 steps (take-off) + 7 x 4 (7 strides [7 x 4] = 28 steps) + 2 steps (landing).

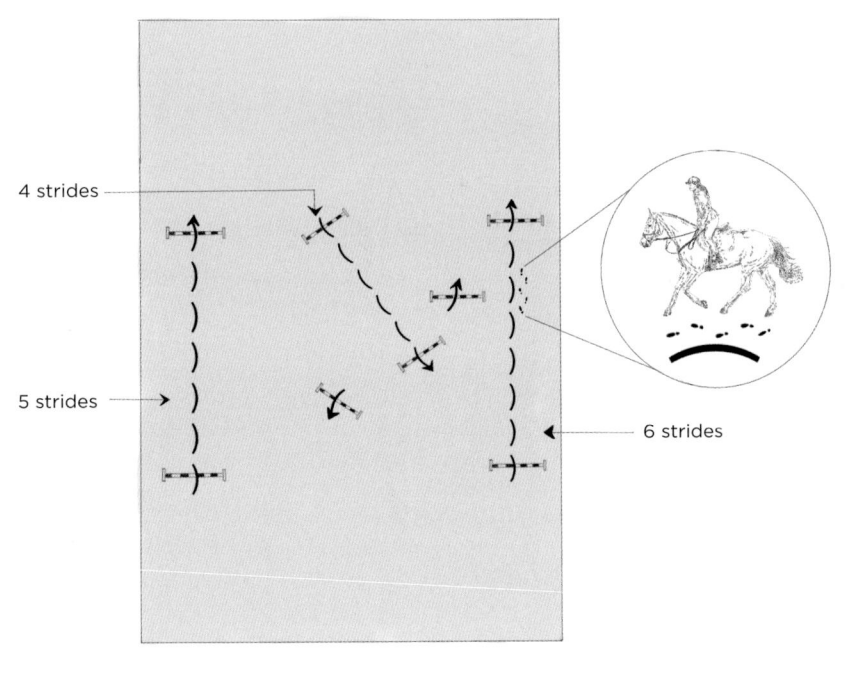

HEIGHT OF JUMP
DEEP DISTANCE
GOOD DISTANCE
Height of jump x 1-1.5
LONG DISTAN

TAKE-OFF AND LANDING DISTANCE: To get a good bascule (the round arc the horse takes over a fence), your horse should take off and land at an equal distance on either side of the fence. To achieve this, the horse should take off within the 'ideal take-off zone'. This zone is positioned on the ground in front of the jump, at about 1 to 1.5 times the height of the fence (usually equal distance, 1:1, for showjumping). As a general rule of thumb, if a jump is set at 1 metre, the horse should ideally take off 1 to 1.5 metres out from the fence.

There are three types of distances:

- **GOOD DISTANCE:** If your horse takes off within the ideal take-off zone, this is a *good* distance. It usually feels very smooth to sit to and allows the horse to correctly bascule over the fence.
- **LONG DISTANCE:** If your horse takes off before the ideal take-off zone, this is a *long* distance. This distance can feel and appear quite jarring, as the horse will have to launch from quite far away from the jump, often causing an inexperienced rider to tip backwards. If the jump is wide, like an oxer or a triple bar, a long distance can also cause the horse to knock the back rail as it will struggle to clear the width of the jump.
- **DEEP DISTANCE:** If your horse takes off after the ideal take-off zone, this is a *deep* distance. This distance may feel like you're being double-bounced on a trampoline, with your body going against the horse's movement as it takes off. This can be because the horse's stride has gotten in too close to the fence, or it may have had to *chip in* (take an abrupt, shorter stride) because it got to an 'impossibly long' distance and had to add a short stride to clear the jump.

Until you develop your eye (the ability to see your take-off distance early, on the approach to the fence) and are able to adjust your horse's canter stride to correct a long or deep distance, your distances may be inconsistent and messy. This is why good flatwork, strength and fitness are so important when it comes to jumping; when a rider is able to produce a good-quality canter and stay on a relaxed rhythm, it becomes much easier to see a distance.

It is important to understand that even at Olympic level, riders still get all three distances. It usually doesn't matter what take-off spot you get, so long as you have a good-quality canter on the approach to the jump to support the distance that your horse gets.

Every horse has its own unique way of going, so it's your job as the rider to gauge any weaknesses your horse may have and improve its canter quality to make its job easier when jumping. This can be achieved by the following.

- **AN ADJUSTABLE STRIDE:** Although horses generally canter on a 12-foot stride, and ponies canter on a 10- or 11-foot stride, you can train your horse to have many different canter lengths by collecting and lengthening its canter during your flatwork and when training over poles. The more adjustable the canter, the easier it will be to lengthen or shorten your horse's canter stride to reach the distance you see.

Top: Example of a good take-off distance, relevant to the height of the jump. Anywhere between 1–1.5 times the height of the jump is the ideal take-off zone, resulting in a *good* distance. Anywhere after that (closer to the jump) is a *deep* distance. Anywhere before that (further away from the jump) is a *long* distance.

Bottom: A correct take-off distance will result in the horse landing equal distance after the fence.

- **A STEADY RHYTHM:** To see the take-off distance from several strides in front of the fence, your horse needs to be able to maintain a steady rhythm. If it speeds up or slows down approaching the fence, it is very hard to see what distance you will get. A steady rhythm should be established in your flatwork, then over poles, before progressing to a course of jumps.
- **A RELAXED HORSE:** An excited or agitated horse will have poor rideability, making it difficult to maintain a rhythm or adjust the length of its stride when needed. It is always important to foster relaxation while training your horse; if it gets tense or worried when being asked to jump, change your focus to flatwork and polework until it can canter around a whole course of poles on a soft contact while keeping a relaxed rhythm (if this doesn't help, do diagnostic work to see if the issues are pain related). Only then are you ready to try jumping again; start with just one jump and once your horse is able to maintain relaxation, progress to a full course.
- **A STRAIGHT APPROACH:** To give yourself the best chance of getting a good distance, it's important to approach the jump on a straight line, without the horse drifting or wobbling. You shouldn't still be turning as the horse takes off; if you try to jump off a turn, your horse will likely drift through its outside shoulder, resulting in it running off the jump or knocking a rail (as the horse's front legs will tuck up unevenly).
- **GOOD CORNERS:** Ride 'square corners' (90-degree angles) whenever possible, to ensure that you have as much time as possible to approach each jump on a straight line. You can teach your horse to ride square corners on the flat, before jumps are introduced, so that your horse understands how to correctly use its body through a turn. If your horse drifts through the corners this will greatly affect your ability to see a distance. When warming up, ensure you ride deep into the corners of the arena to prepare your horse; if you allow your horse to cut corners in its flatwork, you are training it to cut corners while jumping. For horses that anticipate the turn or drift, it can be useful to halt in the corners, to break this habit.

Left: A good corner, with a 90-degree corner, made in plenty of time for the horse to approach the jump on a straight line.

Right: Examples of bad corners.

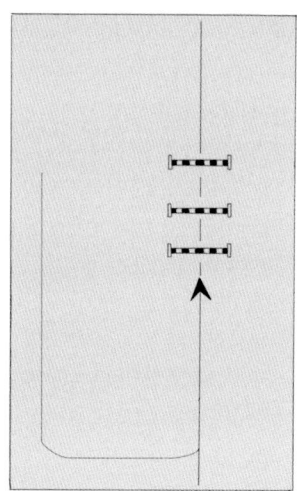
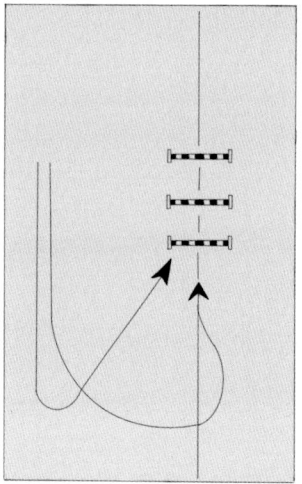

Learning to jump

Whether it's the horse or rider learning to jump, it's important to foster confidence so that jumping becomes enjoyable for you both.

Before you start jumping, you should already:
- Have an independent riding position, with a stable lower leg and steady hands.
- Be able to maintain straightness and rhythm at each pace.
- Be confident working over a course of poles at a trot and canter while changing between the four jumping positions.

Other things to consider, when learning to jump, include the following.
- It's easier for a young or inexperienced horse to learn to jump with an experienced, capable rider.
- It's easier for an inexperienced rider to learn to jump on a schoolmaster or schoolmistress (see page 14).
- Stay within an enclosed paddock or arena while learning how to jump.
- Have an experienced rider or trainer present, to offer instruction as needed.
- Horses don't reach physical maturity until about 6 years old, so any jumping before then needs to be minimal and done within a careful management plan to ensure the horse's long-term soundness (see Development of the equine skeleton, page 42).

How to teach your horse to jump

When you're teaching a young or inexperienced horse to jump, it's important to foster relaxation and straightness from their very first jumping attempt. The following steps work for horses learning to jump (ideally under the guidance of an experienced rider), as well as inexperienced riders wanting to try jumping for the first time (ideally on an experienced horse).

JUMPS AS OBSTACLES

To begin with, treat every jump like an obstacle (see page 293). They should be less than 30 centimetres high and approached from a walk, so that your horse requires only a slightly elevated step to clear it, rather than having to actually jump. More importantly, if your horse refuses, the jump will be small enough that you can ask your horse to walk over it from a halt so it learns how to be 'honest' and trust you enough to attempt something even when it's unsure.

- **LOOK UP:** As you approach the jump or obstacle it is important to look up, beyond the jump, rather than at it. On landing, change your focus to where you are riding next; whether it's to another jump, or to a set point in the distance. Looking down at the jump will encourage your horse to drop its energy and lose impulsion, often resulting in the horse stopping or hesitating on take-off, in mid-air or on landing.
- **KEEP YOUR HORSE STRAIGHT:** To avoid a run out, aim for the middle of the jump and imagine that there is an invisible 'V' fanning out in front of it which

your horse must not cross. If you feel your horse starting to deviate left or right on the approach, use the opposite rein to straighten it. If the horse ignores you and continues to deviate from the straight line, halt and turn it back to the jump (without circling away) while it is only one walking stride wrong, rather than waiting until it has taken several strides in the wrong direction and crosses the invisible 'V'.

- **KEEP YOUR LEG ON**: Once you have your horse in front of the jump, press your legs against its sides on take-off and simultaneously move into your half-seat jumping position, sliding your hands up the horse's neck to crest release (for nervous or inexperienced riders, holding the mane is recommended). Keep your legs gently squeezed on your horse's sides all the way over the jump and on landing so it doesn't lose impulsion over the fence.

SMALL JUMPS

Once your horse can maintain a rhythmical walk over a jump, and you have mastered your jumping position, approach the same fence, at the same height, at the trot.

- **MAINTAIN A STEADY RHYTHM**: Make sure you have an active trot established well before the jump, and maintain a steady rhythm both into and away from the jump. If you allow your horse to slow down or stop on landing, it can start to anticipate the downward transition on its approach to the jump and may start hesitating on take-off. Your energy and focus shouldn't finish at the jump, but rather at the corner after the jump.
- **INCREASE THE HEIGHT**: Once you and your horse are confident, raise the height of the jumps to about 30 to 40 centimetres so that your horse will need to make more effort and properly jump over them. At this early stage, the jumps should still be lower than your horse's knee height so that they are small enough to step over from a standstill if your horse refuses.
- **FOLLOW THE LEADER**: It can be very helpful in the early stages of jumping to play 'follow the leader' around a small course of poles or low jumps; not only will this improve your steering and impulsion, but it will also help your horse gain confidence by following the example of another horse and rider (or even a person walking or running on the ground) in front of you. Your horse will need to learn to work independently, but for the first attempt or two it can be easier on your horse if it can follow someone. Be careful, though, as this can give you a false sense of your ability — it is unlikely that your horse will be able to jump the same height and type of jumps independently as it can when following a horse or person. *Note:* If you are following behind someone, leave at least two horse-lengths between you and them (about 5 metres).
- **ADD VARIETY**: Once your horse is able to confidently navigate logs and uprights you can introduce small oxers, fillers or even cross-country jumps. You don't want to put your horse in a position where it can stop, though, so keep these jumps low (under the height of your horse's knees). If you feel your horse tense, by

Top four: Showing your horse a 'spooky' jump, such as a wall or filler, can build its confidence so it is more likely to jump it on the first attempt, rather than refusing.

Bottom: The rider looks ahead to the next jump.

either hesitating or spooking sideways, slow your horse and approach the jump like it's an obstacle, asking it to walk over it from a standstill if needed.
- **INCREASE IMPULSION:** When your horse is able to maintain straightness and rhythm while trotting over a variety of jumps, progress to trotting in and asking the horse to land in a canter. This may require you to approach the jump with a faster trot so that your horse has enough power to pick up a canter lead. Build on this further by getting your horse to canter into the jumps.

INCREASE THE HEIGHTS

Once you and your horse are able to jump without changing your speed and rhythm in front of the fence, you're ready for something higher. Gradually build up the size of the fences, then allow yourself time to consolidate at each height. A few one-off fences at a higher height is fine, but treat jumping a bit like a yo-yo: if you are confident jumping 70 centimetres, try only a few jumps at 80 centimetres before dropping back to the height you're comfortable with. If you keep pushing your or your horse's comfort zone too quickly, you risk over-facing either yourself or your horse, which will increase the likelihood of refusing, crashing through the jump, taking a rail or losing your confidence.

START COMPETING

Once you are confident jumping at home, you can extend yourself by entering competitions; start with training days, then progress to local competitions (see page 323).

COMPETITION

While becoming a skilled rider and enjoying your horse at home or out on the trails might be your highest level of ambition, others will enjoy the challenge of competition. Competing a horse not only gives you both purpose, allows you to socialise with other horses and riders, changes up your routine and offers you something to strive towards, but it can also strengthen the relationship you have with your horse due to the time spent together training and at competitions.

Many horses have an innate competitiveness and desire to please and, when channelled correctly, the competition arena can allow their unique personalities and talents to shine. Some will excel as allrounders due to their average talent but above-average versatility, while others may show specific traits for a particular discipline; whether it be the movement for dressage, the athleticism for showjumping, the bravery for eventing, the beauty for showing or the rhythm and style for Show Hunter.

While competing can be a huge commitment of your time and money, it fosters many skills which will help you in every facet of your life, including future career options. These include setting goals and upskilling to reach them, problem-solving when things go wrong, organisational skills to manage the time and money involved with entering, preparing and competing at shows, and a high level of presentation and attention to detail.

Competition can also allow the rider's abilities to shine. The further you progress in the sport, the more opportunities there will be for you. Top-level riders can get huge sponsorship endorsements, have the opportunity to represent their country on the world stage, or even turn their love of horses into a successful career.

Entering a show

In New Zealand, the competition season primarily runs in spring, summer and early autumn, with winter series being offered during the off-season. Every region has a local event calendar, featuring a wide range of shows held across different disciplines, so most weekends there will be many options to choose from. While some events allow you to enter on the day, most require you to enter well in advance.

Here are some important things to consider.

- **CALENDAR OF EVENTS**: There are different calendars of events available for both local and national competitions. Visit the Equestrian Sports New Zealand (ESNZ) website for the national calendar or ask your local saddlery or Pony Club where you can access your regional calendar. The calendars will let you know what competitions are on, where they are located, how to enter and the deadline for entries.
- **MAKE SURE YOUR PAPERWORK IS UP TO DATE**: Many disciplines require the horse and rider to have an annual registration with ESNZ, or a height certificate, in order to compete. Make sure your paperwork is up to date at the start of the season.

What to pack for a show

The following packing list will help ensure you have everything you need at a show so you can pack quickly and efficiently. While you may not need everything on this list, depending on your chosen discipline or the level you're competing at, it's a good starting point.

- **PAPERWORK**: A copy of your entries and the schedule, any paperwork required for you or your horse (including height certificates and registration papers), the address of the show, and spare paper and pens.
- **FOR THE RIDER**: Helmet, riding apparel (including jodhpurs or riding tights, riding shirt, jacket, belt, socks, riding boots and/or chaps, gaiters or jodhpur clips, gloves and a hair net), safety vest (required for Cross Country), wet weather gear (including white waterproof riding pants that you can compete in), a sunhat and sunblock, personal items (including make-up, brush, hair ties, hair spray and a mirror), a human first aid kit, drinking water and food (or money to buy food if the show offers food stands), camping chair, torch, casual clothes (to wear when you're not riding) and bedding (if you are staying overnight). Miscellaneous items like safety pins, scissors, a lint roller and a sewing kit may also come in handy.

- **FOR THE HORSE:** Halter and lead (including a spare set in case one breaks), grooming kit (including a range of brushes, hoof pick, braiding supplies, make-up, coat conditioner or baby oil, hoof oil, sponge, shampoo and conditioner, sweat scraper and a towel), saddlery (saddle and saddle cover, saddle pads, girth, bridle and bit, jumping boots, breastplate or martingale, spurs or a whip and leather-care supplies), bandages and leg wraps or stable boots, studs and a stud kit, lunge line and lunge whip, cover and show kit (hood, tail bag, show rug), mucking-out equipment (see box, page 69), buckets, feed (including hard feed, hay and supplements), water and an equine first aid kit.

Preparing for your first competition

Competing at your first show requires careful preparation. This is even more important if your horse has never competed either, as it will need to learn to cope with crowds, trade stands, signage, working in unfamiliar arenas, travelling to the showgrounds (see page 194) and possibly being yarded overnight (see page 199).

INTRODUCING NEW ENVIRONMENTS: Working your horse at local arenas will allow both of you to get used to new environments, and will also give you an opportunity to work through any issues that may develop. If your horse is inexperienced or spooky, begin by letting it look at any jumps, signage and obstacles in the arena, allowing it to approach and sniff anything it might be scared of. From there, ask your horse to maintain a rhythm around the outside of the arena, until you can complete a full lap without it drifting or spooking off any of the sides or corners. At a real competition you usually won't have a chance to do this, so make the most of training opportunities to increase your horse's confidence in unfamiliar environments. Once your horse is confident, continue as if it were a normal training session, working on anything you have been practising at home.

EXPOSURE TO A SHOW ATMOSPHERE: Once your horse is confident leaving your property, it can be beneficial to introduce it to a show environment so it gets used to other horses coming and going around it, as well as the hustle and bustle of people. A good introduction is to take your horse to a local show and lead or ride it between the trucks and trailers, then stand quietly at the ringside while you watch, allowing it to soak in the atmosphere without the added pressure of having to compete. Attending Pony Club or an adult riding club event is also a great way to foster relaxation in a busy environment.

TRAINING DAYS: Once you feel like you're ready for your first competition, start by attending a training day. Something going wrong at a local outing with only a few spectators is going to be less stressful than if it happens in front of a large crowd. These events are usually quite relaxed and if you have issues the show organisers may allow someone into the ring to help you.

If you're planning to jump, enter a class much lower than what you've been practising; generally 10 to 20 centimetres lower than what you're jumping around a full course at home. As you increase in experience you'll be able to enter higher

Previous spread: Amanda and Showtym Viking competing in the Grand Prix at Woodhill Sands, which gains them points towards the ESNZ Grand Prix Series.

Opposite page: Amanda and Woodbine Legacy competing in the 7-Year-Old class at the Tauranga World Cup Finals, which gains them points towards the ESNZ 7-Year-Old Series.

classes. A good gauge for your capabilities is how frequently you are able to jump around a course clear. If you consecutively have three clear rounds at a set height, say 80 centimetres, you're probably ready to try the next height. Extend your horse by jumping 80 centimetres at the next training day in its first round, then step up to 90 centimetres for your second round. Horses should only compete in one to two showjumping classes per day, so drop back to 80 centimetres on the second day of competition (or at the next show) to keep your horse confident. Once you've done this a few times, and are consistently jumping clear at the higher height, you'll be ready to go straight into 90 centimetres without a warm-up class.

LOCAL COMPETITIONS: Pony Club competitions can be a good place to start as they are suited to lower-level riders (including those on a lead rein). They usually have a more relaxed dress code, fewer rules and cheaper entry fees, and are generally held over one day, so you don't have to worry about yarding your horse overnight. They also offer many different disciplines including Ribbon Days (which include both flat and hunter classes), Show Hunter, showjumping, eventing (at Pony Club level these are known as an ODE or One Day Event), dressage and games. Because they cater to riders of all levels, including those just starting out, they are a good place to gain experience, become accustomed to the rules of each discipline, and also discover what type of competitions you most enjoy.

From there, you can attend local shows or mini-circuits (where riders accumulate regional points and prize money over a series of shows). Most local shows are hosted by regional committees and follow the rules of ESNZ, requiring both horse and rider to have an annual registration or to pay a day registration levy.

NATIONAL COMPETITIONS: In many disciplines (including showjumping, Show Hunter, eventing and dressage) there are national series hosted by ESNZ, which offer prize money and also allow horses and riders to accumulate points towards the national leaderboard (or even qualify for prestigious competitions like Horse of the Year). These shows are hosted in every region, with the top riders often travelling the length of the country to follow the national circuit.

ESNZ competitions cater to a wide range of levels, with series classes suited for young horses and junior or amateur riders, right through to professional athletes. At the highest levels, riders can compete in FEI classes (see page 324), which gain you points towards the world rankings, or even earn you the opportunity to represent your country.

INTERNATIONAL COMPETITIONS: When riders reach the highest level of national competition, many will campaign internationally to gain the experience and qualifications needed to represent their country. The most prestigious events to gain qualifications for include the following.

- **OLYMPICS:** The Olympics is held every four years and offers individual and team medals for dressage, showjumping and eventing, as well as para-equestrian dressage.

Vicki winning the 6-Year-Old Horse of the Year title on Equador MVNZ, at the New Zealand Horse of the Year Show. NED DAWSON

- **WORLD EQUESTRIAN GAMES:** WEG is held every four years — in the middle of the Olympics cycle — and combines eight equestrian disciplines, including dressage, showjumping, eventing, driving, vaulting, endurance and reining, as well as para-equestrian dressage.
- **FEI:** The Federation Equestre Internationale is the international governing body of equestrian sports and was founded in 1921. It represents nine equestrian disciplines including dressage, showjumping, eventing, driving, vaulting, reining and endurance, as well as para-dressage and para-driving. Each year it hosts international competitions, in which riders gain points towards the FEI World Ranking, including the FEI World Cup Finals which brings together the best riders in the world.

Etiquette for the warm-up arena

When you are riding in a small area with lots of other horses, like the warm-up arena at a horse show, there are rules you need to follow to keep yourself and your horse safe.

Here are some important rules to help you navigate a crowded ring.

- Try to ride in the same direction as the other riders. If that is not possible, pass left hand to left hand, leaving enough room to ensure that the horse on the outside of the ring doesn't feel crowded.
- Stay a safe distance from other horses at all times. To avoid being kicked, this should be at least two horse lengths, and more if the horse is wearing a coloured ribbon in its tail. *Top tip:* A red ribbon will let other riders know your horse is prone to kicking, while a green ribbon will indicate that your horse is young or inexperienced; both types of horses should be given more space to avoid a potential injury.
- Always keep an eye out for where other people and horses are riding. Never ride behind a jump, or cut in front of a horse approaching a jump.
- If lots of horses are in the ring, call for your practice fence (for example, 'coming to the oxer'), just in case someone else is also aiming at the same jump.
- Never approach a jump if someone is changing the height of the fence, or is standing in front or behind it. Wait until they have finished before approaching.
- Practice jumps will be flagged to indicate which direction they should be jumped from; always jump with the red flag on your right.
- For showjumping, enter the warm-up arena about 8 to 10 horses before your turn (this will generally allow you 20 minutes in the practice ring). Prior to this, your horse should only be walked around or trotted on a loose rein to loosen them up. Spend the first 10 minutes doing flatwork, then move onto jumping a crossbar, followed by a small upright and oxer, and finish by jumping an upright and oxer at the same height as you'll be competing in the ring. Ideally you should only jump six to ten practice fences — any more than this will fatigue your horse or may make it sour.

Types of competition

On the flat

DRESSAGE: Dressage (which means training in French) is an Olympic and FEI sport where the horse is judged on its obedience, flexibility and balance, while performing a series of movements in a dressage arena. At high levels, dressage can be performed to music and will feature intricate movements like the piaffe, passage and tempi changes.

SHOWING: Showing is an equestrian discipline where the horse is judged on its conformation, looks, manners and paces, while working on a circle with other horses and riders. In some classes, the judge will then call the best horses into the middle of the ring to perform an individual workout. The overall picture of the horse and rider should be pleasing to the eye, and the horse should have soft, active and ground-covering strides, good rhythm and impulsion, and work on a contact with a well-rounded topline. There are three main categories in showing, depending on the build of the horse and the thickness of its bones: show horses (fine bone), riding horses (medium bone) or saddle hunters (heavy bone).

Jumping

SHOW HUNTER (ALSO KNOWN AS HUNTER OR HUNTER JUMPER): Show Hunter horses are judged on their style over a fence and their rhythm between the fences. These competitions also include Equitation classes, which are judged primarily on the rider's position and etiquette. Hunters generally jump between 60 centimetres and 1 metre for ponies, and 70 centimetres to 1.15 metres for horses.

SHOWJUMPING (ALSO KNOWN AS JUMPING): Showjumping is an Olympic and FEI sport where the horses are generally judged on speed over a timed course of jumps. Jumpers generally have more energy, power and speed than hunters. The jumps range from 70 centimetres in training classes, through to 1.30 metres for ponies and 1.60 metres for horses at the highest levels.

EVENTING (ALSO KNOWN AS ONE-, TWO- OR THREE-DAY EVENTING): Eventing is an Olympic and FEI sport where riders compete in three disciplines: Dressage, Cross Country and Showjumping. These are generally run as one-day events at Pony Club level or two- or three-day events at higher levels. At one-day events the jumps can range from as low as 40 centimetres to 1.05 metres, while at FEI events they generally range from 80 centimetres through to 1.30 metres.

WORKING HUNTER AND HUNTER CLASSES: Working Hunter and Hunter classes are a part of the showing discipline; horses are judged on their conformation, manners, paces and jumping technique while jumping around a course of walls, brush jumps and wire. Overall, the picture that the horse and rider make should be pleasing to the eye, and the horse should have soft, active and ground-covering strides, good rhythm and impulsion, and work on a contact with a well-rounded topline and a nice bascule over the jumps.

Other types of equestrian competitions

POLO: Polo, known as the Sport of Kings, is a ball game played on horseback by two opposing teams of four riders. Players score goals by using a long-handled wooden mallet to hit a small, hard ball into the opposition's goal. Even though they are traditionally horse-sized, the horses used in polo are referred to as polo ponies. Polo Cross, which has six players per team, is also popular, and combines the concepts of polo and lacrosse.

VAULTING: Equestrian vaulting is an FEI sport, which is the equivalent of gymnastics and dance on horseback. Individuals or teams perform intricate movements on a cantering horse, which is controlled by a person in the centre of a circle, called a lunger. Large, sturdy horses with mild temperaments and rhythmical gaits are ideal for vaulting.

DRIVING (ALSO KNOWN AS COMBINED DRIVING): Driving is an adrenaline-fuelled FEI sport, in which horses or ponies are driven in harness instead of being ridden. Like eventing, driving has three phases: dressage, marathon (where the horse crosses diverse types of terrain, including water) and cones (the horse is driven through a course of cones).

HUNTING (KNOWN AS FOX HUNTING IN USA AND EUROPE): A winter sport in which horses, riders and a pack of hounds chase a hare (or fox) across the countryside, jumping fences and spars to move between paddocks. Participants must follow the Master (who wears a red jacket) and adhere to the traditional rules and etiquette of hunting, including attending a 'breakfast' at the conclusion of the day. In modern times, drag hunting is also popular, in which riders follow the trail of an artificial scent, rather than hunting a live animal.

ENDURANCE: Endurance is an FEI sport, in which horses compete in long-distance races against the clock. The horses need to be very fit and have a high level of stamina, as they cover a wide variety of terrain and will usually travel between 40 and 160 kilometres in a single day of competition. There is a strong emphasis on the welfare of the horses, and they are vet-checked at least every 40 kilometres to ensure they finish each phase in good condition.

WORKING EQUITATION AND COWBOY CHALLENGE: These competitions are designed to test the partnership and communication of horse and rider over a course of obstacles, with marks being awarded for both horsemanship and speed. Working Equitation has Portuguese origins, while Cowboy Challenge has Western origins.

WESTERN REINING: Reining is the only Western riding event to be approved by the FEI, and is often referred to as the dressage equivalent of the western world. In reining competitions, horses complete an intricate and highly difficult pattern of spins, circles, lateral movements, flying changes and sliding stops. It evolved from the cowboy way of life, where ranch horses need to have quick reflexes and be ridden on a light rein. A well-trained reining horse should look effortless and obedient, and be willing, relaxed and able to be guided around the pattern without any resistance to the rider's aids.

There are countless other competitive Western riding events, including cutting,

Top left: Vicki winning the Debutante Saddle Hunter of the Year title at the 2011 Horse of the Year Show.

Top right: Kelly and Showtym Copy Cat competing in the Amateur Rider class, a showjumping series for riders over 21 years old, with the jumps set between 1.10–1.20 metres.

Bottom: Amanda competing Blackstone Fattori NZPH in the cross-country phase of eventing.

barrel racing, Western pleasure, horsemanship, Western trail, working cowhorse and roping. At higher levels, riders usually ride on purpose-bred Quarter Horses and always compete in Western attire and saddlery.

FLAT AND HURDLE RACING: The sport of racing horses at speed around an oval track. Traditionally, these include thoroughbreds ridden by jockeys and raced on the flat or over hurdles (known as Hurdlers or Steeplechasers).

HARNESS RACIING: A type of horse racing in which standardbreds pull a sulky and are guided by a driver. The horses are categorised by their gait; Harness Trotters (which trot) and Harness Pacers (which pace, moving both legs on one side of their body at once, rather than as a diagonal pair).

DISPLAY GOOD SPORTSMANSHIP AT ALL TIMES

Good sportsmanship is a pivotal part of being a successful horse-rider and trainer, and should be exercised at all times. This involves being supportive of fellow riders (even when they are doing better then you), and thanking the volunteers, course builders, judges and show organisers, as well as your own support crew (including parents or spouses that support your riding dreams). If you win a class, it is also important to send a letter or email of appreciation to the show or class sponsors to thank them for their investment into the sport.

Horse riding can be a tough sport, so it's important to encourage others and be polite at all times. This doesn't just go for other people, but also for your horse. You should always treat your horse in a compassionate and empathetic way, even if your round didn't quite go to plan. Riding out of the ring and yanking on your horse's reins or mistreating it is never acceptable and will reflect poorly on yourself, your trainer and the industry as a whole.

Good sportsmanship is vital for every rider, especially for those who want to build a career in the industry, gain potential sponsors, have owners invest money into purchasing top-level horses, or represent their country. First impressions always last, so make sure you treat every person and horse with the respect and consideration they deserve.

Kelly and Amanda with Showtym Viking, who is finally back on New Zealand soil to retire after six years competing in Europe.

EPILOGUE

There was a time, not that long ago, when we were just three girls with a love of horses. Although horses were in our blood, with a legacy of showjumping, polo, hunting and racing on our father's side, and a mother who rode horses, we were, in hindsight, well-meaning horse-owners who still had a lot of learning ahead of us.

Granted, back then we were still very knowledgeable, having tamed wild ponies, started horses under saddle and competed with success at numerous disciplines. But looking back, we can appreciate how much knowledge we have gone on to gain over the last two decades. The more we have learned, the more we have come to realise just how much there is to learn about these beautifully complex creatures. Our only wish is that we could have had access to this information when we were much younger; for although we read books, had lessons when we could afford them and constantly asked questions of the equine experts with whom we crossed paths, it has been a long journey to get to where we are today.

To have a successful career in horses, love is not enough. We have seen many people who love their horses but lack the experience and knowledge needed to ensure their horses' ongoing welfare, and too often it is the horses that silently suffer. And yet, we are bolstered by the fact that most owners want the best for their horses.

Our gift to you now is to share the knowledge we have accumulated from a lifetime with horses so that you can become the type of owner your horse deserves. The more you learn, the better your horses' lives will become and the more meaningful your relations with them will be.

About the Wilson sisters

Vicki, Kelly and Amanda Wilson are three of New Zealand's most prominent equestrian personalities, following their success in the competition arena and high-profile appearances in mainstream media. Their humble upbringing and down-to-earth personalities have also made them admired role models, inspiring and encouraging people of all ages.

The three sisters grew up riding from a young age, competing with great success on the Pony Club and showing circuits. These defining years, in which they tamed wild ponies and retrained difficult ponies that others had given up on — for want of money to buy well-trained ponies — are captured in the bestselling junior fiction series Showtym Adventures. These ponies, through dedication and hard work, inevitably transformed into willing, kind and competitive allrounders, and the sisters started gaining a name for themselves as up-and-coming horsewomen.

In 2002, they turned their attention to showjumping, firmly establishing themselves as some of New Zealand's most competitive riders, with both Vicki and Amanda competing to World Cup level and winning many of the nation's most prestigious classes and national titles. Unlike her sisters, showjumping has always been just a hobby for Kelly, although she has competed to Pony Grand Prix and 1.30-metre level.

In 2012, the Wilson sisters became involved with the plight of New Zealand's wild horses, before going on to tame American Mustangs and Australian Brumbies offshore. Their work is featured in the hit television show *Keeping Up With The Kaimanawas*, as well as in several of Kelly's bestselling books, including *For the Love of Horses*, *Stallion Challenges*, *Mustang Ride*, *Saving the Snowy Brumbies* and *Ranger the Kaimanawa Stallion*.

The sisters, now in their 30s, spend their time pursuing their individual passions within the equestrian world, while also being each other's biggest advocates. They have become highly respected and often headline at leading equestrian events as competitors, ambassadors and clinicians.

From left: Vicki with Showtym Spotlight, Amanda with Woodbine Legacy, and Kelly with Ngahiwi Showtym Dancer.

ABOUT THE AUTHORS

About Kelly

Back in 2012, when their journey with the Kaimanawas began, Kelly had no idea where her affinity for wild horses would take her. Now, alongside a list of bestselling books and award-winning photographs of wild horses, Kelly is the only trainer in the world to have achieved top six finishes in the Extreme Mustang Makeover, Australian Brumby Challenge and Kaimanawa Stallion Challenges.

In recent years, she has continued to advocate for wild horses on a global scale and tamed a further 60 wild Kaimanawas. From 2018 to 2020 she spent several months tracking and photographing wild horses in Canada, the United States of America, Australia, Portugal and New Zealand to observe herd behaviour for her bestselling book *Wild Horses of the World*. She has now had 20 books published.

Kelly also has a passion for training domestic and wild horses at liberty, winning Equidays Top Talent in 2018 and going on to perform at a number of the nation's leading equestrian events. Her extensive knowledge of wild horses, equine behaviour and horsemanship has gained her international recognition and she has become a popular guest on television shows and renowned equestrian podcasts and in magazines.

At her property in Taupō, New Zealand, Kelly spends her time writing; taming wild horses from the annual Kaimanawa horse musters; hosting wild horse, liberty and photography workshops; and advocating for the welfare of the Kaimanawa herd, both on the range and in domestication.

About Amanda

Amanda grew up competing from a young age, and was showjumping at Grand Prix level by the age of 13. In 2009, she crossed paths with Showtym Viking, her pony of a lifetime, and together they went on to win many of the nation's biggest showjumping titles.

Over the years, she has gained a reputation for starting and producing horses through to the highest levels of showjumping. Her career highlights include winning the Pony of the Year, National Pony Grand Prix, ESNZ 5-Year-Old Series and 7-Year-Old Horse of the Year, as well as placing in the Olympic Cup in 2015 and 2016.

Amanda is also a popular clinician, having taught thousands of riders across the country during retreats and clinics, and at New Zealand's biggest equestrian events. She is also a well-known entertainer and has hosted night shows at Equidays, Equifest and Equitana, and is a sought-after motivational speaker.

In 2022, she celebrated the publication of her first book *Showtym Viking*, which she co-wrote with Kelly.

Amanda is a full-time professional rider, and from her property, Blackstone Farm, she breeds, trains and competes a team of showjumpers. In her spare time, she writes, travels the world in search of adventure, and educates people on the effects of unresolved trauma in both humans and horses.

Amanda with Woodbine Legacy and Kelly with Showtym Gossip Girl.

Acknowledgements

First and foremost, thank you to the ponies who shaped our early years and became our greatest teachers, as well as the thousands of horses that have crossed our paths since. Everything shared in this book has been lessons well learnt, many of which are case studies from particular horses that imparted their unique knowledge on to us — to each of these horses, we thank you.

To the many vets, equine dentists, farriers, horse trainers and clinicians that have shared their knowledge with us over the years, we also thank you. The stories you shared were listened to with rapt attention, and your words of wisdom have been woven into the fabric of our belief system, helping develop us into the horsewomen we are today.

The biggest thanks must go to our sister Vicki, who taught us much of what we know. She is without a doubt one of the world's most talented and diverse horsewomen, having won countless national titles in showing, Show Hunter and showjumping to World Cup level, as well as winning back-to-back titles at Road to the Horse, the US$100,000 World Championships of Colt Starting in 2017 and 2018, and more recently training her first winning race horse. Her extensive knowledge of all things equine has seen her receive invitations to attend some of the world's leading equestrian events. Growing up alongside such a well-respected horsewoman gave us access to a wealth of knowledge, and much of the success we enjoy today is due to her paving the way.

Of course, a book like this wouldn't be possible without our parents, who inspired us to chase our dreams and work hard for what we wanted. A special thanks to Mum especially, who has been instrumental in the editing process; not only for this book, but for every book we've published.

A special mention to the many experts — including veterinarians, equine dentists and professional riders and trainers — who fact-checked the contents of this book, especially Warwick and Dianna Behrns (who have been doing our horses' teeth for over 20 years), Holly Jeffares, Lillian Bonner and Lynley Schollum. Your time and attention to detail was appreciated beyond words.

And of course to the entire team at Penguin Random House, most notably Catherine O'Loughlin, Olivia Win-Ricketts and Kelsey Pasco (who did the beautiful illustrations): this book turned out much bigger than expected and took a year longer than planned, but the end result was well worth it. So many horses will benefit from the knowledge we have amassed within these pages.

Watching Vicki ride Showtym Spotlight bridleless was one of our greatest inspirations growing up.

Glossary

ACID-BASE BALANCE — The balance of respiratory and metabolic processes within the body needed to maintain a stable blood pH level.
AGEING — The process of estimating a horse's age by inspecting its teeth.
ALKALOIDS — A class of plant toxin associated with disease in animals.
ARENA — An enclosed area for training or riding horses.
BACK/BACKING — (1) Asking a horse to walk backwards. (2) Getting a wild or untrained horse to accept a human on its back.
BAREFOOT or **UNSHOD** — When a horse does not wear horseshoes.
BASCULE — The natural round arc that a horse's body makes as it goes over a jump.
BIT — An object, usually a metal bar, placed in the mouth of a horse. It is held on by a *bridle* and used with *reins* to direct and guide the animal. It may occasionally be made of other materials, including rubber.
BOG SPAVIN — Swelling of the tibio-tarsal joint (hock) of a horse.
BOLT — When a horse suddenly runs away, with or without a rider.
BONE SPAVIN — Osteoarthritis of the lower hock joints (most commonly the distal inter-tarsal and tarso-metatarsal joints).
BRIDLE — Headgear placed around the head of a horse to hold the *bit* in place in a horse's mouth, with *reins* attached for directing and guiding the animal.
BRIDLE LAMENESS — An unsoundness that is only evident when the horse is being ridden, often caused by pain-related issues from the bridle, saddle or rider's weight.
BUCK/BUCKING — A behaviour where the horse lowers its head and rapidly kicks its hind feet into the air. At liberty, this is seen as an expression of excess energy or high spirits, while under saddle it is generally considered to be disobedience or a sign of pain.
CANTLE — The highest point at the back of the saddle.
CHIP IN — An abrupt half-stride taken by a horse to correct its take-off distance while jumping. It usually happens if the horse doesn't have the correct canter quality to take off from a long distance.
COLIC — Any of several painful digestive disorders, usually involving intestinal displacement or blockage. It is a leading cause of death among horses.
CONDITION — An evaluation of a horse's overall weight and health.
CONFORMATION — The shape and proportion of a horse's body.
CONTACT — Contact refers to the connection between the horse's mouth and the rider's hand, leg and seat. When a horse is working correctly on the contact (also known as working on the bit, or in a frame) its poll should be the highest point of its neck, with the jugular forming the shape of an upside-down 'U'.
CORONET BAND — The junction of the leg's hairline and the hoof, and is the area from which the hoof grows.
CROSSBRED — A horse that is a cross between two or more known breeds.
DOCK — The muscular portion of a horse's tail, where the hair is rooted.
DRESSAGE — An Olympic-level equine sport based on classical principles of horsemanship,

Kelly riding Showtym Sinatra bridleless.

involving tests designed to measure the level of the horse's training in classical dressage. Lower levels of dressage competition are organised by national equestrian organisations, while the higher levels are governed by the *Fédération Équestre Internationale*.

ENGLISH RIDING — A form of horse riding that originated in England and includes many different disciplines, including dressage, eventing, show jumping, showing, hunting, etc. It features English saddles and bridles, with riders holding a rein in each hand.

EQUESTRIAN SPORTS NEW ZEALAND (ESNZ) — The governing body for most national-level equestrian competitions in New Zealand, including showjumping, dressage, eventing, endurance and Paralympics.

EVENTING — A sport-horse discipline with competition that goes as high as Olympic level. It includes three types of riding: dressage, cross-country and showjumping.

FALSE TAIL — A hair extension, made from horsehair, that adds length or fullness to the horse's natural tail.

FARRIER — A professional hoof-care specialist who does hoof trimming and shoeing.

FÉDÉRATION ÉQUESTRE INTERNATIONALE (FEI) — The governing body for most international-level equestrian competitions, including the FEI World Equestrian Games and the Olympics. It recognises and governs 10 disciplines: dressage, combined driving, endurance riding, eventing, horseball, para-equestrian, reining, showjumping, tent pegging and equestrian vaulting.

FETLOCK — The hinge joint above the hoof, corresponding to the upper knuckle of a human finger or toe.

FLANK — The indented area between the horse's ribcage and hindquarters.

FLATWORK — Ridden exercises where the horse is trained on the flat, as opposed to over jumps.

FLEHMEN — A behavioural response, usually in stallions, when a horse detects a particular smell from mares, characterised by a curling of the upper lip and a raising of the head.

FOAL — A young horse of either sex under the age of 1 year. May be qualified by sex: colt foal (male), filly foal (female).

FORM — The style that a horse uses when jumping over fences.

FREE-JUMPING — The practice of jumping a horse without a rider. It is usually done down a lane and used to assess the horse's jumping form and ability.

FROG — A tough, rubbery, triangular part of the underside of a horse hoof. It acts as a shock absorber for the horse's joints and also assists with blood circulation in the lower leg.

GALLOP — The fastest natural horse gait.

GALVAYNE'S GROOVE — The Galvayne's groove is located on the lateral surface of the upper third incisor and is useful in ageing older horses. It appears first near the gum line at about 10 years of age. The groove extends halfway down the tooth at 15 years, and all the way down the tooth by 20 years. By approximately 25 years, the Galvayne's groove is halfway gone, and by 30 years, it has disappeared completely.

GELDING — A castrated male horse of any age.

GIRTH — A wide, flat strap made of leather, or synthetic materials with similar characteristics, used to secure most types of saddle to a horse's back. It is attached to billets (straps secured under the saddle flap) at each end, so that it can be tightened correctly.

GRAND PRIX — The highest level of either showjumping or dressage, generally governed by the rules of the FEI.

GREEN — A horse or rider who is either untrained or has just started training.

GROUND MANNERS — A horse with good ground manners will have been taught correct handling foundations to ensure it knows how to safely interact with people while it is being handled and led.

HACK — *see* horse.

HALTER — A device made of rope or leather straps that fits around the head of a horse and is used to lead or secure the animal.

HANDS (HH OR H) — A measurement used to determine the height of a horse, taken from the ground to the top of the withers. It was originally taken from the size of a grown man's hand, but is now standardised to 4 inches (10 centimetres). The number written after a period represents additional inches, so 15.3 hands ('fifteen-three') would be 15 hands 3 inches — i.e. 15 times 4 inches plus another 3 inches = 63 inches (160 centimetres).

HEAD-SHY — A horse that fears movement near its head, or being touched on the head.

HOCK — The joint between the tarsal and tibia bones, on the horse's hind legs.

HORSE — In general, a member of the species *Equus ferus caballus*. In equestrian terms, a horse that matures to 14.3 hands (148.5 centimetres) or taller. Also known as a hack.

HORSE GRAND PRIX — One of the highest levels of horse showjumping, with the jumps ranging from 1.40 to 1.50 metres.

HUNTER — A competition for horses that are shown around a ring of jumps at an A&P Show; also the name for horses that compete in Show Hunter or Hunter classes.

IMPULSION — The movement of a horse going forward with controlled power.

IN HAND — A type of horse show competition where the horse is led, rather than ridden, and judged on its conformation and movement.

JUMP — A raised obstacle for a horse to jump over. Examples include:
   OXER or **SPREAD**: Two verticals close together to widen the jump.
   CROSSBAR: Two jump poles that form an 'X'.
   COMBINATION: A combination of two or three jumps in a row.
   VERTICAL or **UPRIGHT**: A jump consisting of poles placed vertically on top of each other with no spread (only one set of poles or jump stands, so there is no added width).
   WALL: A solid jump that usually resembles brick or stone, but is made of lightweight material.

LAMINITIS — Inflammation of the sensitive laminae of the hoof (the laminae connect the hoof to the bone). It causes lameness and severe pain and may require colic surgery or euthanasia in extreme cases.

LATERAL WORK — Any movement made by the horse where it is moving in a sideways direction.

LEG-YIELDING — A lateral movement in which the horse travels both forwards and sideways at the same time.

LUNGING — To work or train a horse at the end of a long rope, often used to exercise the horse without a rider.

MARE — A mature female horse, 4 years of age or older.

MARKINGS — This generally refers to white markings on the horse's face and legs, and sometimes the occasional body spot on an otherwise solid-coloured horse.

MOUTHED/MOUTHING — Getting an untrained horse to accept a bit.

MUSTER — The assembling or round-up of livestock.

NAPPING — When a horse is disobedient and refuses to go forwards, sometimes involving bucking or kicking.

NAVICULAR BONE — A small bone in the horse's hoof. Changes to the navicular bone can cause lameness and severe pain. It may require euthanasia in extreme cases.

NEAR SIDE — The left side of a horse. This is the traditional side on which all activities around a horse are done or start being done.

OFF SIDE — The right-hand side of a horse.

ON THE BIT — A horse that is flexed at the poll (the highest point of the skull), moving forwards well, holding the bit without fuss, and responsive to the rider.

ON THE BUCKLE — Holding the reins very loosely; literally, holding the reins only by the buckle that joins the reins together.

OVER-FACING — Overwhelming the rider or horse by asking them to perform a task they aren't capable of or don't have the confidence to complete with ease.

PLACE — In horse shows, any award ranking, particularly other than first place; usually second through to sixth place.

POINTS — Used when referring to the colouring of a horse's head, legs, mane and tail.

POLL — The part of the horse's head immediately behind or between its ears.

PONY — In general, a member of the species *Equus ferus caballus*. A pony is a member of a horse breed that typically matures to 14.2 hands (148 centimetres) or shorter.

PONY GRAND PRIX — The highest level of pony showjumping, with jumps ranging from 1.20 to 1.35 metres.

POVERTY LINES — An indentation that runs between two large muscles on the horse's hindquarters, on either side of the tail. When pronounced, it can indicate a horse is in poor condition.

PRESSURE (AND RELEASE) — Reinforcing behaviours through the use of applying pressure, usually to a halter or bridle, to ask the horse a question, then rewarding the horse by softening the pressure when it provides the correct answer.

QUARTER MARKS — Decorative marks made on the horse's hindquarters, and traditionally seen in showing competitions.

RAIN SCALD — A skin disease caused by infection with actinomycete bacteria, typically caused by persistently rainy conditions.

REIN — An item of horse tack, attached as a pair to either side of a bit in the horse's mouth, and used to direct or guide a horse for riding.

REIN-BACK — A two-beat movement in which the horse walks backwards.

RINGBONE — Progressive arthritic changes of the pastern or coffin bone, causing new bone growths.

SADDLE — A device placed on the back of a horse (or other equine) for the rider to sit on. It is designed to support and stabilise a rider.

SHOW — A competitive event or series of events where horses are judged.

SHOW HUNTER — A jumping competition in which the horse is judged on its style and rhythm over fences.

SHOWJUMPING — A jumping competition in which the horse is judged on both the number of jumps it clears on the course and the time it takes to complete it.

SOFTENING — A horse that gives to pressure, normally to contact applied to the halter or bridle.

SOUND/SOUNDNESS — A sound horse is one that has no lameness or illness.

SPLINTS — Ossification (additional bone growth) of the second and fourth metacarpal or metatarsal bones in the leg of the horse, which often occurs after impact injury to the area (such as from a kick). An injury may ossify into blemishes with no effect on soundness, depending on its location.

STALLION — A mature, uncastrated male horse, 4 years old or older.

STANDING SQUARE — Standing still, with all four hooves placed evenly under the horse's body.

STARTING — Teaching a wild or untrained horse to be ridden, usually under saddle.

STIRRUPS — Pairs of small, light frames that a rider puts their feet in. They are attached to each side of the *saddle* by straps called stirrup leathers, and are used to assist with mounting and as a support while riding.

STRIDE — The distance from the imprint of a horse's forefoot until the same foot hits the ground again.

STUD PILES — Mounds of manure left by stallions to mark their territory.

SURCINGLE — A piece of training equipment which is buckled around the barrel (middle part) of the horse.

TACK — The term for all the equipment that horses wear, such as *saddles*, *bridles* and *halters*, and other horse-care equipment.

TACK ROOM — A room where tack is kept.

THOROUGHPIN — Swelling of the tarsal sheath around the deep digital flexor tendon, as it passes over the hock.

TOPLINE — The muscles over the horse's wither, back and rump.

UNSOUND/UNSOUNDNESS — A horse with significant lameness or other health problems.

WEANLING — A young horse that has been weaned, usually between six months and 1 year old.

WESTERN RIDING — A form of horse riding based on the cowboy way of life, including the disciplines of reining, Western dressage, barrel racing, roping, team penning, cutting, etc. It features Western saddles and bridles, and at more advanced levels riders only use one hand to hold the reins (with the horses trained to neck rein). The horses are also shorter and more compact than those traditionally seen in English riding, with the American Quarter Horse being the most common. The horses' gaits are known as walk, jog (trot) and lope (canter).

WITHERS — The ridge between the shoulder blades of a horse. It is the tallest point of the body, and is the standard place to measure the animal's height.

YEARLING — A horse between 1 and 2 years old.

Index

360-degree turn 298

abortion 89
abscesses, hoof 117, 129
acid, stomach 40–41 — see also gastric ulcers
adrenaline 38
age of horse 30–34
   how to age from teeth 33–34
aids, riding 6, 7, 258, 259, 278–283, 327
alignment, correct for riding 256–258, 261, 266, 268, 302
allergies 67, 136
alternative therapies 127, 128
American Mustang 27
American Quarter Horse 18, 20, 328
Andalusian 20
anti-rub vest 189, 190
Appaloosa 24
Arabian 20, 46
arthritis — see osteoarthritis
artificial aids 282 — see also spurs, whips
ascarids 110
azoturia — see tying-up

back at knees 49
back, faults 52
backing (preparing for saddle) 44, 273
balage, as feed 85, 90, 103, 137
bandages 126
bandages, travel 196, 200
barbed wire 82
bareback riding 266, 268

bascule 230, 301, 311, 325
base wide or narrow 49, 50
bathing horse 176–179
BCS — see Body Condition Score
beaches, riding on 273
bedding 67, 69, 119, 195,
behavioural problems 10, 113, 137, 138, 166–167, 168, 204, 206, 214, 226, 259, 265, 275, 277, 291, 306
bend 289, 292
benefits of horse ownership 7
birthday, official 33
bit rings 223–225
biting 56–58, 204
bitless riding 145, 220, 226, 281
bits 220, 221, 222–228, 235, 238, 240
   bit size 228
   issues caused by incorrect bits 226
   types of bit 223–225
blood tests 14, 89, 96, 132, 134
Body Condition Score 75, 98, 101, 105, 136, 275
body control 44, 152, 156, 298
body language, horse 54–59, 151–152, 293–295
body language, human 142, 151–152
bog spavin 50
bone and spinal development 29, 32, 42, 44, 48, 313
bone chips 49, 96
bone density 42

bone spavin 50
boots, riding 243, 246, 317
   — see also specific types
bot fly 77, 106, 107, 110, 170
bounce (jump) 308
bowed hocks 50
boxy hoof 52
bran 94
branding 26–27
breastplate/breast collar 230, 248, 321
breeds of horse 18–21
bridle lameness 131, 204
bridle maintenance 236, 238
bridles 218–220, 236, 240
   assembly 240
bridling 235
broken wind 136
browband 221, 235, 240, 247, 248
Brumby 27
brush jump 305
brushes and combs 170, 172
buying a horse 9–15
   questions to ask when buying 10
   red flags 12
buying a saddle 206

calcium, as supplement 89, 94, 96
calendar, competition 317
cancer 137, 146
canes 247, 265
canter 14, 44, 113, 136, 146, 156, 204, 212, 261, 265, 266, 268, 275, 277, 282, 283, 285–287, 288, 289, 300, 302, 306, 308, 309, 311, 312, 313, 316, 327

capillary refill time test 72
caps (teeth) 33
catching horses 151–152
cattle guards 82
cavaletti 303
cavesson noseband 218, 220
cellulitis 134
chaff 73, 91, 104
change in feed 15, 131
change of rein 289
cheek teeth 33
Cherry Roller bit 223
chipping in 311
chloride, as supplement 96
chlorinated water 73
choke 91, 113, 125, 133
cipher brand 27
circles, working in 289, 327
circulatory system 39
clipping coat 134, 136, 170, 176, 177, 179, 182–183
  clip patterns 183
clothing 241, 243, 246–250
clothing, for competitions 246–250, 317
  specific competitions 247–250
club hoof 52
Clydesdale 18, 20
coffin joint inflammation 52
cold compresses 127
cold hosing 127
cold-blooded breeds 20, 21
colic 59, 71, 72, 79, 87, 89, 91, 98, 106, 110, 113, 125, 126, 131–132
colic, impaction 42, 70, 110
collection 259, 279, 289, 291, 293
colours of horse 23–24
  colour and temperament 23
combinations 303, 306–308
combs and brushes 170, 172
commercial feed mixes 91, 94
companionship for horses 64, 73, 75, 138, 151
competing 316–328
  clothing, for competitions 246–250, 317

etiquette, when competing 324
grooming, for competitions 247, 248, 250
jumping in competition 321–323, 324
types of competition 325–328
warming-up for competition 324
concentrates — *see* hard feed
conformation 35, 45–53, 138, 325
Connemara 27
contact, working on 42, 44, 111, 113, 258, 259, 275, 277, 279, 280, 281, 289, 291, 293, 312, 325
contracted hooves 117
contracts, purchase 14
copra 91, 133
cornering 279, 292, 300, 312
coronet 26, 114
correction 162, 166, 295, 302
corrective shoeing 120, 129
corrective trimming 48, 49, 52, 117
cortisol 38
costs of horse ownership 8
counter canter 285
cover rub 190
cover, saddle 236
covered yards 67
covers, fitting 189–190
cow hocks 50
Cowboy Challenge 296, 327
crab biting 138
cracked heels — *see* mud fever
cracks, hoof 117
crest release 301, 302
crossbar/crossrail 303
Cross Country (eventing) 216, 232, 246, 247, 250, 296, 305, 314, 317, 325
cross-country jumps 305, 314
cross-grazing 77, 107
cues, visual 160, 168
cues, vocal 162, 283 — *see also* aids
curbs 50

Cushing's 89, 134

deer netting 82
dehydration 42, 70, 72–73, 137
dental development 33–34
dental health 40, 101, 103, 111–113, 131, 226
dental issues 111–113, 167, 226, 306
development and growth of skeleton 29, 32
diagonal (trotting) 283–285, 289
diarrhoea 79, 89, 106, 110, 125, 137
digestive system 40–41, 85, 91, 111, 131
dismounting 254
disunited canter 287
DNA testing 20
double bridle 218–220
double or triple jumps 308
draught horses 20, 138
dressage 20, 46, 120, 158, 180, 206, 214, 216, 218, 228, 230, 232, 246, 247, 248, 250, 261, 277, 287, 289, 316, 323, 324, 325, 327
dressage girth 214
dressage saddle 206, 247
driving (sport) 326
driving seat 298, 300

ears, body language signs 56
ears, cleaning and trimming 179
ear–shoulder–hip–heel alignment 254, 256, 261, 266, 300, 302
eggbutt bit ring 223
electric fences 81, 84
electric tape (fencing) 77, 81, 82
electrocardiogram 14
electrocution 81
electrolytes 73, 96, 132
emergency plans and kits 67, 84, 148, 196

endocrine system 38, 39
endoscopy 14
endurance 327
English Riding Pony 20
English-style competition 31
Equestrian Sports NZ 317, 323
equine gastric ulcer syndrome (EGUS) — *see* gastric ulcers
Equitation 158, 296, 325, 327
Equiwire 80, 81, 82, 84
etiquette, when competing 324
eventing 20, 120, 216, 232, 247, 250, 303, 305, 316, 323, 324, 325, 327
eventing boots 230
ewe neck (upside-down neck) 46, 105
exercise rug 189
expectations of young horses 44
eye injuries 129
eye rolling 58
eyes, body language signs 58
eyes, cleaning 170, 177
eyesight, horse 38–39

face mask 135, 146
faecal egg count (FEC) 106
fake-pulling mane 180, 182, 251
false mane 251
false tail 247, 251
farrier care 48, 49, 52, 101, 115, 117, 119, 142, 170
fascia system 38
fatty liver 104
faults, conformation 46–52, 138
feathers' 180
Fédération Equestre International (FEI) 27, 323, 324, 325, 326
feed buckets 69, 70
feed mixes 91
feed room 69
feed, change in 15
feeding 85–98

after exercise 86
for healthy hooves 115
feel and timing 151, 168
FEI (Fédération Equestre International) 27, 323, 324, 325, 326
FEI World Cup 324
fences — *see also* jumps
fencing 80–84
fertiliser, on pasture 89
figure eight 289
fillers 303, 314
Fillis irons 216
finding the right horse 9
first-aid kit 125–126, 145, 196, 317, 321
first-aid, basic 126–127
fitting a cover 189–90
fitting a halter 147
fitting a rug 193
flat-seat saddles — *see* jumping saddles
flatwork 44, 206, 216, 270, 277–278, 279, 289–292, 311, 312, 324
flehmen 58
flight, fight, freeze 6, 38, 54, 58, 60, 127, 168, 293
fly mask 146
fly sheets 187
flying changes 285, 289, 327
'follow the leader' 314
following hips 266, 282
food rewards 166
footwear 142, 243 — *see also* boots
foreleg conformation and faults 48–49
founder — *see* laminitis
fractures 129
free-access shelters 67
freeze-branding 27
full seat 298, 300

gag bit rings 223
gaining weight 103
gaits 283–287, 289 — *see also* walk, trot, canter, gallop
gallop 44, 71, 136, 232, 283, 287, 300

Galvayne's groove 33
gamgee 126, 200
gastric ulcers 12, 15, 41, 70, 85, 86–87, 89, 91, 94, 98, 103–04, 132, 167, 199
gates (jumps) 296, 305
gates, safe 82, 84, 98, 100, 142
geldings 32, 173
gender of horse 30
general-purpose saddles 206, 214, 250
German Scales of Training 289–293
girth 214, 232–235, 254, 263
adjusting 263
girth galls 214
glandular ulcers 87 — *see also* gastric ulcers
gloves 246, 317
glue-on shoes 120
grains, as feed 91
grass growth 64, 67
grass or sand cracks 117
grass-affected 10, 88, 89, 167
grazing — *see* paddocking
grazing muzzle 85, 104
'greedy' horses 85
'green' horses 12, 31
grids 303, 308
grooming 170–183
grooming, for competitions 247, 248, 250
grooming kit 170, 317
grooming mitt 172
ground manners 152–158
groundwork 145, 270 — *see also* flatwork
groups of horses 64 — *see also* companionship
growth and development of skeleton 29, 32
'guitar' metaphor 280–281
gums 72, 125
Gypsy Cob 20

hair accessories 246, 317
half seat 298, 300
half-halt 288
halter accessories 146

halters 145–147, 151, 235, 281, 317
   fitting 147
   halter types 145
   safety concerns 146
hand aids 280–281
handling, safe 142–145
hands (height) 27–29
Hanoverian 18, 20
Happy Mouth bit 225
hard feed 69, 90–91, 103, 104
harrowing 77
hay net 69, 70, 85, 98, 100, 104, 107
hay, as feed 87, 89–90, 98, 103
hay, weighing 88
head injuries 242
head, body language signs 55, 56, 113
head, conformation and faults 46
health, horse 101–113, 124–138
hearing, horse 38
heartbeat 39, 124
hedges 67, 82
height certificate 26, 29, 317
height conversion chart 28
Height Measuring Day 29
helmets 142, 241–242, 246, 247, 248, 271, 317
herd hierarchy 75, 98
hill work 277
hills, riding up and down 271
hind leg conformation and faults 49–50
hindquarter yield 156, 281
Hippo Health 135
hips, following 266, 282
history of horses 18
hogsback jump 305
holding reins 258, 265
Holstein 18
hood 179, 187, 189
hoof boots 115, 120
hoof care 48, 49, 52, 114–123
hoof issues 117–119

hoof protection 115
hoof trimming 48, 49, 52, 115, 173
hoof, function of 119
hooves 50–52
   grooming 173
   oiling 115, 173
   picking out 115, 170, 173
horse breeds 18–21
horse colours 23–24
horse identification 26–27
horse markings 24–25, 26
Horse of the Year 323
horse ownership, benefits 7
horse ownership, costs 8
horse ownership, principles 6
horse versus pony 27–28
   when to up-horse 30
horses, history 18
hot oil wash 177
hot-blooded breeds 20, 21
Hunter class 180, 214, 218, 228, 247, 248, 250, 287, 303, 316, 323, 325 — *see also* Show Hunter, Saddle Hunter
hunting/fox hunting 327
hydration 70, 73, 104
   after exercise 71
hyperflexion 291
hypothermia 67

ice boots 127
Icelandic horses 27
icy conditions 70
identification of horses 26–27
illnesses, common 124–125, 131–138
impaction colic 42, 70, 110, 131
impulsion 156, 281, 289, 291, 292, 313, 314, 316, 325
in-hand gallop 287
injuries, common 128–131
injury prevention, fences and gates 81, 82, 84, 100
instinctive behaviour — *see* flight, fight, freeze
insulin dysregulation 89

insurance 14–15, 124
internal systems 35–42

jacket, riding 246, 247, 248, 250
'jockeys' 238
jodhpur boots 243
jodhpurs 243, 246, 247, 248, 250
joint or tendon injuries 128–129
jointed bit 223
jumping boots 123, 230, 248
jumping girths 214
jumping in competition 321–323, 324 — *see also* showjumping
jumping positions 298, 300, 301, 302, 256–258, 261, 266, 268, 302, 306, 313
jumping saddles 206, 250
jumping training 270, 298–316
jumping, does your horse like it? 306
jumps 296
   cross-country 305
   parts of 303
   types of 303–305
juvenile horses 30–31, 33, 44

Kaimanawa horses 27
kidney failure 70, 72
kissing spine 52, 137

lameness 49, 50, 117, 129–131, 204
laminitis 54, 89, 96, 101, 117, 119, 120, 131, 134
lateral movements 280–281, 327
lead (when cantering) 285, 289, 316
lead ropes 146
leading a horse 154–156
leather maintenance 236, 238
leg aids 278–279, 280–281, 314
legumes, as feed 88, 89, 90, 133

length, stirrups 261, 263
lice 136
light seat 298, 300
liniment 126
Liverpool 303
loading horses 196–197, 293
loneliness in horses 75
long back 52
losing weight, horse 104
lunging 146, 156, 268, 275, 283
lymphangitis 40
lymphatic system 40

magnesium, as supplement 77, 89, 94–96, 133
make-up, horse 247, 251
mane, fake-pulled 180, 182, 250
mane, false 251
mane, grooming and trimming 173, 180, 182
mane, plaiting 180, 182, 247, 248, 251
mane, pulled 173
mānuka honey 126, 134, 135
manure 41, 54, 59, 69, 107, 110, 132 — *see also* mucking out
markings 24–25, 26
martingales 230
mature horses 32, 33
measuring horses 29
melanoma 137
mesh gates 82
microchipping 27, 29
minerals 69, 89, 90, 133
monkey mouth (underbite) 46
mouldy hay 90
mounting 254
mounting block 254, 256
moxidectin 110
muck heap 69
mucking out 65, 67, 69, 77, 199
mud fever 96, 135
mullen mouth bit 223
musculoskeletal system 35
Mustang 27
mycotoxins 89, 133

navicular syndrome 129
neck conformation and faults 46
negative reinforcement 164
nervous system 35–38
new horse, settling in 15
nitrogen 89
nose guard 135, 146
nose, cleaning 170, 177
nosebands 218, 220, 221, 240
number brands 27
numnahs 216, 218

obstacles 197, 270, 293–298, 313
types of obstacles 296–298
oedema 40
official birthday 33
offset knees 49
oiling hooves 115, 173
Olympic Games 17, 20, 32, 311, 323, 324, 325
One Day Event 323, 325 — *see also* eventing, Pony Club
osteoarthritis 49, 50, 130, 138
over or back at knees 49
overbite (parrot mouth) 46, 112
overgrazing 77, 107
overreach boots 123, 230
overweight horses 73, 101, 103, 105
overworking 42, 44, 273
oxer 303–05, 308, 311, 314, 324

paddling 49
paddock maintenance 77–79
paddock rotation 64, 107
paddocking 64–67, 77–79
pain-related issues 12, 103, 137, 166, 167, 168, 204, 211, 214, 275, 287, 291, 306, 312
parasites 77, 103, 106–110
parrot mouth (overbite) 46, 112
parts of a horse jump 303

passport, horse 26, 27
pastern axis 52, 114
pasture (grass) as feed 88–89, 137 — *see also* grass-affected
pasture improvement 77, 107
'pecking order' 75, 98
Pelham bit 225
Percheron 20
periosteum 35
phenylbutazone 86
phosphorus 94
picking out hooves 115, 170, 173, 317
pinch test 72
pinworms 106, 110
plaiting 49
plaiting mane 180, 182, 247, 248, 251
pneumonia 136
points of the horse 35, 36–37
poisoning 79, 131, 133
poisonous plants 39, 79, 82, 133
polework 270, 277, 302, 306, 312, 313
polo 327
Pony Club 31, 45, 194, 250, 303, 317, 321, 323, 325
position, correct for riding 256–258, 261, 266, 268, 302, 306
positions, jumping 298, 300, 301, 302, 306
positive reinforcement 164–166
post-and-rail fencing 80
post-legged 50
posturing 59
potassium 89, 96
poultices 126
poverty lines 101, 105
praise, vocal 166
pressure 7, 278, 282
pressure scale 158–162, 164, 278
pricked hoof 130
principles of horse ownership 6
pulled mane 173, 250, 251 — *see also* fake-pulling

pulse — *see* heartbeat
PVC planks 81

Quarter Horse 18, 20, 328
quarter marks 247, 251
quick-release knot 100, 142, 148
quick-release stirrups 216
quidding 112

rails 303
rainscald 134
ramp (jump) 305
ramps 111
RAS Lifetime Certificate 27, 29
red flags when buying 12
redworms 110
rein back 156, 160, 280, 298
rein, change of 289
reinforcement, negative 164
reinforcement, positive 164–166
reins 228–230, 235, 240, 265
    how to hold 258, 265
related lines 303, 308
relaxation, signs of 54
respiratory issues 136
respiratory system 40
rewards 7, 158, 160, 164–166, 293, 295
rhythm 266, 277, 281, 283, 285, 287, 289, 291, 293, 306, 311, 312, 313, 314, 316, 321, 325, 327
Ribbon Day 303, 323
ribbons, coloured 324
ridden adventures 270–271, 277
rideability, and breed 21
riding aids — *see* aids
riding alone 271
riding bareback 266, 268
riding boots 243, 246, 317
riding jacket 246, 247, 248, 250
riding on roads 271
riding position 256–258, 261, 266, 268, 302, 306
ringbone 49, 120

ringworm 134
roach back 52
'roaring' 40, 136
roll back 298
rolling 59, 132, 179
rolling paddocks 77
Rollkur 131, 291
rope halter 145, 147
rotation of paddocks 64, 77
roughage 40, 41, 64, 85, 86, 87–90, 91, 103, 104, 199
roundworms 110
routine, feeding 85, 98
rug fitting 193
rugs and rugging 179, 182, 184–189, 196
    rug sizing 186
    rug weight 187
    types of rugs 185–187

sacrifice paddocks 64–65, 77
saddle accessories 214–218
saddle blanket 210, 216, 248
saddle cover 236
saddle fit and fitting 15, 52, 137, 167, 204–212, 258, 265, 275, 306
saddle pads 216–218, 232, 247, 248
Saddle Hunter 228, 247, 250, 287, 325,
saddle tree 208, 236
saddles 204–212, 321
    buying 206
    types of saddle 206–208
saddling horse 232–235
safety stirrups 216
safety vest 246, 247, 317
salt supplements 73
sand colic 131
sarcoids 137
schooling 270, 276–278
schoolmaster/mistress 12, 14, 32, 313
seat aids 281–282
seats (jumping positions) 298, 300
seedy toe 117
selenium, as supplement 96
Selle Francis 20

sense of smell, horse 38
sense of taste, horse 39
sensory system 38
serpentine 289
settling in a new horse 15
shampooing 176
sheared heels 119
sheath, cleaning 173–176
sheep netting 82
shelter 67–69, 182, 184, 185
Shire 20
shivers 138
shoeing 115, 119–120, 129, 173
short back 52
shoulder conformation and faults 46
shoulder slope 46
shoulder/forehand yield 156–158, 281
Show Hunter 180, 214, 218, 228, 248, 303, 316, 323, 325
show rugs 187, 196
showing 180, 206, 214, 218, 220, 228, 230, 246, 250, 251, 277, 316, 325
showjumping 20, 120, 215, 230, 232, 246–48, 303, 311, 316, 323, 324, 325, 327 — *see also* jumping
shows, what to pack 317–321
sickle hocks 50
side-pass 158, 160–162, 281, 298
signs of relaxation 54
signs of tension 54, 58
Silver Whinny Sox 135
size, horses and ponies 27–29
sizing, bits 228 stronger bits 228
skeletal development 29, 32, 42, 44, 48, 313
smegma 176
snaffle bridle 218, 221, 235, 247, 248, 265
snaking 55
soaking hay and feed 73
sodium, as supplement 89, 96, 133

soil in paddocks 77
soundness 14, 120, 313
sounds horses make 59 — *see also* body language
spinal and bone development 29, 32, 42, 44, 48
spooking 55, 56, 73, 89, 94, 113, 128, 142, 263, 293, 295, 298, 300, 316, 321
sportsmanship 328
spurs 238, 278, 282
squamous cell carcinoma 146
squamous ulcers 87 — *see also* gastric ulcers
stable rugs 187
stables 67, 71
staggers 10, 133
stallions 32, 55, 58–59, 64, 84, 176
Standardbred 18, 27
'steady hands' 265
stifle lock 138
stirrup irons 216, 238, 254, 256, 261, 268
stirrup leathers 216
stirrup length 261, 263
stirrups, adjusting 263
stocks and ties 247, 248
stomach acid 40–41
straight or sickle hocks 50
straightness 156, 289, 291, 292, 293, 295, 312, 313, 316
straw 90, 104
stress colic 131
stress, effects on horses 86, 87, 131, 137, 138
strides, measuring 309
striking 54, 59
stringhalt 138
strip-grazing 77, 81
strongyles 110
stud books 20
stud guards 123, 214, 248
stud piles 54, 59
stud register 26
studding, on horseshoes 120–123, 214, 248
Suffolk 20
sugar beet 91, 133
summer sheets 187

sun photosensitivity 135
sulphur, as supplement 96
supplements 69
supplements, minerals 94
suppleness 156, 277, 278, 288, 289, 291, 292, 306
survival response 6, 38, 127, 166, 293 — *see also* flight, fight, freeze
sway back 52
sweating 54, 59, 96, 125, 131–33, 146, 176, 182, 187, 196, 273, 277
swimming, horses 277

tack room 69
tack storage and maintenance 236, 238
tacking up 232–235
tail bag 179, 187, 189
tail wrap 196
tail, false 247, 251
tail, grooming and washing 172–173, 177
tail, trimming 179–180
take-off distance 306, 309–311
tapeworms 106, 110
teeth, in ageing horses 33–34
temperament, and horse colour 23
temperature, taking 124
tendon and ligament injuries 130
tension, signs of 54
tetanus 128
Thoroughbred 18, 20, 27
thoroughpin 50
Three Day Event — *see* eventing
thrust, in hooves 117–119
ties and stocks 247, 248
timing and feel 151, 168
TMJ disorders 111–113
toeing in or out 48–49
topline 44, 52, 89, 105, 218, 275–277, 278, 289, 325
topping of paddocks 77
Training Days 170, 316, 321, 323

transitions 285, 288–289 — *see also* gaits
transporting 15, 194–200
 negative effects 15, 194
travel bandages 196, 200
travel boots 196
travel sickness 136
treats, feeding 166
trees 67 — *see also* shelter
trembling 58–59
trimming 179 — *see also* clipping
trimming, hoof 48
triple bar (jump) 303
trot 14, 44, 45, 138, 146, 156, 162, 168, 212, 265, 266, 268, 273, 275, 277, 283, 285, 287, 288, 289, 302, 306, 308, 313, 314, 316, 324
tubbing 126–127
TuffRock GI 126, 132
tying hay net 100
tying up 147–148, 196, 232
tying-up (azoturia) 96, 132
types of obstacles 296–298
types of saddle 206, 208

ulcers — *see* gastric ulcers
ultrasound 14
underbite (monkey mouth) 46
underweight horses 101, 103, 105, 275
up-horsing 30
upright 303, 314, 324
upside-down neck (ewe neck) 46, 105
urea 89
urinary system 42
UV protection 135, 146

vaccination 128
vaccination record 27
vaulting 327
vehicle safety 195, 197
vertical 303, 314, 324
vet care 14, 101, 106, 107, 117, 119, 124–38, 142, 176

vices — *see* behavioural problems
visual cues 160, 168
vitamins 96, 134, 135
vocal cues 162, 283 — *see also* aids
vocal praise 166
vocalising 59
voice aids 283

walk 14, 44, 45, 79, 138, 152, 156, 162, 164, 197, 199, 242, 265, 266, 271, 282, 283, 285, 288, 289, 295, 298, 302, 306, 313, 314, 324
wall (jump) 303
wall eye 25
waratahs 84
warm-blooded breeds 20, 138, 218
warming-up for competition 324
wash, hot oil 177
wash-down bay 69
washing horse 176–179
water buckets 69, 70
water jump 305
water, how much horses need 70, 71
Waterford bit 223
watering 71, 73
weaving 138
weeds 77
weighing hay 88
weight aids 281–282
weight of rider 28, 52, 137, 210
weight, gaining 103
weight, losing 104
weight, rug 187
Welsh 20
Western riding 327–328
Weymouth bit 225
Weymouth bridle 218–220
what to pack for a show 317–321
whips 278, 282
whites of eyes showing 58
whorls 26

wild horses 18, 64, 67, 114, 119, 184
Wilson sisters 5–6,
windsucking 103, 138
winter coat 183, 185
wolf teeth 111
Working Equitation 158, 295, 327
Working Hunter 287, 325
World Equestrian Games 324
worming treatment 106, 109
worms 64, 69, 77, 106–110, 131, 137 — *see also* parasites
wounds and cuts 128
wrap, tail 196

x-rays 14, 129, 130, 137

yards 65, 67, 71 — *see also* paddocking
yawning 56
yield, hindquarter 156
yield, shoulder/forehand 156–158

PENGUIN

UK | USA | Canada | Ireland | Australia
India | New Zealand | South Africa | China

Penguin is an imprint of the Penguin Random House group of companies,
whose addresses can be found at global.penguinrandomhouse.com.

First published by Penguin Random House New Zealand, 2023

1 3 5 7 9 10 8 6 4 2

Text © Kelly Wilson and Amanda Wilson, 2023
Photography © Kelly Wilson, 2023, unless otherwise credited, except
the following on page 78: Foxglove (Unsplash); Avocado (Pexels);
Yew (Unsplash); Oak (Unsplash); Rhododendron (Unsplash); Oleander
(Unsplash); Hemlock (iStock); Mexican devil (iStock); Bracken (iStock);
Privet (iStock); Sycamore (iStock); Ngaio (iStock); Tutu (iStock).

The moral right of the authors has been asserted.

All rights reserved. Without limiting the rights under copyright reserved above,
no part of this publication may be reproduced, stored in or introduced into
a retrieval system, or transmitted, in any form or by any means (electronic,
mechanical, photocopying, recording or otherwise), without the prior written
permission of both the copyright owner and the above publisher of this book.

Design by Megan van Staden © Penguin Random House New Zealand
Illustrations by Kelsey Pasco © Penguin Random House New Zealand
Prepress by Soar Communications Group
Printed and bound in China by 1010 Printing

Disclaimer: While the information in this book has been checked by equine
experts and veterinarians, it is not intended to replace expert care and advice.
If you have any concerns about the behaviour or well-being of your horse or
pony, you should always consult your vet or relevant equine specialist.

A catalogue record for this book is available from
the National Library of New Zealand.

ISBN 978-0-14-377616-1

penguin.co.nz